A Practical Approach to PG Dissertation

....a handbook of research methodology for postgraduate students ....

Second Edition

A Practical Approach to PG Dissertation

....a handbook of research methodology for postgraduate students ....

Second Edition

Dr. R. Raveendran, M.D., Dip. Clin. Pharmacol.
Professor of Pharmacology,
Jawaharlal Institute of Postgraduate Medical
Education and Research (JIPMER), Puducherry 605 006

Dr. B.Gitanjali, M.D., Ph.D.
Professor of Pharmacology,
Jawaharlal Institute of Postgraduate Medical
Education and Research (JIPMER), Puducherry 605 006

and

Dr. S.Manikandan, M.D., DNB., MNAMS
Asst Professor of Pharmacology,
Indira Gandhi Medical College &
Research Institute (IGMC&RI), Puducherry 605 009

PharmaMed Press
An imprint of BSP Books Pvt. Ltd.
4-4-309/316, Giriraj Lane,
Sultan Bazar, Hyderabad - 500 095.

A Practical Approach to PG Dissertation, Second Edition
by R. Raveendran, B. Gitanjali and S. Manikandan

Second Edition

Sixth Reprint, 2024

Published by

PharmaMed Press
An imprint of BSP Books Pvt. Ltd.
4-4-309/316, Giriraj Lane, Sultan Bazar, Hyderabad - 500 095.
Phone: 040-23445600; Fax: 91+40-23445611
E-mail: info@pharmamedpress.com
www.pharmamedpress.com/pharmamedpress.net

Cartoons
Idea, design & dialog : Authors
Illustration : Icon Animation Academy, Chennai

Printed at
Repro India Limited.

Price: Rs. 395.00
ISBN: 978-93-81075-65-4 (Paperback)

Dedicated to

All postgraduates

Who have suffered at the hands of incompetent guides

and

All guides

Who are frustrated by the insincerity of their students

Acknowledgements

Our heartfelt thanks are due to Icon Animation Academy, Chennai for making our cartoon ideas a reality.

We thank Natural News, Canadian Journal of Psychiatry and a number of others who have placed in the public domain their creative writings which we have reproduced in the book as light reading matter at the beginning of each chapter.

- Authors

Before we begin…

> ***"I have always believed that writing advertisements is the second most profitable form of writing. The first, of course, is ransom notes..."*** **- Philip Dusenberry**

The second edition of "A Practical Approach to PG Dissertation" was long overdue. When we started writing the first edition in 1994, research methodology was not a topic that was very much discussed by postgraduate students (PGs) and their teachers. There was a feeling that "learning from masters" and "learning by doing" were the only ways to become skilled at research. Things have drastically changed since then. PGs are under pressure not only to conduct good quality research but also to try and publish the work they have done since many agencies have started using publications as a yardstick of competence.

Many universities in India have made the PG dissertation compulsory because it is believed that PGs in medicine and allied sciences should be proficient not only in clinical medicine but also in research. What we have presented here is not a complete book on research methodology but mainly a skeletal framework on how to carry out a dissertation and write it up. Some of the difficulties PGs face during their dissertation work tends to put them off research forever. We believe these difficulties stem from a poor understanding of research methodology which is never taught to many PGs.

Therefore, in this edition we have tried to give our readers an overall view of the latest tools available for conducting and publishing research. This ranges from the use of bibliographic software to manage references to consulting standardized reporting guidelines when writing up. We believe that this will give the readers of this book that little extra edge which is necessary in today's world. No book including this one is a substitute for sheer hard work, honesty, perseverance and discipline which forms the foundation for any research work.

The book touches almost all basic aspects of research connected to medicine, though some are not covered in great detail mainly to avoid creating confusion to PGs who are beginners to the field of research. The chapters are organized in the order of steps of a research project. For this reason, the statistical aspects of research are not clubbed together in a single chapter but spread out over different chapters. Only the required information on statistics for a particular stage is given in each chapter.

Examples are given in many places for better understanding. The data used in the examples are hypothetical.

The readers who have read the first edition would notice a couple of new additions to the second edition. Each chapter starts with a light reading matter such as jokes, quotes or anecdotes and has at least one medical cartoon. We believe these additions add to the joy of reading. The ideas for all the cartoons are of the authors; a couple of them were inspired by the jokes available on the net. Included are the problems/tasks at the end of many chapters to enhance the practical approach to learn research methodology. The serious readers can solve the problems/tasks. Is there a better way to justify the title of the book?!?!

This edition also has a new author, Dr.S.Manikandan, who gives the book the fresh insight it needed from a postgraduate's point of view. We continue to keep the book jargon-free and as compact as possible to keep it reader-friendly. However, we once again caution our readers that the book aims to only introduce you to the intricacies and nuances of research. It is mandatory for PGs to read up relevant details from textbooks or the internet, which hosts many websites that give a large amount of factual information. The book is the fruit of our own desperation, when, as young postgraduates and later as residents we could not find information on research methodology in a language which was familiar to us. Our email IDs given below are open invitations to whosoever wants further help on any of the chapters. We hope, that this book will continue to be the first book which a postgraduate would read to understand the basics of research methodology.

R. Raveendran (dr.ravee@gmail.com)

B. Gitanjali (gitabatman@gmail.com)

S. Manikandan (drsmanikandan001@gmail.com)

Contents

Chapter 1

Research and Postgraduation

You might be a scientist.......

If your wrist watch has more computing power than an Intel Core i5.

If your ideal evening consists of fast-forwarding through the latest sci-fi movie looking for technical inaccuracies.

If you carry on a one-hour debate over the expected results of a test that actually takes five minutes to run.

If you have never backed-up your hard drive.

If you can remember 7 computer passwords but not your wedding anniversary.

If you can type 70 words a minute but can't read your own handwriting.

If you have more friends on the internet than in real life.

If you think that when people around you yawn, it's because they didn't get enough sleep.

If your three year old son asks why the sky is blue and you try to explain atmospheric absorption theory.

From http://www.xs4all.nl/~jcdverha/scijokes/8.html#might.be_6

1. Research and Postgraduation

Research

Importance of research

Aims and objectives of PG dissertation

Difference between a thesis and a dissertation

Outcome of PG dissertation

Role of universities

Role of guides

Role of PG students

Research

Research is a systematic and organised scientific process to find answers to questions. For example *a question is raised : Can prazosin prevent deaths in children stung by scorpion?* Assuming the question is not answered already in the whole of medical literature, it can be answered by conducting a scientific study. Such a study, if conducted is systematic because there is a definite set of procedures and steps to be followed in a specified order. It is organized in the sense it is a planned process and not an impulsive one. The above question is the basis and a starting point of research. If there is no question there is no research. Answer(s) to question(s) is the endpoint of research. The answer may be negative (*"Prazosin cannot prevent deaths"*) but it is still an answer.

Research generates new knowledge that can be used to solve a problem or improve the existing status of a process. A sociologist questioning villagers about their food habits, a statistician doing a meta analysis of clinical trials, a geneticist encoding a protein sequence - are all doing research though using different instruments to attain their objectives i.e., *a pencil and paper by the sociologist, a computer by the statistician and molecular probes by the geneticist*. Research uses the scientific method to discover facts and their interrelationships and the new knowledge obtained is applied in practical settings. Research may provide a fresh understanding of a disease process, or mechanism of action of a drug or it may provide new tools for disease management such as vaccines or it may generate information on the health problems of a community to plan health care strategies.

Importance of research

Knowledge is power and research is essential for generating information and understanding problems that can enable the community to achieve a better quality of life. In the context of medicine, research is undertaken to promote health. There are four important reasons why research should be undertaken:

(a) Promotes basic knowledge: This is the infrastructure upon which drug treatment, disease management, or health care reforms depend.

(b) Development of new tools: These may be drugs, vaccines, a diagnostic aid, pesticides, an operative technique, an instrument or rating scales. These are all weapons in the war against disease.

(c) Informs public: In the industrialized countries substantial improvements in health have resulted from changes in life style, diet and activity - all of which are due to health promotion on the basis of the outcomes of research.

(d) Effective planning: Research provides the data for better management of scarce resources and can guide health policies and actions.

The pursuit of research depends on systematic analyses, creativity, exploration and commitment to truth. The benefits of research, both social and monetary stimulate a demand for it and result in faster progress for the mutual benefit of society.

Box 1.1 **Why do research?**

If we	
Do research	**Don't do research**
1. We ourselves can solve our problems.	We have to depend on others to solve our problems.
2. We can attain intellectual independence and stay in front	We will be depending on others for information and knowledge.
3. We can commercially exploit the fruits of research leading to economic growth.	We will be buying technology and equipment and become poorer.

Having read the importance of research, it is natural that a question arises in our minds; where do we, the Indian researchers, stand in the international arena of medical research? How many new drugs have we developed and introduced in the market? How many new medical devices have we designed and marketed? How many diseases, syndromes and treatment regimens were described by Indian doctors? How many scientists in India got Nobel Prize for medicine? Sadly we are not in a position to proudly answer these questions holding our head high. We are far behind our Western counterparts. Many of us like to believe that the Westerners do research because they have better facilities. The reverse is, in fact true. They create facilities because they want to do research and not that they do research because the facilities are already existing. The facilities were/are developed/created by them and were/are not gifted to them by their Gods from heaven. We do not show adequate interest in research and hence we have not established better facilities either. We have miserably failed to create a favorable environment for research. There is a misguided belief that our doctors and scientists are no inferior to those in the West. When most of the original work and scientific inventions emanate from the West and our contribution is very little so far or nothing to speak of, we wonder how we can call ourselves equals. At the most we are good photocopies. Even though a photocopy looks better than the original, still it is a photocopy i.e., *the value attached to it is much less than that of the original.* This is one reason why we should make adequate original contributions if we really want to be considered equals. This is not something impossible and we can do it, if we desire.

Research has become the last priority for many medical teachers whose dictum is patient first, teaching next and research last (or no research). Many clinicians are happy publishing case reports as a way of increasing the number of publications in their respective curriculum vitae. We have reached a stage where we expect our Western counterparts to solve most if not all our problems including some which are exclusive to our country. Why would a Western scientist be interested in finding an effective treatment for leprosy which is not a problem of the West? Many believe that meaningful research can only be done in the West and we need not or cannot do good research. Nothing could be more unfortunate for medical science in India.

At last we have developed an elephant model for elephantiasis. Now we should start testing new drugs on elephants.......

The most deplorable state is lack or non-availability or inaccessibility of medical data even on a common disease or some important aspect of medicine. We have come across many theses and dissertations done in India which typically quote statistics of USA or Europe; not that of India. The stock answer for this malady is "the Indian data are not available or accessible". When one of us was examining a PhD thesis from an institute in India, the candidate was asked why he quoted statistics of USA instead of India. The answer was "the data were not available". When it was suggested that he could have mentioned at least the data from his hospital, his answer was the same. The thesis was on schizophrenia and the institute was exclusively for mental disorders.

This situation is not irreversible. Though there are many reasons for the pitiable state of medical research in our country – lack of training and lackadaisical attitude towards research among the medical fraternity are the major ones. Proper training of postgraduate students (PGs) on research methodology and changing their attitude by generating interest in research will go a long way in tilting the scales favorably even though this process may take decades.

Aims and objectives of a postgraduate (PG) dissertation

Many universities in India have made dissertation work a part of PG curriculum. The aim is to teach a PG student the fundamentals of research methodology and stimulate an interest in research. A PG student, at the end of his course, should be capable of planning and carrying out an independent research project. It also helps him develop the necessary skills required to do research. Such skills will also assist him to critically analyze medical literature. He may not be able to assess the relative merits and demerits of new drugs and new treatment modalities, unless he is familiar with the basics of research.

Dissertation and thesis

Dissertation is not very different from thesis. A thesis as The Oxford English dictionary (Oxford University Press, London, 1933 & 1961) says is `a proposition laid down or stated especially as a theme to be discussed and proved or to be maintained against attack'. It is an 'in depth' study of a particular topic which contributes new information/knowledge in the field. In contrast, a dissertation is `a spoken or written discourse upon or treatment of a subject in which it is discussed at length'. At the postgraduate level one is expected to do a dissertation and what research scholars (Ph.D.) produce is called thesis. The length of a thesis is usually much longer than that of a dissertation. There is no specific length prescribed, though a dissertation should be at least 50 typed pages. It is also generally expected that original work is done as a part of a thesis (as mentioned in the definition). The same is true for the dissertation too but the volume of work is smaller than that of a thesis. Ph.D. is a full time research course extending for at least three years whereas dissertation work is only part-time for medical PG students and the duration of work does not normally extend beyond two years. Hence the rigors of a thesis are not usually expected of a dissertation.

Advantages of PG dissertation

The reasons for doing a PG dissertation are many :

1. Learning research methodology: PGs learn and get trained in research methodology.
2. Development of scientific attitude: A doctor must think scientifically and develop scientific attitude towards patient management (evidence based medicine) and research. Such attitude is useful in assessing new approaches to management of patients/community health.
3. Chance for in depth study: Dissertation work offers the PGs an opportunity to study a topic in depth and earn experience in a particular field.
4. Critical reading: The PGs learn how to collect literature on a topic and analyze it critically instead of blindly accepting whatever is

published. They get to know how to use the library and the internet for literature search.

5. Special skills: In the course of a dissertation, PGs may develop special skills and interests which they could put to good use in future.
6. Imparting new information: Contributing new knowledge, however small it may be, is exciting and satisfying.
7. Curricular requirement: In many universities/institutes, dissertation is a part of the curriculum to earn a postgraduate degree.
8. Publication: Dissertation work can be published in journals and publications are very important for a successful academic career.

The role of universities

Universities insist on PG dissertation. What they do not insist on are the minimum standards for a dissertation. When a dissertation is submitted to the university it is sent to the examiners who are appointed for that particular session. The examiner is expected to evaluate the dissertation and either approve or not approve it. If the dissertation is not approved, the candidate is asked to revise the dissertation along the lines suggested by the examiners. The candidate is, however, allowed to sit for the examination but his results will be withheld until the dissertation is revised and resubmitted (Some universities do not allow students to take the examination till the dissertation is approved). During the oral examination the candidate is asked to defend his dissertation. The time devoted to the dissertation in an examination is very little and examiners tend to point out very obvious errors and do not discuss it in detail. There can be no better way of diminishing the importance of research.

Many times the universities send the copies of the dissertation to the examiners at the last moment. The examiner has no time to even read the summary of the dissertation. At some centers there are 10-15 candidates appearing for the examination. It is not humanely possible for any examiner to critically go through all the dissertations in one or two weeks (sometimes they are given only one or two days time). Indeed, there have been examiners who have come for the examination without even opening the parcel containing the dissertations sent from the university.

What can universities do to improve this current scenario? If research is to be given importance then universities should insist on dissertation being given due weightage during the final examination. A specific number of marks for the dissertation will certainly ensure that more effort will be spent on it. At the end of one and a half years (if the course is of three years) an assessment of the progress of the work should be done. The university could recruit a team of people (two or three) to conduct an open viva-voce on the progress made. The candidate will then be forced to carry out some work before this evaluation and hence one can expect the dissertation to be planned and understood better by the candidate and assessed better by the examiners. Universities should also insist on orientation/training courses in research methodology and statistics for the first year PGs before they choose the topics and submit their protocols. An examination on research methodology and statistics will at least force the PGs to learn these subjects. Currently the PGs in dental and allied medical courses undergo these courses and examinations. It is a mystery why the medical PG courses have been left out.

The role of guides

*Many of us are (were) not lucky enough to have erudite, research-*oriented, enthusiastic guides. Some guides take on the mentoring of PGs as a cross to bear which comes with the job. Some take it as an opportunity to have one more paper and as a statistic to be added to their biodata. Some simply do not bother at all. They leave it up to the PGs to do everything and simply sit back and sign the certificate at the end of the whole thing. Between these extremes, there are varying shades of interest shown by guides.

But do we always have only the guides to blame? The same attitude is prevalent (and at times endemic) among PGs too. There are those who meet the guides and co-guides for the first time with the draft of their dissertation, not having taken the trouble to contact them before this stage leading to an inevitable stand-off between the two.

The guide is expected to supervise the candidate at all stages of the dissertation. From defining a problem to finally approving and signing the dissertation he should be involved in all stages. This does not mean that the guide should sit with the candidate and do the experiments or finally write the dissertation (though there are many instances where guides have done so). The guide is expected to teach the PGs the basics of research methodology, cut through the red tape, smoothen administrative problems and help the candidate procure the necessary drugs or instruments and offer general help in the conduct of the study. During this process one hopes that some of the guide's enthusiasm (or disinterest) for research will rub off on the student.

The guide should also take it as a challenge to identify relevant areas of research, define challenging problems and ask the PGs to seek answers to problems facing our health care. This is easier said than done. Some guides have problems selecting a topic and ask students to "look" at dissertations from other colleges and quickly plagiarize the topic with a regional feel. Of course the justification is easy. We do not have data from our population. While there is nothing wrong with this line of thinking, it stifles imagination and does not permit the students to think out of the box.

Box 1.2 **Guides**

Qualities of an ideal guide	**Problems with the guides**
Available and approachable	Too busy and no/little time for the student
Knowledgeable, competent and encouraging	Unethical
Considerable interest in research	Lack of interest in research
Expertise in the field of interest	Poor knowledge about research methodology and statistics
Good communication and feedback	Poor communication skills
Solves administrative problems	Lack of problem solving skills
Critical but flexible and listens to student	Lack of confidence and commitment
Courteous and respectful	Selfish and rude

There is no universally accepted norm to be nominated as a guide. It appears any faculty member with three years experience after a PG degree can become a guide. Senior faculty members are allotted students not because they are proficient in research but because of their seniority. One wonders why universities cannot scrutinize the research background of a faculty member before declaring him a qualified guide. Guideship must be earned and not conferred. Universities should ask the individual institutes to conduct a course on research methodology for their faculty and conduct examinations (written and viva) for those aspiring to become guides. In some departments the staff student ratio is very low. In such instances it is very difficult for a guide to think of 3-4 topics per year and guide his PGs. There have been instances of dissertations being copied verbatim from other universities (or sometimes the same university) and being submitted with the approval of the guide.

These "misguides" and the mass production of dissertations have led to waning enthusiasm among faculty members and the apathy is transmitted to the PGs.

The role of PGs

Most PGs think that research is a waste of time and they try to finish their dissertation as quickly as possible so as to have more time to devote to their books. This has led to a lot of malpractice, with data being cooked up, statistics being manipulated and large portions of the text being copied verbatim from other sources. One of the reasons for this state of affairs is that PGs are unable to relate the need for a dissertation with their clinical goals. They believe that research can be carried out only in teaching institutions and since most PGs do not opt for academics (after getting the degree) they believe it to be a waste of time. Research enriches one's understanding of medicine and gives him the knowledge to critically assess scientific literature. It allows one to form his own opinion of drugs and treatments and grants the freedom to be able to scientifically assess the true worth of new discoveries. It is also possible to do research in private practice or in a primary health center (PHC). Certainly there will be some/many constraints and limitations in such settings. But these obstacles can be overcome by choosing a viable research project with careful planning.

It is time that PGs realized the importance of research and became truly involved in their dissertation projects working sincerely to make the best use of the opportunity to learn research methodology, gain the practical knowledge and skills of organizing and conducting the work and have a firsthand experience of learning scientific writing – a skill which is required more and more in today's world. They should also insist on more involvement from their guides. Since it is customary for the postgraduate student to be the first author of publications which evolve from the dissertation work, he has to accept responsibility for the same. It is probably the first time he will be held accountable for their actions. Unless PGs take pride in presenting a good dissertation and guides are challenged to select better topics for their students, mediocrity will be the norm.

Therefore, a dissertation is like a well choreographed dance. Unless the guide asks the student to come and dance with him it is bound to be full of wrong moves. It is time both the guides and PGs look upon the dissertation as an opportunity to learn and add to knowledge.

Chapter 2

Where and how to Start?

What they said about 'idea'?

Ideas are like wandering sons. They show up when you least expect them. - **Bern Williams**

If at first, the idea is not absurd, then there is no hope for it.
- **Albert Einstein**

The man with a new *idea* is a crank until the *idea* succeeds.
- ***Mark Twain***

Don't worry about people stealing your ideas. If your ideas are any good, you'll have to ram them down people's throat - **Howard Aiken**

In science the credit goes to the man who convinces the world, not to the man to whom the idea first occurs **- Sir Francis Darwin**

When you start in science, you are brainwashed into believing how careful you must be, and how difficult it is to discover things. There's something that might be called the "graduate student syndrome"; graduate students hardly believe they can make a discovery
- Francis Henry Compton Crick

2. Where and how to Start?

Idea and hypothesis formation

Defining objectives

Requirements and feasibility

Other considerations on practical difficulties

Idea

How to get an idea for research? This is a million dollar question for which there is no straightforward simple answer. It all depends on one's knowledge, intelligence, interest and research experience in the field concerned. When a researcher encounters a problem, or believe that the current understanding of the problem is inadequate, or is intrigued by some observation, he may start thinking deeply about it. Subsequently he may look for more information regarding the particular topic. In due course of time he may get some ideas for overcoming the problems and also think he can try out those ideas. This is the nucleus of an idea. At this point he may have to take some time to define the problem (it is not as easy as it sounds though).

Box 2.1 **Getting an idea/ a topic for research**

Encounter a problem → An idea to solve it strikes

Lack of information about a topic → Desire to fill in the vacuum arises

Unanswered questions → An idea/a plan to find an answer strikes

Desire to acquire more knowledge → Inquisitiveness and the desire to explore develops

More knowledge leading to more questions → Yearning to find answers for questions develops

Many guides give postgraduates some time to outline an idea for their own dissertation. Ninety five percent of the time the PGs do not have any idea of their own. It is not that PGs are short of ideas. It is simply that our education system kills originality right from the start. Invariably, the idea for PG dissertation work comes from the guide. There is nothing wrong in this since the guide is capable of assessing the adequacy of facilities and resources available and the capabilities and limitations of PGs. He will certainly be in a better position to choose a good topic. For many PGs, the dissertation work is their maiden attempt in the area of research. Some of them may have worked in small projects during their undergraduate days and have some good ideas to try. But their guides may not have adequate experience or working knowledge in that field. This would make it difficult for them to guide a student. Any guide would like to give his students topics with which he is familiar. Moreover the ideas suggested by the PGs may not be feasible to carry out for want of finance or sophisticated equipment. In such situations, it is better for PGs to accept the topic suggested by their guides.

What exactly is an idea for research? An example can illustrate it. *A surgeon who had a special interest in gastrointestinal surgery read an article from a pharmacology journal that erythromycin increases upper gastro-intestinal tract (GIT) motility by stimulating motilin receptors and not by stimulation of nerves. This information was relatively new to the field and so he read up the various cross references to get a better understanding of the picture. He wondered whether erythromycin could be useful in relieving gastric stasis occurring due to complete vagotomy. He wanted to try out this idea. This was only a rough idea and there were so many issues to be sorted out before he could start finding the answers. Naturally he outlined his idea to the next PG student and asked him or her to work on it.*

Formulation of hypothesis

Hypothesis is nothing but an idea which is yet to be proved. From the above example one can formulate the following hypothesis:

'Erythromycin relieves gastric stasis due to complete vagotomy'

Now the investigator has to prove or disprove the above hypothesis by designing and carrying out an experiment. This hypothesis is called `research hypothesis'. One can formulate a hypothesis from his/her experiences also. For example, *an experienced and alert physician may have noticed that a few patients with Alzheimer's disease who received drug X for some other unrelated problem, clinically improved. So his hypothesis could be*

'Drug X improves the symptoms of Alzheimer's disease'

The responsibility of proving or disproving rests solely on him.

Research question

Can any study start without a hypothesis? In other words, is it a must for a study to have a hypothesis at the beginning? Some studies do not have *a priori* hypothesis but are likely to end with one. Exploratory studies do not have a pre-defined hypothesis but when the data are collected and analysed a hypothesis or two may be formulated from the data. On the other hand, experimental studies start with a definite hypothesis and conclude whether the hypothesis is proved or disproved. If an exploratory study does not have a hypothesis then what does it start with? If the reader is able to recall, it was said earlier there is no research without questions. Exploratory studies start with questions. For example *a researcher may happen to ask a question such as "What happens to cellular organelles when drug X enters a cell?", if the knowledge of events that may occur when drug X enters a cell is lacking.* He may conduct a molecular study without formulating any hypothesis, observe the cellular events and draw conclusions. Some of these conclusions may be in the form of hypotheses which need to be proved by further studies. Hence a study may or may not have a pre-defined hypothesis but all studies start from a question which is called 'research question'. Hypothesis can also be written in the form of a research question. In the example given above the research question will be "*Can erythromycin relieve gastric stasis due to vagotomy?*"

Defining an objective

At this stage only vague objectives can be formed. To define them precisely more information may be needed. If we take the same example of gastric stasis and erythromycin the aim at this stage is to find out whether erythromycin will be effective in relieving gastric stasis in patients who have undergone vagotomy. Next step is to search for available literature on the topic. Literature search is discussed in detail in chapter 3. A thorough reading of pharmacology text books on erythromycin will be helpful. Cross references from original articles should be gathered. One should also find out whether similar and related work has already been carried out and published elsewhere. This knowledge would certainly help the investigator avoid duplicating the work which someone has already carried out. It also gives him an edge over the other investigators. This aspect is discussed in detail in the following chapter.

After acquiring adequate information through literature search the objective(s) can be defined with a little more precision. If the literature search reveals that the idea has already been tested by many, one has to drop the idea and go for another one. Or if the researcher realizes that all the other workers have missed an important aspect, the study can be modified with an objective to explore that important point. Make the objectives simple, unambiguous and precise and do not exceed two or three. Use verbs to define objectives. If the objectives are complex and more in numbers, more time may be needed to complete the work. One must remember that time available for dissertation work is limited.

After the literature search, the objective in our example may now be framed as ***"to evaluate the effect of erythromycin on gastric emptying time in patients who have undergone esophageal resection".***

Difference between aims and objectives

There is no real difference between an aim and an objective. Aims point out the general purpose of the study, whereas objectives spell out exactly what one intends to do in the study. In the above example the aim of the study would be ***"to study the effect of erythromycin on gastric stasis after esophagectomy"*** and the objectives would be ***"to evaluate the effect of erythromycin on gastric emptying time after esophagectomy using a gamma camera"*** and ***"to compare the effect of erythromycin with cisapride on gastric emptying in these patients"***. As one can see, the objectives clearly state what the researcher plans to do.

Justification for the study

In any study, the objectives must be justifiable and the investigator must be able to defend it. He cannot and should not do a study just for the sake of doing it. There is no justification for doing a double blind placebo controlled clinical trial of some drug in India just because no such trial has been conducted in India (unless required by the regulatory authorities). If it is believed that Indians would handle the drug differently, then the researcher is justified in carrying out the study but there must be some basis for the belief. One cannot carry out a study to find out the efficacy of paracetamol in Alzheimer's disease unless otherwise there is some suggestion from earlier work (need not necessarily be related to the disease) or one's own experience. In the example described above, esophageal resection necessitates complete vagotomy leading to gastric stasis and other problems like heartburn and dumping syndrome in the post-operative period. Erythromycin was reported to increase upper gastrointestinal motility. Since no one had tried it in patients who underwent esophagectomy there was ample justification to try the idea with the belief that it might benefit these patients.

Sham research

Do not duplicate studies in various species of animals just for the sake of "doing something". We have seen dissertations where studies published in some journal on the effect of a drug on rats are reproduced on mice, guinea pigs, frogs and so on. When asked why such studies are undertaken we are given the stock answer that a dissertation is only meant to teach research methodology to the PGs and therefore the content of the research work does not matter. This is like building a house and living in it without any furniture. The content does matter. After all it is the content which differentiates good from bad research. It is just not enough for the student to go through all the motions of research. Unless a challenging and legitimate topic is chosen it will only result in "sham research".

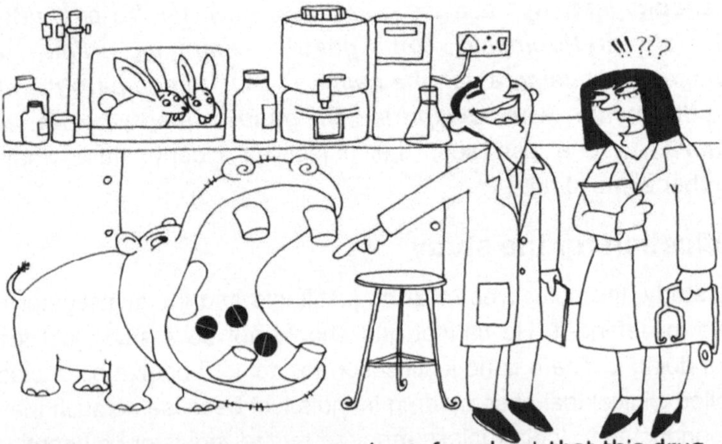

After extensive literature search we found out that this drug was not tested in hippopotamus and we will be the first one to report the analgesic effect of the drug in hippopotamus......

Requirements

Research is not a path strewn with roses. There are many constraints which may force the researcher give up an idea and choose another. The first and foremost constraint as regards to PG dissertation is the knowledge and the experience of the guide in the topic chosen for research. If the guide is really competent, it will save the student a lot of trouble. In many instances, since the guides themselves choose the topic one should not expect any problems. A good guide is the single most important basic requirement for a PG dissertation work.

It is better to list the requirements including the subjects/animals for the study and find out whether they are available easily. Patients who are undergoing esophagectomy in a hospital per year may not be many and the number may not exceed 3 per year. In such a situation the researcher may have to modify his objectives or include patients from a nearby bigger hospital (in which case permission from the Medical Superintendent of that hospital may be needed). Make sure the equipment required and investigational facilities are available within reach. One may require radio-active compounds and a gamma camera for measuring gastric emptying. Or there may be simpler procedures for which both expertise and instruments are available in the department. The procedure one chooses depends mainly on the availability and their advantages and disadvantages over the other.

Box 2.2 **Requirements for a PG dissertation**

1. Competent guide
2. Subjects or animals (in adequate numbers)
3. Time
4. Instruments and expertise to operate them properly
5. Consumables like syringes, needles, kits and chemicals
6. Drugs (if any used)
7. Institutional Review Board and/or Ethics Committee
8. Access to literature (print and electronic)

Another important aspect is time. Generally the time allotted for PG dissertation work will not exceed 2 years and the PG student is expected to do his dissertation work when he finds time amidst his routine work. So the researcher has to be conscious about the time available and should plan accordingly. If he plans to use any drugs or chemicals, it is necessary to find out whether they are available in the department or college and/or easily procurable in India whenever he needs them.

Practical difficulties

A PG student can neither choose his guide nor change him even if he is convinced of the guide's inability to guide him. What can one do when he is allotted an incompetent and egoistic guide? In the Indian set up he cannot complain to higher ups. Even if he does the authorities almost always take the side of the guide who generally happens to be a senior faculty member. The best way out of this tricky situation is to find out who else is capable of guiding. Certainly there will be someone in the department, other unit or discipline who is capable, experienced and friendly enough to help the PG. He should utilize him to the fullest extent but should not forget to satisfy his guide's ego on and off. Unless he manages this problem with a certain amount of tact, life will be miserable.

Keep the guide informed about the dissertation work. Meet him and discuss with him regularly the problems, the work carried out and the results obtained. This will help the guide assess the progress of work and offer suggestions if required. Otherwise there is a possibility that he might suspect the authenticity of work when the PG presents the whole bunch of results suddenly a few days or weeks before the deadline. It is better to fix up a weekly/monthly meeting with the guide exclusively to discuss the dissertation work.

As far as possible restrict the work within one's own department. This is not always possible since one may need to use the facilities from other departments. In such a situation ask the guide to talk to the department concerned and make it official if they are willing to collaborate. Name someone from the collaborating department as a co-guide to your work and this arrangement makes things easier to access facilities available in the other department. Try to avoid using facilities available in other departments unofficially. If interdepartmental relationship is not good, the investigator will be the sufferer.

The required quantity of consumables such as drugs, chemicals and kits must be worked out at the beginning and arrangements should be made for procuring them as early as possible or in some cases as and when required. Since institutions, especially the government organizations have to complete a lot of procedures such as calling for quotations before placing an order, it may take a couple of months to procure the necessary consumables.

In case the work needs animals, contact the person in charge of the animal house to find out how many days in advance they should be informed when the animals are needed. If the study is limited to a particular group of animals (pregnant mice or new-born animals) there may be some difficulty in obtaining all animals needed at one time. Hence sort out matters like where to house the animals, who will clean the cages, feed them and so on.

Human studies will have its own problems and one must anticipate and devise the strategies to overcome them. The number of patients expected to be available during the study period must be considerably more than the sample size estimated. Not all patients with the disease will be suitable for the study. Not all suitable patients will be willing to participate in the study. Not all patients participating in the study will complete the study (if the study requires follow-up visits) without dropping out. Hence it is better not to choose a condition that is rare or will fetch you a relatively small number of patients. Also it is better to design a study requiring a few or no follow-up examinations since the 'drop out' rate is directly proportional to number of follow-up visits required.

Ethics committees (for both animal and human studies) are a must. One cannot proceed with the study before it is cleared by the institutional ethics committee. What if your institute does not have an ethics committee? Ask your guide to speak to the administrators to set up one. For human studies, the services of independent ethics committees available in the country may be availed but they charge a fee. Find out the frequency of the ethics committee meetings and the date of next meeting. Submit the application before the deadline and get the approval in time so that the dissertation can be completed within the stipulated period.

Any institute worth its name should provide good library services which in today's parlance include access to print and digital (electronic) information. If the library services are poor, try a nearby institute which has good facilities.

Dissertation work demands time and hard work. One must be prepared to put in extra effort and time since the routine clinical/departmental work will not be allowed to suffer for the sake of dissertation work. Hence it is in ones best interest to plan personal or family commitments/duties/responsibilities such as marriage and child birth in such a way they do not disrupt the dissertation work.

One should maintain a log book where all events pertaining to dissertation work can be entered. A log book is nothing but a register of 12" × 8" size in which one can note down the details of volunteers, drugs procured and quantity available and data obtained from experiments conducted. It is a bad practice to use loose sheets of papers to note down some important events as there are more chances to misplace it. Keep the log book safely as this is the document which will bail the researcher out later if he is challenged regarding the credibility of the work.

Post-reading Exercises

Read the following text and carry out the tasks given below :

A. *Cleistanthus collinus* is a toxic plant and its leaves are consumed for suicidal purpose. The patients who have taken *Cleistanthus collinus* consistently experience cardiovascular and/or respiratory toxicity. One of the common findings in these patients is hypotension which could not be reversed by adrenergic agonists. Cleistanthin A and cleistanthin B are the major constituents of the plant and these compounds are responsible for the toxicity.

B. About 10,000 snake bites are reported yearly. Antivenom (hyperimmune immunoglobulin) is the only specific antidote but it can cause anaphylactic or anaphylactoid reactions in 87% of the patients. The occurrence of such reactions depends on the type of antivenom, dose and mode of administration and it is difficult to predict them by sensitivity tests. Bronchospasm and shock may occur leading to death.

   It has been suggested that prophylaxis with antihistamines (H_1 blockers with or without H_2 blockers) is effective against anaphylactic or anaphylactoid reaction. However, no properly controlled studies have been conducted so far.

Tasks (common for A and B):

1. **Do you get any idea to do research from the above information?**
2. **If so, write it down and formulate a hypothesis based on the idea for research.**
3. **Frame the objectives of the study to be carried out to prove the hypothesis.**
4. **What is the justification for the study?**

Chapter 3

Literature Search

All about articles

Photocopying is not the same as reading.

The printed word is no guarantee of truth.

The article that is misplaced is the article you need.

You may download an article and read it too!!!!

An article in the hand is worth two on the Net!

An article a day keeps your boss away!!

Too many authors spoil the article.

You can't remember what you never read.

'Never-read-journals' do no harm.

Look for your external's papers and put them on the bibliography.

From http://www.xs4all.nl/~jcdverha/scijokes/8_11.html

3. Literature Search

Definition

Reasons for literature search

Sources of literature

Methods of search

After the search

What is a literature search?

Literature search is a systematic review of all scientific resources both published (i.e. *journals, databases and textbooks*) and non-published (i.e. *registry, dissertation and thesis*) in order to gain information in an area of one's interest.

Literature search is not a one-time task but a continuous process. It starts when a researcher is looking for a researchable problem in the area of his interest and gets repeated throughout the study from writing the protocol to publishing the results so that he can update himself about the new information on the topic of interest.

Why review literature?

The first step one should do while planning a study is to do a literature search. Because it helps the researcher find out the lacunae in an area and identify a research problem. Sometimes one may stumble upon an exciting researchable problem but there is a possibility that the same has been already studied in detail and published. Unless a literature search is carried out it is not possible to recognise whether the proposed research work has already been done or not. This would effectively prevent duplication of the work which is a waste of time, energy and resources. One will probably end up reinventing the wheel if a literature search is not carried out.

There are a few definite advantages in reviewing literature :

1. A review of literature will reveal which aspects related to a topic were researched and which were not. Unresearched topics can be chosen for the dissertation work.
2. The pitfalls / weaknesses in others' studies can be identified and can be rectified in the proposed work.
3. The difficulties faced by the other workers may be avoided by foreseeing or finding out solutions for some of them in advance.

Some papers may offer solutions to the problems encountered in another study.

4. Some workers may have described a modified procedure instead of the standard one. The modification may be the better one and may very well suit the purpose.
5. It will be of great help if the researcher does not have adequate details of the experimental procedure of the study. The technical know-how can be obtained by searching the literature.
6. It can give an idea about the dose of drugs, animal models, number of subjects and statistical methods. These details can help the researcher design the study.
7. The published data can be used for calculating the sample size for the proposed project.
8. One can get an idea whether the study can be completed within the stipulated time period.
9. Review of literature also helps the authors write an effective discussion of their manuscript.

Where to search?

There are various sources for literature search. Every effort should be made to perform a thorough search of all the sources.

Primary sources:

The journals are the primary source for a literature search. Journal articles provide the latest information and help us update our knowledge in pathophysiology, treatment regimens and newer developments in the area of interest apart from providing the details of design and methodology. Literature search should be conducted in indexed as well as non-indexed journals. The limitation is that all journals are not freely accessible.

Secondary sources:

Abstracting services like PubMed, EMBASE, Biosis and IndMed are the secondary sources. It is possible to do an effective and quick search of the literature using the secondary sources. Abstracts should never be used as a primary source since it can lead to misinterpretation. The abstracting services are useful for initial search.

Every abstracting agency has a limited number of journals only and not all journals in the world. So it is prudent to search more than one abstracting agency. Yet another limitation is that the abstracts may not be available for all the articles, viz – editorial, research letter, case report and letter to the editor.

Tertiary sources:

Text books are the tertiary sources and are easily available. One should not hesitate to refer to all the available textbooks to find out what has been said about the chosen topic. The drug that is to be used in the study may be exhaustively covered in pharmacology textbooks. If the study is on a disease, it would be wise to read not only the general textbooks but also the reference books. It is important that one should read the most recent edition of a book. It is also a good practice to read the older editions which sometimes describe the historical background of a disease, drug or procedure. The newer editions omit such information for want of space. Limitations of tertiary sources include the absence of the most recent developments as it takes several years to publish a new edition of the textbook.

How to do a literature search?

The following steps describe a systematic approach to literature searching.

Identify keywords

The first step for an effective literature search is identifying keywords. The following steps can guide the reader in selecting the keywords for a study.

1. Define the researchable problem as specifically as possible.
2. Break it into small topics.
3. Think carefully about each topic and select all possible keywords.
4. Synonyms of the keywords should be included e.g. *cancer, tumor, carcinoma, malignancy, neoplasia.*
5. Alternative and related terms should also be used e.g. *adrenaline, epinephrine.*
6. Alternative spelling should also be used e.g. *oedema, edema*. Its worth remembering that U.S and U.K spellings for many biomedical terms differ. The use of just one spelling may fail to pick up the papers with alternative spelling.
7. Older terms/terminology should also be used e.g. *For 'type 2 diabetes mellitus', one can also use 'Type II diabetes mellitus' and 'Non-insulin dependent diabetes mellitus'.*

8. Acronyms should also be used e.g. *AIDS, HIV.*
9. Scientific and common name should be used e.g. *Ascaris lumbricoides, round worm.*
10. Singular and plural should also be used e.g. *mouse, mice; testis, testes.*
11. Change of place name should also be considered e.g. *Bombay, Mumbai.*

Search all sources

Once the list of keywords is made, start making a list of sources. Every effort should be made to search all the sources. The search can start with the textbooks in the library. Once an article relevant to the topic is obtained, list of references given in the article should be carefully read and the important relevant references picked up and searched. This is one way of extending the search. The search then must be conducted on the internet. A cautionary note here is there are many layman websites, the sites maintained by individuals and the information given in them need not be reliable. The researcher should use his discretion before using or quoting such information. Literature search on the internet should essentially include a search of the abstracting database like PubMed. Abstracting agencies give only the abstract and every effort should be made to get the full text of the article. Internet search can also be made on the websites of professional organisations like World Health Organisation (WHO) and professional associations, say for diabetes – American Diabetes Association (ADA).

Use wide range of search techniques

Searching by a phrase

If the identified key word is a phrase, (e.g) adverse drug reaction, the phrase should be mentioned within quotes while searching.

Boolean searching

Once a list of keywords for searching is ready, a way to link the keywords together must be worked out. The linking is usually done by three terms – AND, OR, NOT. These terms are called Boolean operators. The Boolean operators are always written in the upper case (full capitals). A search using Boolean operators (Boolean searching) may help to narrow down or widen the search.

AND: used for narrowing the search. The search results should contain all the terms joined with this e.g. *the search "asthma AND children" leaves out all the studies conducted in adult patients and narrows down the search to asthmatic children.*

OR: used for broadening the search. The results contain any or all of the terms linked.

NOT: used to refine the search by narrowing it. The search "edema NOT heart failure" displays all studies on edema but NOT those due to heart failure.

Truncation and wildcard searching

A part of the keyword is replaced by a symbol, usually *. If the last part of the keyword is replaced by * it is called as truncation searching e.g. *a truncation search with the keyword sedat* will carry out a search on sedative and sedation.* When letters inside a keyword are replaced with the symbol then it is called a wild card search e.g. *the keyword am*biasis will look for both amoebiasis and amebiasis.*

Focused searching

The search can be focused or refined by giving limits to the search. A few ways of limiting the search are to include the following limits in the search:

- Experimental / clinical study
- Age, gender of the participants of the study
- Design of study – randomised controlled trial, observational study
- Type of publication – meta analysis, review, original research, case report
- Date of publication

What to do after the initial search is over?

Once the initial search in all the sources is over, record the date of search, key terms used, methods followed and results obtained. Carefully go through the results obtained for relevance, quality and quantity. All the relevant results should be retained and saved. If it is a textbook, necessary pages along with the first two pages (where one can find the year of publication and the details of the publisher) should be photocopied and filed. If it is a chapter in a book, the whole chapter should be photocopied and filed. All the materials saved in electronic format (PDF of articles, web pages) should preferably be printed out and filed. The hard copy as a backup is essential since the hard disk can crash or the memory disks (CD, pen drive) can get lost or corrupted. On the print out of the web page, the name of the home page, URL and date of access should be mentioned and filed.

Start reading

After filing the search results, one should start reading them. This will improve the knowledge on the topic which will naturally help the researcher plan and conduct the study better.

Keep searching

Literature search is a dynamic process and continues throughout the study. It should be carried out at frequent intervals. This is one way by which a researcher can keep in touch with the recent developments in the topic of interest. PGs can subscribe to e-mail alerts to the contents of the journal issues in their field and e-alerts from abstracting agencies like PubMed.

Some tips

1. If you are looking for a specific article, log on to the journal website and download the article/abstract. Google can be used to locate the journal website.
2. Search at least PubMed, Google Scholar and IndMed (http://indmed.nic.in/). While PubMed database includes only the articles from the journals indexed, the Google Scholar can pick up articles from anywhere in the cyberspace. IndMed includes also the Indian journals not indexed by PubMed. Searching PubMed alone is not enough.
3. Plan a search strategy. Start with a broad term and if the number of articles listed is enormous, narrow down the search using the relevant keywords and Boolean operators to end up with relevant articles without missing the important ones.
4. Get the full text of articles relevant to the topic. Open access journals offer full text free of cost immediately after publication. The Directory of Open Access Journals (www.doaj.org) and the Free Medical Journals (www.freemedicaljournals.com) list the open/free access journals and give links to their websites.
5. If your institute subscribes databases such as EBSCO or Science Direct, the full text of the article may be obtained from them.
6. It would be good idea to email the authors of the articles for an electronic copy (PDF file). The email ID can be obtained from the affiliation of the author mentioned in the abstract either in PubMed or journal website. One can also get the email IDs of the authors from their university websites. Many respond positively and promptly.
7. The National Medical Library, New Delhi subscribes to a large number of print journals and one may be able to get photocopies of the desired articles by post on payment of prescribed fees.
8. Ask your friends abroad whether they could send the article by email.
9. Cochrane reviews on different topics are available from the Cochrane Library free of cost (http://www.cochrane.org/)
10. Avoid collecting technical/medical information from websites meant for general public (e.g. Wikipedia).

Post-reading Exercises

Task 1:

Vitamins and blood pressure

- Is there a relationship between vitamins and blood pressure?
- Can vitamin deficiency cause hypertension?
- Can vitamin B_6 be used to treat hypertension?

Do a literature search to answer the above questions. Having done so, answer the following questions :

1. Explain your search strategy.
2. What keywords did you use?
3. How did you choose the keywords?
4. Which databases did you search?

Task 2 :

Do a PubMed search to find out the articles on randomised controlled clinical trials on aspirin between 2001-2010. The title of the articles should include the words 'infarction' and 'aspirin' but not 'myocardial'.

Explain how you did it.

Chapter 4

Study Designs

Sir Austin Bradford Hill

Sir Austin Bradford Hill (1897 - 1991) a famous epidemiologist and statistician in the United Kingdom introduced the randomized clinical trial. As a member of the study team (MRC Tuberculosis Research Unit), he brought in the random allocation technique for the first time in a clinical trial on the use of streptomycin in treating tuberculosis (1947-48). But the trial was neither double blinded nor placebo controlled (BMJ 1999;319:572–3). He along with Richard Doll published a case-control study in 1950 comparing lung cancer patients with matched controls. His team also started a long term prospective cohort study (1951-2001) to establish the increased risk of lung cancer by smoking. The "Bradford Hill criteria' to determine a causal link to a disease were originally presented by him.

4. Study Designs

Importance of study design

Types of studies

Advantages and limitations

Methods to eliminate bias

Design issues

Why is study design important?

Having framed the aims and objectives, one should look for a suitable study design that can answer the research question(s) raised in the beginning. If the study design is found to be wrong at later date, the project cannot be salvaged and entire effort goes waste.

Criteria for research designs

Any design should satisfy the following criteria :

It should

1. be able to test the research hypothesis properly
2. control for extraneous variables like bias, confounders and sampling errors.
3. allow generalization of results of the study to the population.

While designing the research all these three criteria should be taken into account. It should be noted that sometimes, there is no single correct design for the hypothesis and more than one design may be appropriate for the hypothesis.

Types of study designs

Study designs can be broadly classified into either observational or experimental (Table 4.1).

Observational studies

The subjects of the study are just observed for the parameters to be measured and no active intervention is done. Based on the time frame, the observational studies can be divided into cross sectional and longitudinal (Table 4.1). The longitudinal studies are further divided into case control (retrospective) and cohort (prospective) studies. The observational studies can also be classified as descriptive study, where the characteristics are described and analytical study, where analysis is carried out to ascertain an association between two factors.

Table 4.1 **Study designs**

Observational studies		**Experimental studies**
Cross sectional	**Longitudinal**	
Survey *Prevalence studies*	*Case control(retrospective)* *Cohort (prospective) studies*	*Clinical trials* *Animal experiments* *Quasi experimental studies*
Descriptive	**Analytical**	
Case report *Case series* *Survey*	*Case control(retrospective)* *Cohort (prospective) studies* *Cross sectional*	

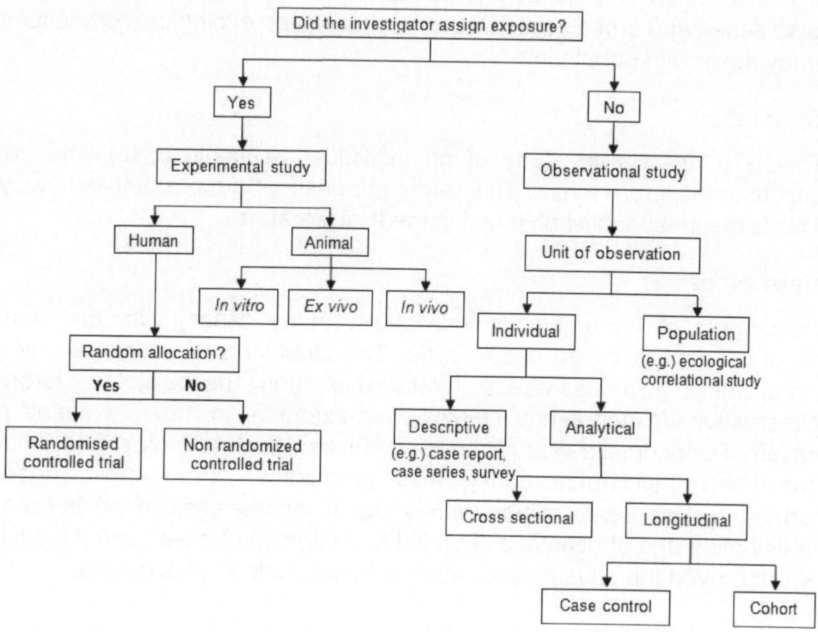

Figure 4.1 **Study designs**

Descriptive Study

A descriptive study is done to describe the various characteristics of the study subjects without a causation or hypothesis testing. A good descriptive study should answer the questions like who, when, what, where, why and more importantly "so what". An important point which should be borne in mind while designing a descriptive study is the need for a specific and stringent criteria for case definition. For example, a descriptive study is designed to describe the characteristics of the distribution of a rare disease in relation to

Person – *age, gender, occupation, personal/socioeconomic characteristics*

Place – *geographic variation*

Time – *seasonal/diurnal variation.*

Types of descriptive study

Descriptive studies can be classified based on whether the study deals with individuals or population. Individuals are observed in case report, case series and cross sectional study whereas an ecological correlational study deals with population.

Case report

This is a descriptive study of an individual (a single case) who has encountered a rare event. This forms the basis of a more detailed study. This is the least publishable unit in medical literature.

Case series

Description of a number of individuals (many cases) with the same disease/event is called case series. The clustering of cases can be a signal for a cause-effect relationship and necessitates further observational/experimental studies. For example, in 1961, a series of cases of phocomelia was reported in children born to mothers who had consumed thalidomide during their pregnancy. These case reports formed a case series which was a signal for the association between thalidomide and phocomelia. This led to designing of case control studies which proved the causal association of thalidomide to phocomelia.

Cross sectional study

It involves the study of a random sample of population or a group of patients at a single time point. Cross sectional studies are the best design to study the prevalence of a disease. That is why they are also called as prevalence studies. These studies can identify the health needs/attitudes and help in planning and implementation of various health programs. One of the limitations of this design is that it does not take into account the temporal relationship between exposure and outcome as both are measured at the same time point. A cautionary note in these studies involving patients is the potential for selection bias.

For example, a cross sectional study on malnutrition may wish to establish

(a) *percentage of malnourished children*

(b) *Socioeconomic, physical, political variables that influence the availability of food*

(c) *Feeding practices*

(d) *Knowledge, beliefs and opinions that influence these practices*

By comparing malnourished and well nourished children, the study can determine which independent variable *(i.e. socioeconomic, behavioural)* contributed to malnutrition.

Ecological correlation study

This is called ecological study because the analysis is at the level of the entire population and not at the individual level. In this type of study, the suspected risk factor is measured in various population and compared with the incidence of the disease to generate a hypothesis about the risk factor and disease. An important limitation of this design is that it can establish association only and not a causal relationship. For example, the number of safe deliveries is related to regular antenatal visits by the mother.

When to do a descriptive study

A descriptive study can be undertaken when the disease is new or rare and much is not known about the etiology, symptoms and disease characteristics. Descriptive study is the first approach to research in a new event. For example, a decade ago SARS was virtually unknown and the initial descriptive studies on the symptomatology and presentation paved way for further research.

Uses of descriptive studies

1. Provide data regarding the magnitude and types of disease in the community.
2. Provide clues to disease etiology and help in formulation of an etiological hypothesis.

3. Provide background data for planning, organising and evaluating preventive and curative services.
4. Used to describe variations in disease occurrence by time, place and person.

Limitations of descriptive study

1. Does not account for chance variation. For example, the improvement or worsening of a disease can be due to the fluctuating course of the disease or due to chance/inter-individual variation. This cannot be ruled out as there is no control group.
2. Cannot account for bias.
3. Cannot account for confounders.

Case control study

A group of patients with disease (cases) is compared with a group of individuals without disease (controls). Both the groups are followed backwards in time to determine the association with the risk factor (Figure 4.2). So this is also called retrospective study.

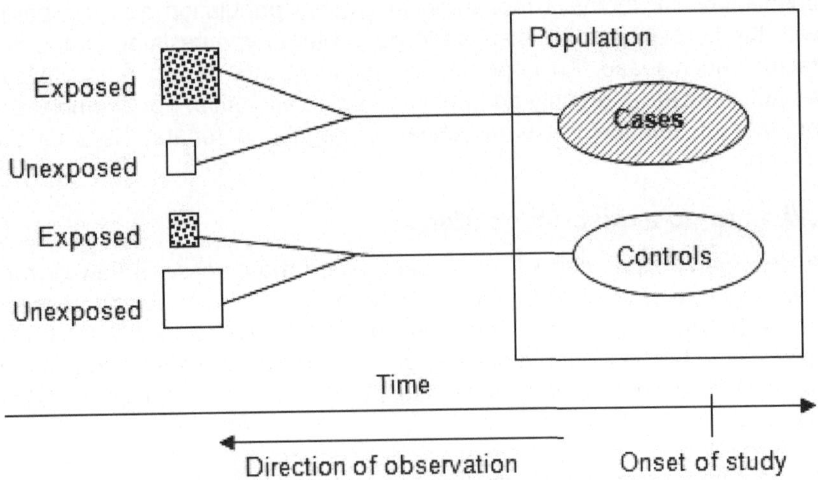

Figure 4.2 **Case control study**

Example: *Pregnant women at term with (a) foetal malformation and (b) normal foetus are selected for the study and traced back to find out whether they took a particular drug during the first trimester.*

When to do a case control study

1. It is an efficient design for the study of rare diseases. (A cohort study will be very difficult for such diseases as large number of people have to be followed to identify one with an outcome)
2. It can be employed for studies in diseases with long latency period like AIDS, cancer. Cohort is not an ideal design for this as the researcher has to follow up for a long period before the disease manifests.

Design issues

Selection of cases and controls

The case and the source population (population from which cases arise) should be well defined. Previously existing cases are not preferred, as diagnostic criteria changes with time and the exposure may affect the prognosis and duration of the disease.

The validity of a case control study depends on the selection of controls. They should be selected from the same population as cases and it should be independent of exposure. Increasing the number of controls increases the power of the study but increasing beyond four controls per case has no change in the power.

Matching

Generally each case is matched to a control by gender and age. Matching helps to remove the confounders. Matching for too many factors is also not advisable as it may restrict the availability of suitable controls.

Blinding

The data gatherers should not be aware of the status of the participants (case/control) and the study hypothesis. As the cases and controls differ in recollecting the exposure, the data gatherers should be trained to elicit history of exposure in a similar manner in cases and controls. This helps to eliminate bias.

Advantages

1. Quick, cheap and easy to conduct.
2. Requires smaller sample size than other designs.
3. Many risk factors can be investigated.

Limitations

1. Case control study is susceptible to bias.
2. They are inefficient if the frequency of exposure is low.
3. Can never prove causality, but helps to formulate hypothesis of association.

Cohort study

In this type of study design, the researcher assembles a group of people (cohort) and follows them forward in time. The exposure status to a risk factor and the outcome are observed in this cohort (Figure 4.3). In Roman military, a group of 300-600 soldiers marching forwards was called a cohort. As this study proceeds forward from exposure to outcome, it was named so.

In general, all cohort studies are prospective. The readers should not to confuse this with 'retrospective cohort'. In this type of study, the researcher goes back in time to form a group of people from the case records/registry and observes them for outcomes. In this type of study also, the direction of observation is always forwards. (But in case control study, the direction of observation is backward, hence it is called a retrospective study). e.g., *a retrospective cohort can be designed to describe the natural course and risk factors for rupture of aortic aneurysm. Patients with aortic aneurysm are identified from the case records of the hospital and the data on various risk factors at the time of diagnosis were noted. They are then followed forwards in time to determine the outcome of aneurysm.*

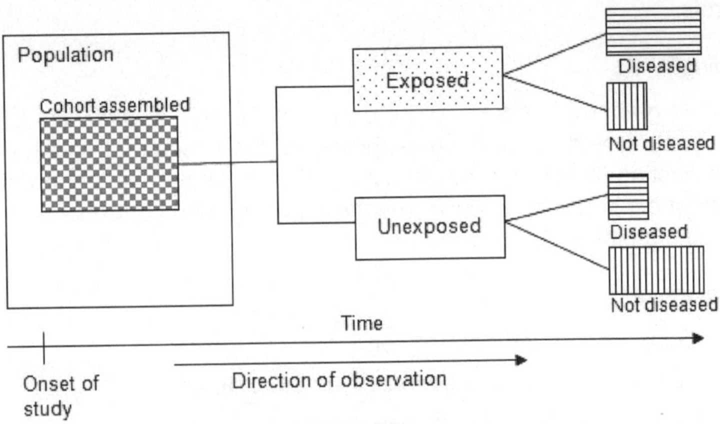

Figure 4.3 **Cohort study**

Design issues

1. Cohort study is susceptible to selection bias. e.g., *in a cohort to determine the effect of jogging on cardiovascular events, the researcher should be careful in selecting the subjects as people who jog are more health conscious and their lifestyle and dietary habits may also differ.*
2. The outcome should be defined clearly and the person/researcher who measures the outcome should be unaware of the status of exposure of the subjects (blinding).

Strengths

1. It is the best design to establish the natural history and incidence of a disease. Relative risk can also be calculated.
2. Establishes the time sequence of events (temporal association) and this strengthens the inference.
3. Multiple outcomes of a particular exposure can be studied.

Limitations

1. Time consuming and costly.
2. Requires large sample size hence not suitable for study of rare diseases.
3. 'Lost to follow up' is an important problem. This can be tackled at the time of designing by restriction (only those subjects who are judged as likely to complete the study should be recruited).
4. The exposure status of the subjects can change in the course of time.

Experimental studies

An experimental study should satisfy the following criteria:

1. There should be an intervention (i.e. drug therapy / exercise / yoga / surgery).
2. It should include a control group.
3. The participants / animals should be randomly assigned to different groups

If one or more criteria are not satisfied, then it is known as quasi experimental study. Experimental studies can be broadly divided into animal studies and human studies.

Animal studies

Animal studies can be *in vitro* (experiment or reaction occurring outside the body in a test tube / culture medium), *in vivo* (experiments on intact animals) or *ex vivo* (tissues / cells are removed from the animal and experiments are carried out on it by maintaining it in a viable state).

Human studies

Clinical trials

Clinical trials are carefully designed experiments to answer specific questions or to test a hypothesis. It consists of a group subjected to an intervention / drug and the other group as a concurrent control. It can be non-randomized or randomized (Figure 4.4). Randomized control trials (RCTs) are the gold standard to evaluate an intervention / treatment.

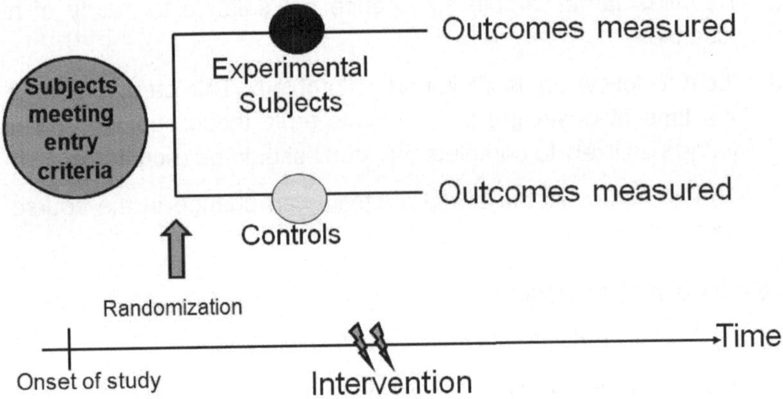

Figure 4.4 **Randomized control trial**

In this study we have used a novel design - "semi-randomised, animal controlled, clinical trial" in which the control group comprises of 10 animals and the test group 10 randomly allocated patients...

(i) *Parallel design*

In this design (Box 4.1) two separate groups are treated concurrently by two different ways (standard drug / new drug). This design is commonly used.

Box 4.1 **Parallel design**

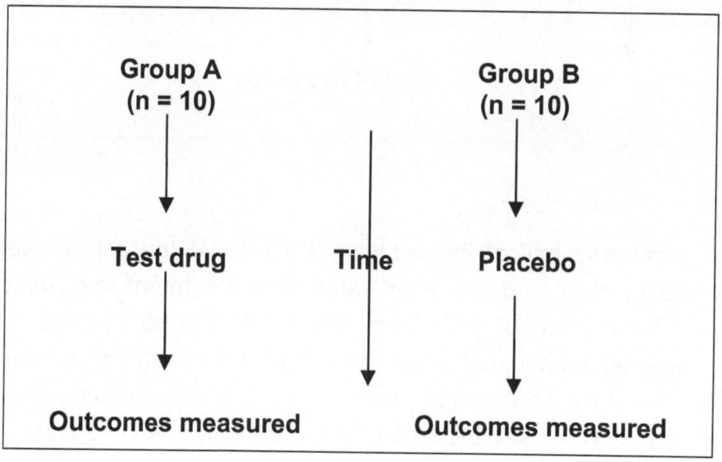

(ii) *Paired design*

Only one group is used (say n=10). After measuring the baseline values in all subjects, an intervention (e.g. drug) is introduced. After giving sufficient time for the intervention to act, measurements are taken again and the data obtained before and after the intervention are compared (Box 4.2).

Box 4.2 **Paired design**

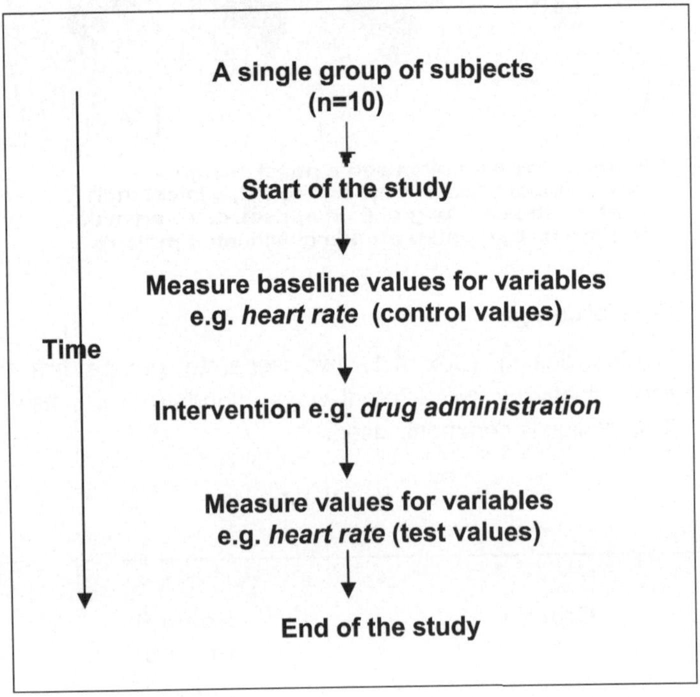

(iii) *Crossover design*

Here one half of the subjects will receive the active treatment (e.g., *drug*) and the other half control treatment (e.g., *placebo*). After a washout period, the treatments will be crossed over so that all the subjects will receive both the treatments in sequence (Box 4.3). This design takes care of not only the inter-individual variation but also the time-effect and the carry-over effect.

Box 4.3 **Crossover design**

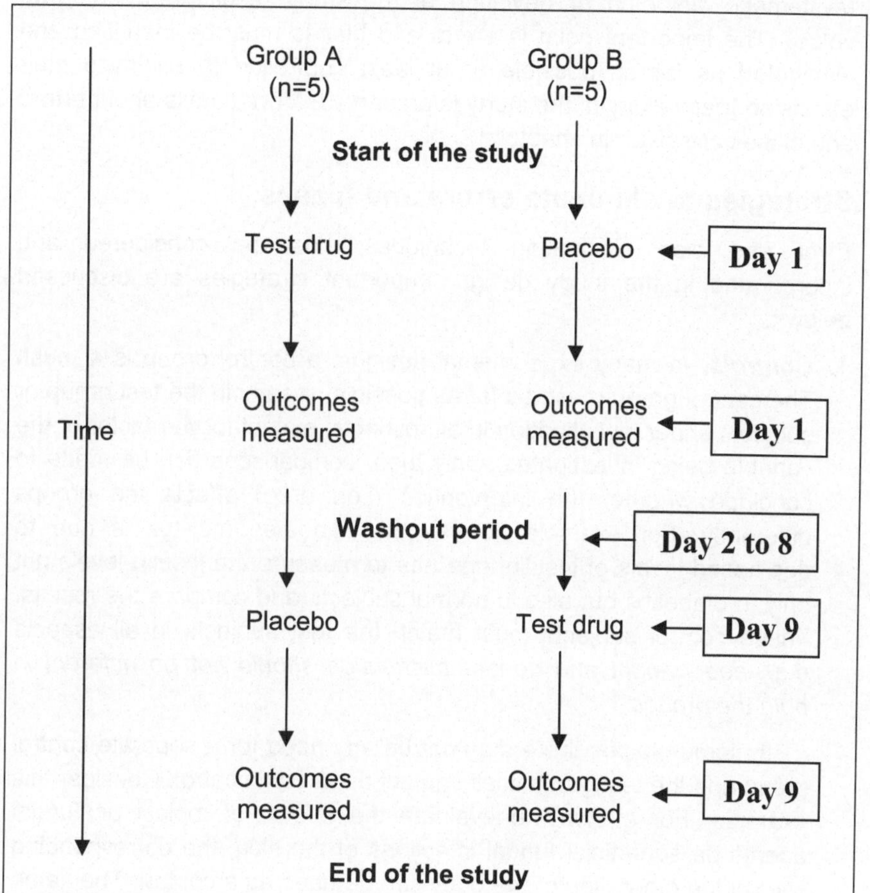

(each subject receives both the interventions i.e. each intervention is given to 10 subjects)

Errors and biases

Errors in measurements can occur in any study and they can adversely affect the outcome. These errors may be random or systematic. The systematic error is called bias and random error is simply known as error. Random error is two sided and bias is one sided. For example the readings of a balance show $\pm$ 0.1 g of real weight of the objects weighed whereas another balance always shows 2 g more than the real weight. The first one is error and it is random since the error can be on the positive or negative side. The other balance is biased (may be due to zero error which was not adjusted) since the error is always one sided (systematic distortion or deviation of the study results from the true value). The important point is errors and biases must be identified and eliminated as far as possible or at least controlled to minimize their effects so that validity of the study is preserved. More details about errors and biases are given in chapter 12.

Strategies to eliminate errors and biases

Error and bias eliminating techniques must be considered and incorporated in the study design. Important strategies are discussed below :

1. ***Controls:*** In many experimental designs, a control group is a must. The control group must, as far as possible, resemble the test group or subjects under investigation in all respects, except for the factor or the variable being investigated. Only then, comparisons can be made to conclude whether the intervention (i.e., drug) affects the groups differently. For example, to say that diabetes mellitus is due to decreased levels of insulin, one has to measure the insulin levels not only in diabetics but also in normal subjects and compare the results. These control subjects must match the test subjects in all aspects e.g., *age, weight and gender distribution should not be different in both the groups.*

   In some studies there may not be any need for a separate control group and the test group itself can act as its own control. Consider this example. For a study to evaluate the effects of topical antifungal agents on superficial fungal infections of the skin, the corresponding site on the other side of the body can be used as a control. The same design is applicable in ophthalmological studies.

   Historical controls are subjects whose data are obtained from old records and used as control values for subjects being treated now. Historical controls are usually not preferred except in tightly controlled situations of advanced diseases like cancer.

2. ***Randomization:*** Randomization (or random allocation) is the process by which every participant has an equal chance of getting any intervention. Hence randomization ensures that the participant gets the intervention purely by chance, not choice. There are two important reasons for advocating randomization. It helps in distributing the various characteristics (which can affect the outcome) randomly between the groups. This reduces selection bias.

Secondly, most of the statistical tests are based on the assumption of random sampling. Even though in most clinical trials convenience sampling is followed, the process of random allocation makes the groups behave as if they were randomly sampled from a single population.

There are many types of randomization and simple randomization is commonly used in postgraduate dissertation / small clinical trials. Randomization is done by random number tables or computer generated random numbers. Software packages like Rando and Random Allocation can be used for this purpose (see chapter 29).

Randomization sequence generation should be done by a person who is not involved in recruiting the participants to the study. For a postgraduate dissertation, it can be done by the guide as the student only will be recruiting patients for the study. It can also be done by some other faculty in the same or another department.

3. ***Allocation concealment:*** The allocation sequence (randomization sequence) generated should be concealed i.e., the investigator / recruiter should not know which intervention the next participant is going to get / which group the next participant is going to be allotted to. For example, if the person who recruits knows that the next participant is going to get a test drug, he might unduly prepone or postpone the participant's entry. This is called selection bias and to avoid it allocation concealment is practised.

   Previously allocation concealment was done by 'sealed envelope technique'. Now most of the multicentric trials follow a central telephone (interactive voice response) randomization system. For the small clinical trials, allocation concealment can be implemented by the pharmacy. In this method the drugs are sealed in serially numbered containers according to the random sequence generated and issued at the pharmacy. Patient no. 1 gets container no.1 and patient no. 2 gets container no. 2 and so on. Neither the recruiter nor the pharmacist knows whether a container contains test drug or placebo. The recruiter simply chooses the suitable patient, issues a number to the patient serially and sends him to the pharmacy to get the drug.

4. ***Placebo:*** As we are aware, many, if not all drugs have a placebo component in their efficacy. This component may or may not contribute significantly to the total effect of a drug. But one has to make sure (in research) that placebo effect does not affect the conclusions drawn. That is why control group is given placebo and the effect it produces is compared with that in the test group so that the real effect of a drug or a treatment can be measured.

In case the drug used in the investigation is a parenteral preparation, normal saline should be injected as a placebo (if the drug is colourless). If the study involves giving two or more drugs, make sure matching placebos for each drug are procured and they are administered in exactly the same time schedule as the drugs.

One should consider ethical aspects while planning to institute a placebo control. Administering placebos to normal healthy volunteers is perfectly alright. But giving them to patients, while withholding the accepted standard treatment is unethical.

In animal studies, drug solutions are usually freshly prepared prior to the experiment. If the drug is dissolved in distilled water or propylene glycol, then the same vehicle should be used for the control animals. If the drug injected has a slightly high or low pH, then the controls should also be matched accordingly. In experiments involving a surgical procedure, control animals should undergo a 'sham operation', where the animal is given anaesthesia and the skin incision is made and sutured.

5. ***Blinding:*** Blinding or masking is a process to make the patient and/or researcher unaware of the nature of intervention (standard drug / new drug) provided to the participant. It can be single blind (either the patient or the investigator alone is blinded) or double blind (both patient and investigator are blinded) or triple blind (patient, investigator and the person who analyses the data are blinded). Blinding eliminates ascertainment bias.

   To make blinding effective, the placebo or standard drug is made to resemble the test drug (shape, size, colour, weight and odour). If both the interventions were given by different routes, then a 'double dummy technique' can be followed. For example, if a new oral drug has to be compared with the standard parenteral drug, then the group receiving new oral drug will also receive a parenteral injection (placebo) similar to the standard drug. The group receiving the parenteral standard drug will also receive a placebo tablet which is similar to the new oral drug.

   Even though blinding and masking mean the same, some researchers prefer the term masking (especially ophthalmologists!). Sometimes it is not practical to implement blinding i.e., when two surgical procedures are compared. Ethical objections may also be raised since the treating physician may not know the nature of intervention if the patient needs to be treated for an adverse event during the trial.

6. ***Standardisation:*** The experiment/ the procedures/ the analytical techniques have to be standardized so that the results are reproducible. The process is repeatedly carried out by the researcher till he gets reproducible results. This reduces error and bias if any.
7. ***Replication:*** Replication reduces errors. The measurements are made in duplicates or triplicates and the mean value is used.
8. ***Study design:*** Some study designs inherently take care of error and bias. Crossover design and paired design described above are examples of such designs.
9. ***Restriction, matching and stratification:*** Confounders can be tackled using these techniques. Confounder is not a bias but an extraneous factor (confounding variable, lurking variable) that is related to both the variables under study. For example, in India the number of cars sold have gone up and so also divorces. Neither is the cause of the other. The growth in economy is the cause of increase in both the variables and hence economy is the confounder in this example. If an association between yellow finger nails and oral cancer could be found, it does not mean the yellow finger nails are the cause of oral cancer. Smoking is the confounder which stains nails and is a risk factor for oral cancer. Confounder should not be confused with bias; the latter results in defective measurement of a variable but confounder leads to error in interpretation even if the measurement is flawless.

Bias or confounder?

Confounders can be eliminated by modifying the design of the study (restriction and matching) and if this not possible, data analysis may be used to adjust, control and correct for confounders (stratification/multivariate analysis). Age is a common confounder. If patients belonging to only a narrow age group (say 40 to 50 yr) is included in the study, it is restriction. Matching ensures no difference between patient and control groups with respect to confounder variable i.e., 54 yr old patient with cirrhosis is matched by including a 54 yr old normal subject in the control group. Stratified analysis involves comparing the groups divided into different strata based on a confounder say age i.e., the patients of 40-50 yr are compared with those control subjects in same age group, the 50-60 yr old patients are compared with control subjects of same age and so on and so forth. These techniques are useful in case-control and cohort studies.

Selection of sample

Animal studies

In animal experiments, it is important to choose the species most suited to the work. So a researcher should be careful in selecting the correct species. There are different strains in a species and selection of a particular strain depends on the study.

Human studies

Selection of healthy volunteers or patients involves not only suitability for experiment but ethical issues as well. The criteria for selection must be laid down in such a way that it should not attract any ethical issues. In general, the volunteers must be willing, and able enough to participate in the study. The seriously ill and the terminally ill must not, normally be included in the study. Any procedure that is applied must not worsen the existing condition of patients.

Selection criteria

It should include a precise and unambiguous definition of all the inclusion criteria (eligibility criteria) as well as all the exclusion criteria. First, the disease to be studied must be precisely defined (if the study includes patients). The subject characteristics such as age limits, gender and profession and other activities if relevant must be defined. The subjects who do not meet these criteria must not be included. However, those who meet these criteria may still not be included if they fall under exclusion category. For example, a patient may be suffering from a disease which you want to study but it is possible that he may have another concurrent disease which may influence the outcome of research. So one has to define the exclusion criteria which will exclude subjects, who should not be included even if they meet all characteristics defined by inclusion criteria. Examples of the criteria of ineligibility are concurrent illnesses, concomitant treatments the patient is receiving and pregnancy (in many but not all studies). As already said the eligibility and ineligibility criteria are different for different studies and there are no general criteria. One has to work out these criteria depending on the objectives. The following may be borne in mind while drafting the criteria:

1. The samples (subjects) to be selected must be true representatives of a population to be studied. For example, when a study on diabetes mellitus is conducted the patients should be typical cases and not have rare complications (unless you are planning to study them). So the eligibility criteria must define the disease status precisely. It is not sufficient just to say type 1 or type 2 diabetes mellitus, but blood sugar levels, glycosylated haemoglobin (HbA_{1C}) levels (range) and duration of diabetes should also be specified.
2. The subjects selected must be sufficiently uniform, i.e., homogenous group.
3. The groups to be compared should be comparable with regard to age, weight range and gender distribution.
4. The personal habits of subjects must be taken into account, if they tend to affect the outcome. Alcoholism, smoking and food habits usually affect drug kinetics. Exclude all smokers from the study if the outcome is likely to be affected by smoking.

Other details

Having decided the type of study and error eliminating techniques to be followed, other details should be worked out. One must decide how many groups to be studied and how to measure the various parameters. There may be more than one method to measure a parameter. The method chosen should depend on the instrument available and the advantages and disadvantages of a method. The technical details of the method used, dose of the drug, time and route of administration, age range of participants and the parameters to be measured will have to be worked out. Details to be considered while designing a study are listed in Box 4.4.

Box 4.4 **Points to be considered while designing a study**

1. Type of study and error eliminating techniques
2. Number of groups (how many test and control groups?)
3. Number of subjects/animals in each group (sample size)
4. Selection of subjects – inclusion and exclusion criteria
5. Parameters to be measured
6. Technical details of experiment/data collection
   a. Subject/animal preparation for experiment (e.g., *fasting*)
   b. Instructions to be given to subjects
   c. Blood/tissue sampling
      - Time schedule
      - Amount to be collected
      - Investigations to be done
   d. Drug dose
      - Route of administration
      - Time of administration
7. Statistical method(s) to be used for data analysis

Post-reading Exercises

What design/method will you choose for the following studies?

1. A new antibiotic developed for typhoid fever is expected to be superior to the existing drugs. How will you establish this?
2. The bioavailability (blood levels) of intramuscular formulation of a drug manufactured by two drug companies (A & B) is to be compared. What design will you choose?
3. Serum phenytoin is measured by a HPLC method. A simple, cheap colorimetric method is developed and is claimed to be useful. You are asked to test it.
4. Self medication is rampant in our country. What are the reasons? How will you find out?
5. A plant product is used by traditional physicians for rabies. It appears to be effective and you would like to try. How will you proceed?
6. A single dose of a new long acting drug (t-half=9 years) is claimed to prevent AIDS, if taken before HIV infection. How will you study the efficacy of the drug?
7. A new kind of minor congenital birth defect starts appearing. A qualitative study conducted on a few cases hypothesised that a drug taken during pregnancy is the cause. How will you investigate?

Chapter 5

Statistics and its Importance in Biomedical Research

(Mis)understanding statisticians

The reasons why statisticians are misunderstood

1. They speak only the Greek/Latin language.
2. They usually have long threatening names such as Bonferonni, Tchebycheff, Schatzoff, Hotelling, and Godambe. Where are the statisticians with names such as Smith, Brown, or Johnson?
3. They are fond of all snakes and typically own as a pet a large South American snake called an ANCOVA.
4. They are frequently seen in their back yards on clear nights gazing through powerful amateur telescopes looking for distant star constellations called ANOVA's.
5. They are 99% confident that sleep cannot be induced in an introductory statistics class by lecturing on z-scores.
6. Their idea of a scenic and exotic trip is traveling three standard deviations above the mean in a normal distribution.
7. They manifest many psychological disorders because as young statisticians many of their statistical hypotheses were rejected.
8. They express a deep-seated fear that society will someday construct tests that will enable everyone to make the same score. Without variation or individual differences the field of statistics has no real function and a statistician becomes a penniless ward of the state.

From http://www.xs4all.nl/~jcdverha/scijokes/1_2.html#subindex

5. Statistics and its importance in biomedical research

- Need for statistics
- Definition of statistics
- Uses of statistics
- Medical students hate statistics
- When to use statistics
- Scope

Why do we need statistics?

Modern day research methodology is based on the principles of statistics. Determination of sample size, sampling techniques, bias eliminating methods (such as randomization), summarizing data and interpretation of data are all based on statistical principles. Why is it so? Let us go back in time and ask how our forefathers described events that were occurring around them, drew conclusions and made decisions. Research methodology and statistics are relatively recent tools but does that mean man did not draw conclusions in the past? There were methods available to him for making decisions :

In the past :

Pure Imagination

[There is another world above the sky; A snake chews off the moon daily and that is why the moon disappears]

Simple Observation

[Earth is flat; Sun revolves around the earth]

Planned Experiments

[Heavy or light, all objects fall at the same speed]

In the present :

Modern day research methodology combines planned experiments and statistical methods which are used in every step of research including analysis of results.

In the future :

The present day research methodology and statistics are not 100% perfect tools. That is why we do not consider it unwise to predict that a better method would evolve in future though it is beyond our imagination what/how it would be.

Why should research methods need the support of statistics? How and why does it make a difference when compared to older methods of drawing conclusions? Remember the dynamic nature of the universe brings in two important characteristics to each and every sphere of life i.e., *uncertainty and variability*. Let us suppose a physician prescribes a well-known drug and effective cure for a disease. Yet how certain can he be that the drug would cure the disease? The answer will be 'most likely' which means he is not 100% certain. Even in patients in whom the drug is effective, will the extent of effect 'same' in all patients? The answer is 'no, the effect will be variable'. One is not 'certain' that the drug will be effective and even if he is, he knows that the effect is 'variable'. These characteristics are applicable not only for the old drugs but also new drugs (for that matter any drug) under investigation. Then will these characteristics not interfere in prediction? How does anyone know a drug will be useful or not, if he cannot control 'uncertainty' and 'variability' when he is experimenting with the drug? To predict the effect of a drug, generally a 'sample' is tested but conclusions are drawn about a 'population'. How 'certain' are we that sample results are applicable to the whole population?

Here is where, statistics comes handy. It is not possible to eliminate 'uncertainty' and 'variability' but these two can be measured. Uncertainty is measured in terms of 'probability' (P) and variability in terms of standard deviation (SD). Predictions can be made in the light of probability and standard deviation measured using statistical methods. The fundamental principle of biomedical research methodology is "test a sample to draw conclusions about the population" which means a small, selected number of subjects/animals/objects (sample) is experimented upon and conclusions are drawn about the entire population from which the sample is drawn. The question is whether the conclusion is valid or not i.e., *whether it is truly applicable to the population*. For example *will a drug which is highly effective in a sample yield similar results when used in the population?*

Think of an experiment as a diagnostic kit. We are well aware that a diagnostic kit can lead to four different outcomes :

Kit Test Result *HIV*	Reality *HIV*	Outcome
Positive	Negative	False positive
Negative	Positive	False negative
Positive	Positive	True positive
Negative	Negative	True negative

Similarly a biomedical experiment can also lead to false positive and false negative results. A sample may show a positive result but the population may not.

Sample *[Is the new drug for AIDS effective?]*	**Population** *[Is the new drug for AIDS effective?]*	**Outcome**
Yes	No	False positive
No	Yes	False negative
Yes	Yes	True positive
No	No	True negative

Since uncertainty and variability are inherent in every event, how do we know the results obtained from a sample will be applicable to the population also (i.e., *will the results be same if the entire population is tested?*). Statistical methods can measure uncertainty and variability using the sample data and also help us draw conclusions depending on the degree of uncertainty and variability. If these characteristics do not exceed certain level in a sample, we conclude that sample results are applicable to population (from which the sample was drawn) too. In research, statistics helps us understand the role of ***uncertainty*** and ***variation*** and aids in providing a rational explanation for observations.

What is statistics?

The word 'statistics' is derived from Latin word "statisticus" which means "of state affairs". The definitions of statistics are given below :

> "a way of taming uncertainty, of turning raw data into arguments that can resolve profound questions" - *T. Amabile*
>
> "a collection of procedures and principles for gaining information in order to make decisions when faced with uncertainty" - J. Utts

"the science of gaining information from numerical data " - D.S. Moore

"the science of collecting, summarizing, presenting and interpreting data and of using them to test hypotheses." - *B. Kirkwood*

The readers may notice that these definitions mention 'uncertainty', 'gaining information' and 'making decisions'. It is a must for a researcher to understand and apply the principles of statistics to do good research. No useful research can be done ignoring statistical methods.

What use is it to us?

Statistical methods are useful in :

(a) reducing the variation in experimental material.

(b) providing valid inferences, based on which one can draw reasonable conclusions from a study.

(c) comparing the effectiveness of a therapeutic regime with that of another.

Why do medical students hate statistics?

It is said that in the UK, statistics as a subject is disliked by students (*BMJ* 1998;316:713) but when they become doctors they like statistics (*BMJ* 1998;316:1674). Many postgraduate students too loath statistics.

We believe the dislike for statistics stems from blindly following the steps of statistical methods for data analysis without understanding the principles behind the procedures. Many think statistics is a subject of pure mathematics and full of formulas studded with obscure Latin characters. It is true in the past the researchers had to work out complex calculations manually using statistical formulas. With the advent of computers and statistical software, actual calculation has become a child's play and now all one should be concerned about is clear understanding of principles of statistical procedures and proper application of the same to data.

When do you use statistics?

It is a common belief among postgraduate students that statistics is something that is done at the end of a study to find out the t and P values which would tell us whether the difference between two groups is significant or not. It is very common among researchers to go after a statistician after completing data collection to consult him or her on the type of statistical test to be used. What they do not realize is that statistics has an important role in planning a study too. One should consult a statistician at the very beginning, i.e., *during the stage of planning*. Because if the study design is flawed or inadequate sample size is used nothing can be done to rectify it at a later date.

Scope

Biomedical statistics is a vast branch and it is not within the scope of this book to consider it in great detail. In the following chapters, some basic concepts of statistics and elementary statistical methods which the postgraduate students are most likely to use are dealt with. To do justice to the title of the book, a practical approach is given importance rather than theory. However, the formulas and actual calculations are not described since the readers are expected to use computer software packages. Readers are encouraged to consult books on biomedical statistics to learn more.

Chapter 6

Nuances of Data

An unwritten footnote in a paper

A copy of the data is available from the authors. This is in the form of a binary dataset on an Atari disk which can be read by any COBOL compiler earlier than 1972. As we are at present upgrading our copy of SAS, we will be unable to handle any requests for data for the next five years, at which time we hope to have carried all the manuals upstairs into the office (if they haven't collapsed inwards under their own mass and formed a neutron star). Please write to us then. ("Thank you for your belated inquiry about our data. Unfortunately they have been discarded because they are more than 5 years old" - The Authors).

Edwin A. Locke, Ronan M Conroy and others

From http://www.xs4all.nl/~jcdverha/scijokes/8_2.html

6. Nuances of Data

Data and variable

Types of data

Scales of measurement

Distribution of data

Importance of distribution

An investigator must have some basic knowledge about the data which he is contemplating to collect. This will help him undertake appropriate analysis of data leading to valid conclusions because the type of data determines the type of statistical analysis.

What are data?

Data (singular: datum) are nothing but numerical or descriptive information held by a variable. Variable is an identifier that holds values which can be numbers, characters, text or non-text materials (e.g., *pictures*). As the name suggests, the values it holds vary from one another (see Table 6.1).

Table 6.1 **Variable and data**

Variable	**Data (obtained from 5 patients)**
Heart rate (per minute)	89, 102, 74, 44, 83
Chest pain (severity)	Severe, Mild, Severe, Moderate, Very severe

Types of data

Data can be classified as given in Table 6.2.

What is the importance of classifying data into different types? As already said, the type of statistical analysis varies with the type of data. Whatever be the type, the data should be converted or summarized to numerical data only. Because statistical calculations are not capable of dealing with names or categories but only numbers.

Table 6.2 **Types data**

Categorical or Qualitative	The individual is grouped into a category based on some qualitative character. Names of categories or labels will form the dataset.	Nominal	As the term suggests, names and labels are called nominal data (Latin: Nomen – Name)	e.g., *Eye color : black, brown, blue* *Religion : Hindu, Muslim, Sikh*
		Ordinal	Categories which imply grading fall into this group	e.g., *Cancer : Stage I, II, III, IV* *Severity : Mild, Moderate, Severe.*
Numerical or Quantitative	The individual is measured for a parameter based on some quantitative character. Only numbers will form the dataset.	Discrete	Some variables can take only full numbers (integers) and not fractions (decimals). Such data are called discrete	e.g., *No. of patients attending a clinic = 245 (it cannot be 245.4 or 123.23)*
		Continuous	Some variables can hold any number i.e., *integers as well as decimals*	e.g., *The weight is 45.4 kg (it can be 45.45, 45.453 or 46.0)*
Other types : Dichotomous or binary data	Some data are binary in nature i.e., *they fall into one of two categories only.*	e.g., *Smoker or non-smoker,* *Is the drug effective – Yes or No?*		

Table 6.3 depicts examples how the different types of data are summarized. The statistical analysis for comparing groups is different for means, medians and proportions.

Table 6.3 **Conversion / summary of data**

Data type	Converted to	Summarized as	Example
Nominal	Counts	Proportion	*Hindus –240- 80%, Muslims –45- 15% Christians –15- 5%*
Ordinal	Ranks or Scores	Median, Mode	*No pain – 0, Mild – 1, Moderate – 2, Severe – 3 Median of chest pain in 12 patients = 2.5*
Discrete	----	Mean	*Mean no. of patients attending a clinic daily = 180*
Continuous	----	Mean	*Mean weight 44.6 kg*

Scales of measurement

Traditionally the following are the 4 scales of measurement of data:

1. Nominal
2. Ordinal
3. Interval
4. Ratio

The nominal and ordinal scales are already described. The interval and ratio scales represent numerical unit of measurement. Any two points of these scales will have a clear interval when compared to ordinal data. For example *it is difficult to say 'very severe' pain is twice stronger than 'moderate pain'*. Similarly it is not possible to conclude stage II cancer is 25% more severe than stage I. Further the interval between stage I and II is not the same as that between stage III and IV. However, 10 g% hemoglobin is twice larger than 5 g% hemoglobin. The difference in temperature between 23° and 25° C is same as that between 33° and 35°C.

The main difference between the interval and ratio scales is that the former does not have a true zero i.e., *the temperature can be below zero (-12°C)*. The ratio scale, however starts at zero and hence it does have a true zero. The hemoglobin value starts at zero and does not go below. Since ratio scale has absolute zero, meaningful ratios exist i.e., *if blood sugar value is 0, it means sugar is absent in blood.* On the other hand, 0° C does not indicate absence of temperature or heat.

Normal distribution of data

One of the characteristics of the continuous data is normal distribution. When data are plotted using a frequency histogram, a distinct shape can be seen on the plot. For example *let us say heart rate of 1024 adult males are collected, categorised and tabulated as follows:*

Heart rate (beats per min)	<40	40 - 45	>45 - 50	>50-55	>55-60	>60-65	>65 -70	>70-75	>75-80	>80 -85	>85-90	>90-95	>95-100	>100 -105	>105
Observed frequency (no. of subjects)	3	4	21	48	82	119	154	160	150	120	84	50	19	6	4

If the above data are plotted (as seen in Figure 6.1) and the mid points of each bar are connected, a bell shaped curve can emerge. If the dataset is adequately large and the sampling is random (i.e., *individual member in a sample is randomly chosen from a population*), a smooth bell shaped and symmetrical curve emerges (Figure 6.1). Hence if a set of data assumes a bell shaped and symmetrical curve on a frequency plot, the data are said to be normally distributed. The figure depicts a peak at the centre and troughs both the sides. The troughs are called 'tails' representing extreme values. It can be inferred from the figure that the extreme values are found in fewer number of subjects, whereas common values are found around the peak. Data of most bodily variables such as blood glucose levels, blood pressure and heart rate are normally distributed. Remember these data are of continuous type. On the contrary, the number of times a person with diarrhoea passes stools may not be normally distributed. Normal distribution is also called Gaussian distribution as it was first described by Carl Friedrich Gauss in 1809.

How do we know whether a set of data follow the normal distribution or not? As already said continuous data from most bodily parameters are normally distributed; it is assumed so, when statistical analysis is carried out. Of course, there is a statistical test to find out whether the data a researcher has collected are normally distributed or not. This test is called normality test or Kolmogorov-Smirnov test; but it is not without limitations.

The word 'normal' has a statistical connotation and it has nothing to do with the clinical normality or disease. Data which are not normally distributed are not 'abnormal' but 'non-normal'. The examples of non-normal distributions include Poisson distribution and Binomial distribution. Generally data types such as scores and ranks are considered to be non-normally distributed.

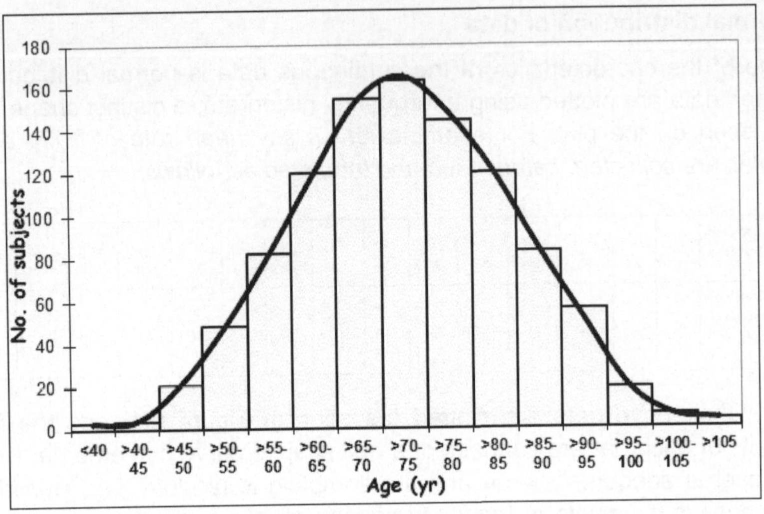

Figure 6.1 **Frequency distribution of heart rates of 1024 normal subjects**

She claims to have collected data from a large number of politicians and says none of the variables follows any known data distribution. So she is into creating a new model of distribution that can fit the body parameters from politicians.....

Skewed distribution

When one tail in a distribution curve is longer than the other, the distribution is no longer normal but skewed (see Figure 6.2). Symmetry and the shape which define the normal distribution are lost. Skew may occur either on the right side (positive) or left side (negative). Right sided skews are said to be more common. Skewed distribution may be converted to normal using transformation methods (discussed later).

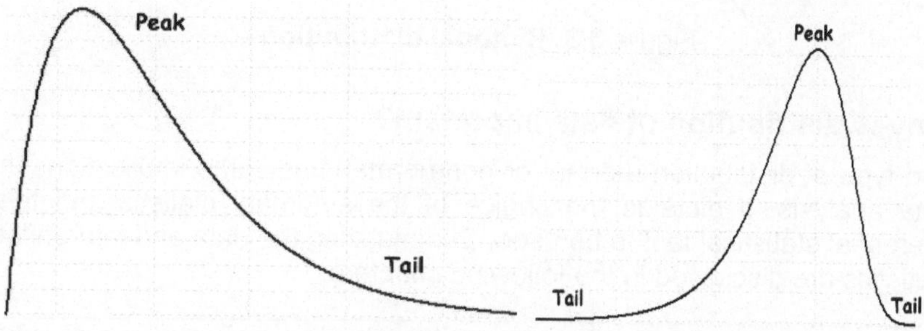

Figure 6.2 a **Positive skewing** Figure 6.2 b **Negative skewing**

Bimodal distribution

For some variables when the data are plotted on a frequency distribution graph, two distinct curves instead of one will emerge (see Figure 6.3). This indicates there are two distinct groups in the sample (based on the parameter for which the data are collected) and hence the sample is not homogenous (as far as the parameter is concerned). As shown in Figure 6.3 for example *estrogen levels measured in a mixed sample of males and females are plotted.* Estrogen levels are low in males and high in females. Even among males some will have relatively higher or lower values of estrogen when compared to majority of males. That is why there are two peaks. The smaller curve indicates the distribution of estrogen in males and the larger one in females. Of course there is an area of merger which indicates some males have higher estrogen levels and some females have lower levels of estrogen.

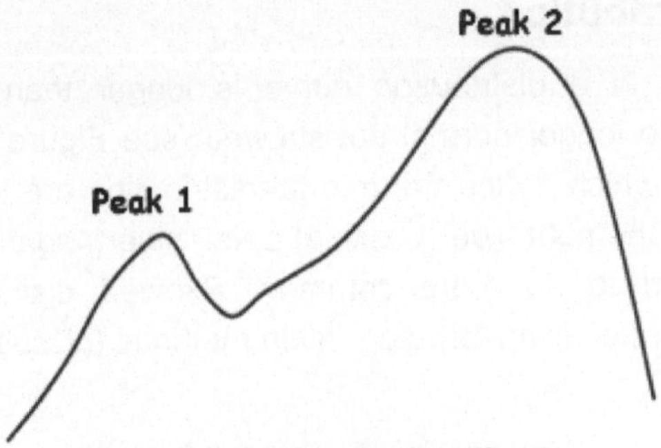

Figure 6.3 **Bimodal distribution**

Why is distribution of data important?

The type of distribution (normal or non-normal) has some implications in data analysis. It dictates the choice of the summary statistic and the inferential statistical test to be used. Summarizing the data and inferential statistics are discussed in the following chapters.

Post-reading Exercises

Identify the scale, the type and the distribution of data for the given variable :

Variable	Scale	Type	Converted to	Summarized as
Hear rate (beats/min)				
Pain				
No. of patients operated/day				
Blood sugar level mg%				
APGAR				
Presence of ADR				
Religion				
Temperature (Centigrade)				
Death				
Antibody titre				
Stage of cancer				

Scales : Nominal, Ordinal, Interval, Ratio

Type : Categorical/Qualitative, Numerical/Quantitative, Discrete, Continuous, Binomial

Converted to : Counts, Ranks/Scores, Not applicable

Summarized as : Proportion, Mean, Median, Mode

Chapter 7

Sample Size

Sampling explained

A statistics professor was describing sampling theory to his class, explaining how a sample can be studied and used to generalize to a population.

One of the students in the back of the room kept shaking his head. "What's the matter?" asked the professor. "I don't believe it," said the student, "why not study the whole population in the first place?"

The professor continued explaining the ideas of random and representative samples. The student still shook his head. The professor launched into the mechanics of proportional stratified samples, randomized cluster sampling, the standard error of the mean, and the central limit theorem.

The student remained unconvinced saying, "Too much theory, too risky, I couldn't trust just a few numbers in place of ALL of them." Attempting a more practical example, the professor then explained the scientific rigor and meticulous sample selection of the Nielsen television ratings which are used to determine how multiple millions of advertising dollars are spent.

The student remained unimpressed saying, "You mean that just a sample of a few thousand can tell us exactly what over 250 MILLION people are doing?"

Finally, the professor, somewhat disgruntled with the scepticism, replied, "Well, the next time you go to the campus clinic and they want to do a blood test...tell them that's not good enough ...tell them to TAKE IT ALL!!"

Kenn Finstuen

From http://my.ilstu.edu/~gcramsey/Gallery.html

7. Sample size

Importance of sample size

Factors affecting sample size

Calculation of sample size

Sample size (n)

One of the important aspects of planning a research project is calculation of sample size. The term 'sample size' refers to the number of subjects or animals required to be used in each group. It is denoted by the alphabet 'n'. The purpose of any medical research study is to draw one or more 'valid' conclusions about the population studied. Here the term population does not mean the general population but all the subjects (who have one or more common characteristics) being studied. For example *when hypertension is studied, all those suffering from hypertension will form the study population.* If Swiss albino rats are chosen for a study, then 'population' refers to these animals. Population varies according to the context in which it is used and one has to define the population which he wants to study.

Typically, a sample consisting of a certain number of subjects/animals is drawn, experimented upon and conclusions about the population are arrived at i.e., *test the 'sample' to conclude about the 'population'.* It would be ideal if one could study the whole population in order to draw valid conclusions about it. However this is an impossible and unnecessary task. That is why 'samples' are chosen from a population and tested to prove (or disprove) a hypothesis. The analogy is `checking a single grain of rice to see whether a whole pot full of rice is cooked or not'. Only one grain is taken as a sample and this is enough to come to a conclusion about a pot full of rice. Unfortunately, the same does not hold good in case of humans because of varying degrees of inter-individual variations. No conclusion can be arrived at just by testing a single subject. In the pot-rice analogy, one should remember, generally only one type of rice is used (e.g., *Basmati, Ponni or IR-8*) and hence most grains are almost similar in size, consistency and other characteristics. Suppose we mix three types of rice in equal parts, is it enough to test a single grain? If not, how many grains do we need to test? In human subjects where no two individuals are similar, how many subjects do we need to test to draw a realistic conclusion about a population?

For example *how many patients with 'type 1 diabetes mellitus' (DM) will have to be studied to conclude that all (or most) patients with DM lack insulin and hence the disease*? It is not possible to study all patients with DM in a country or the world. Then what is the minimum number of DM patients to be investigated to find out this correlation? As you may be aware just studying one or two patients will not offer definite conclusions since the observed findings (if any) may be due to chance and chance alone. One may not come across similar findings (observed in just two patients) in another set of similar patients. But if a finding is present in ten patients then there is a good chance of observing the same in most patients. So if the number is small, chances of finding out the truth is also small. To increase the chances of finding out the truth, one should have an adequate sample size which can be calculated using statistical methods.

Importance of sample size

Inappropriate sample size leads to problems (see Box 7.1). If the sample size is inadequate the investigator will end up drawing wrong conclusions. The whole study becomes futile and a waste of time and resources. If the size is more than adequate then too the resources are wasted. Wasting resources and unnecessarily subjecting patients or animals to experimentation is unethical. Choosing a correct sample size is one among the many factors that help the researcher successfully complete a study and draw valid conclusions without wasting resources and time.

Box 7.1 **Consequences of incorrect sample size**

1. Wrong conclusions
2. Poor quality research
3. Waste of resources (manpower, time and material)
4. Loss of money
5. Ethical problems
6. Delay in completion

Factors influencing the sample size

The factors which alter the number of required subjects in a study are listed in Box 7.2. The expected difference between groups (or the difference the researcher wants to detect) is one of the major factors. The question of how much difference one should expect must be answered by the researcher alone. Generally the minimum difference that is clinically useful (the difference which affects clinical considerations) to detect must be taken as the expected difference. For example *the researcher decides that a drug which reduces the diastolic blood pressure by at least 10 mm of Hg will be clinically useful in hypertension*. In this situation the minimum expected difference is 10 mm of Hg.

How to decide on the expected difference? This question is difficult to answer. The expected difference varies from study to study and decided on various practical aspects concerning the disease and the treatment. For example, *if you are a physician, will you be using an antihypertensive which when given in maximum dose reduces the blood pressure by only 2 mm Hg? If not, what about 4 mm Hg? If you are still not satisfied, will 6 mm Hg be sufficient? Keep on escalating the figure till the 'minimum' effect that satisfies you so that you can use the drug. That will give you the expected difference. It must be noted that it is a 'minimum' difference that satisfies the investigator and not the 'maximum' difference the drug can produce.*

Box 7.2 **Factors affecting sample size**

1. Minimum difference expected
2. Degree of variation among subjects
3. The level of significance desired
4. Power of the study desired
5. Drop-out rate
6. Non-compliance to treatment

If the expected difference is large, then a small number of subjects may be enough. If a small difference is expected then a large number of subjects have to be included in order to detect the difference successfully. To illustrate this, let us take an example of *two drugs which increase the heart rate. They are to be studied in two independent research projects. The minimum difference expected for the first drug is 10 beats per minute (bpm) and the second is 40 bpm which is comparatively larger than the first one. If other factors are comparably same, then the sample size needed for the first trial would be larger than that needed for the second one because small differences are difficult to detect*. An analogy could perhaps help. *We can easily see macro organisms with our naked eyes. For micro organisms we need powerful lenses since the power of our eye lens is not adequate to appreciate the smaller organisms*. The same holds good for sample size estimation too.

Another factor which influences the sample size is the variability of the data to be collected. If the data obtained from one patient to another patient vary very little, far fewer patients would be required than when inter-individual variability is high. For a given difference (10 bpm or 40 bpm) the size may be reduced if the `variation' in the heart rate among subjects is reduced by all possible means (selecting homogeneous subjects in a group is one way of reducing the variation). When variation is low, the deviation from the mean value is reduced in both control and test groups so that the overlapping of the values of both groups (within the study) is reduced. This allows the statistical test to successfully detect the difference (if it exists) even if the difference is small. Let us consider a hypothetical situation. Suppose there is a community where all males are identical in all characteristics. There is no difference whatsoever between the individuals in the height, weight, age, genetic factors and every other parameter. If we want to test the effect of a drug in the community, how many males do we need to recruit? The answer is just one. At the most 2, if we want to be doubly sure. Of course we know that such a community cannot exist unless its members are factory made clones belonging to a single batch.

The level of significance (alpha error) and beta error one wishes to tolerate are also important in determining the sample size. These are described in detail later (see example of sample size calculation). These errors are nothing but false positive rate and false negative rate of an experiment though in statistical parlance these are called alpha error and beta error respectively. When using a diagnostic kit, two important factors we keep in mind is its false positive rate and false negative rate. These errors can cause havoc, if the results are interpreted without taking them into consideration. Hence the manufacturers of diagnostic kits are concerned about these errors and try to reduce them by all means to keep them under a certain level. Similarly these errors occurring in an experiment have a direct bearing on the conclusions. It is not possible to predict the magnitude of the errors before the study but they can be calculated after the data collection is over. What researchers can do is to try to keep these errors under control by choosing an adequate sample size, instituting an appropriate study design and using techniques to eliminate bias. The maximum level that is acceptable for each of these errors is set before the study and this information is used to estimate the sample size. The actual level of errors occurring in a study is known after the study is over and if the actual levels exceed the levels set before, it is generally considered that the study has failed to show the difference between groups.

The drop out rate also should be taken into account when determining the size of the sample. This rate may vary with disease, treatment and place and may be estimated from ones own experience or published studies which make a mention of it. It is discussed in detail at the end of this chapter. Non-compliance to treatment by study subjects will increase the variability. This will necessitate the inclusion of more subjects to arrive at a valid conclusion.

Methods of sample size determination

Often, two "magic" numbers are used as sample size. Six if the study involves animals and eight (or 10 in some cases) in human experiments. This is a bad practice, albeit widely followed. But there are situations (dealt below) where one is forced to use arbitrary numbers. Another method is to find out from literature how many subjects were used in similar studies by others. The indiscriminate use of this practice must be discouraged since one may end up choosing an incorrect sample size for the study. Tables and nomograms are also available for estimating sample size. They are useful but they lack flexibility because they provide sample sizes for fixed levels of alpha and beta. The most appropriate and flexible method is to use the statistical formulae to calculate sample size. One can do it manually or use computer software packages and internet sites which can estimate sample size for a given situation.

She is very lucky. Using a sample size calculation software, she managed to show that the sample size needed is 0 and started writing the final report without doing the experiment.

Issues in calculation of sample size

Sample size determination may be ideal but in some situations it may not be possible, since the calculations are not straightforward. There are many formulae to calculate the sample size and the choice of a formula depends on the type of study and its design. Further, some prior data (like standard deviation of the variable or incidence of the disease studied) are required for calculating the size. If such data are not available, published studies of similar nature can be consulted and data from such studies may be used. Alternatively, pilot studies may be conducted to gather such data. There are some situations where sample size can only be guessed but not calculated. Examples include *pilot studies and exploratory studies*. In the former a small arbitrary number is chosen and in the latter a medium or a large sample size depending on the availability of cases, time required and other factors.

The expected difference which is used in sample size estimation is determined by its clinical, biological or practical importance. It may be difficult to determine such a difference if the compound under investigation is absolutely new and its importance is yet to be established. Initial studies with such compounds will be exploratory and an arbitrary sample size is used.

Toxicity studies in animals and phase I clinical trials guided by regulatory authorities do not follow the methods used for sample size calculation for studies testing hypothesis. It must be noted that such studies dictate researchers to follow the methods prescribed to meet the objectives of the study.

Example of sample size calculation

It is hypothesized that the dose of drug X needs to be adjusted when administered to Indians since the plasma half life ($t_{½}$) is higher in Indians when compared to Europeans. The investigator wants to test the hypothesis and calculate the sample size required. He needs the following information :

1. Variation of $t_{½}$ in Europeans (This information may be available from published papers which give mean $t_{½}$ and its standard deviation. If not, the investigator will have to conduct a pilot study.)

2. Variation of $t_{½}$ in Indians. (Either a pilot study to find out the variation needs to be performed or one should assume that the variation is not much different from that in Europeans and use the same value)

3. The difference one would like to detect.

   Suppose the $t_{½}$ in Europeans is 50 h and the investigator feels that the question of dosage adjustment would arise only if it is increased to at least 70 h in Indians. So he would like to detect a difference if it exceeds or equals 20 h. If the real difference is less than 20 h he does not want to detect it, since the detection is not going to be of any use as it may not require dosage adjustment.

4. The alpha or type I error one wishes to tolerate.

   Every study is prone for two types of errors i.e., *type I and type II*. What are the chances of the difference between two groups detected in the study being false positive? If the chances are less than 5% then it can be tolerated, since we consider 5% as low and tolerable. This type of error is called alpha error or type I error. The limit of probability of finding a difference when there is no real difference (false positive) must be decided at the beginning of the study. This is called significance level, i.e., *the level at which you consider your P values (probability values) significant.*

5. Power of the study.

   Power is the probability of finding out the difference between groups when it really exists. There are chances that the investigator may miss a real difference in a study and conclude that there is no difference when there really is one (type II error or false negative). The chances of this happening is more when the sample size is small. To find out the chances of detecting a real difference, power is calculated using the formula:

   Power = 100-type II error (beta)

   When the type II error is limited to 5% or 10% level, the power of the study will be 95% or 90% respectively. If the power is less than 80%, one may not be able to draw valid conclusions in a study, especially clinical trials comparing the efficacy of two treatments or drugs in patients.

"*The animals are different*" - Type I error is committed

"*The animals do NOT differ*" - Type II error is committed

In the above example the investigator would like to detect a difference of 20 h at a significance level of 5% (alpha error) with 90% probability of achieving statistical significance (power). The literature shows that the mean ± standard deviation of $t_{½}$ in Europeans is 49.8 ± 12.4h. The deviation in Indians is not available and assumed to be similar to that in Europeans i.e., *SD=12.4*. With this information the sample size can be calculated using the following formula.

$$n = \frac{(u+v)^2 \times (SD1^2 + SD2^2)}{(\mu 1 - \mu 2)^2}$$

Where

u is `one-sided' percentage point of the normal distribution corresponding to 100%-the power, for e.g., *if power = 90%, u = 1.28*

v is the percentage point of normal distribution corresponding to the (two sided) significance level, for e.g., *if significance level = 5%, v = 1.96* (see Table 7.1)

SD1 is the standard deviation of group 1 (12.4)

SD2 is the standard deviation of group 2 (12.4)

μ1- μ2 (i.e. *mean 1 - mean 2*) is the expected difference between the means (20)

$$n_{\text{(in each group)}} = \frac{(1.96+1.28)^2 \times (12.4^2 + 12.4^2)}{20^2}$$

$$= \frac{10.49 \times 307.52}{400}$$

$$= \frac{3325.88}{400}$$

$$= 8.06$$

So 8 volunteers are needed in each group to detect a difference of 20 h $t_{½}$ with 90% power at 5% significance level.

The above formula is useful only if sample is unpaired i.e., *two different groups and the variable is continuous (e.g., blood pressure) and not dichotomous* (e.g., *those which answer YES or NO. Does a drug produce a particular adverse effect or not?*). If a paired sample is used (e.g., *measurement of blood pressure in one group of volunteers before and after giving a drug*) the formula is slightly different. It is as follows:

$$n = \frac{(u+v)^2 \times (\text{SD of difference})^2}{(\mu 1 - \mu 2)^2}$$

The essential difference between the previous formula and this one is the standard deviation of difference to be observed in a sample is used in the later. For example, *the difference in measurement of blood pressure before and after drug administration in each individual is found out and standard deviation of this difference is calculated.*

The formulae for other situations such as epidemiological studies and the studies involving dichotomous variables are different and the readers are expected to refer to text books on statistics if they wish to calculate sample size for these studies.

From the above example it is evident that the sample size can be small when a large difference between means is expected. But one should not set the difference at a higher level for the sole purpose of reducing the sample size. One must work out the practically useful minimum difference to decide the difference he wants to detect. Otherwise the conclusions of the study may not be of any use in practice.

A flow chart for sample size determination is given below :

Determine the expected difference

↓

Find out the standard deviations of both groups

↓

Set the alpha error to be tolerated

↓

Decide the power of the study desired

↓

Select the appropriate formula

↓

Calculate the sample size using the formula

↓

Determine the drop out rate

↓

Give allowance for drop out rate

↓

Give allowance for non-compliance of treatment if possible

Table 7.1 **Percentage points for the standard normal distribution**

	% points	
P Value	One sided	Two sided
0.1	1.28	1.64
0.05	1.64	1.96
0.02	2.05	2.33
0.01	2.33	2.58
0.001	3.09	3.29

Drop outs

After the sample size is statistically calculated, drop-out rate of samples must be taken into account. When a study which extends over a period of a few weeks or months is carried out, the subjects/patients may drop out in the middle of it voluntarily (it is their right to drop out) or they may not turn up for a follow up session for some reason. In animals studies too, a few animals may die either due to natural causes or due to the experiment. Therefore the drop out rate must be calculated while deciding the size of the sample at the beginning to give allowance for drop out. This is not easy. If a pilot study is conducted, some idea of drop out rate may be obtained. Otherwise one has to use his experience to decide on the percentage of drop-out and the total number of subjects must be adjusted accordingly.

When a patient drops out it is the duty of the investigator to find out why he discontinued and record his response. This must be mentioned in the dissertation as well as the publication. The responses of volunteers may offer some clues on the adverse side of the experiment. If the volunteers/patients do not turn up for a follow up or subsequent sessions one should make sincere attempts to trace them. When the volunteers/patients cannot be traced, this information too must be mentioned in the write up.

After a study is completed....

When a study is completed and statistical analysis of significance between groups is carried out, one has to calculate the sample size again to see whether the size he has used is enough to draw a valid conclusion. This is because certain parameters are assumed or taken from another study (pilot study). The assumed values may vary from those actually obtained in the study. For example *it is assumed in the example cited above that in Indians the standard deviation of the variable to be studied is 12.4 (or this value may be obtained from a pilot study).* There is no guarantee that one would get a similar value in the study. Since the sample size is calculated using an assumed value, the actual size required could be different if the actual variation is very much different from the assumed one. So the sample size has to be calculated again using the values obtained in the study. If the results (of statistical test) are positive (significant difference between groups) one need not bother. If the results are negative (no difference between groups) and the sample size is inadequate one may not be able to draw any valid conclusion from the data since the power may be low. In such cases power of the study must be calculated to see if it is above 80%. If it is less than 80% one cannot conclude that there is 'no difference' but 'the study could not detect the difference' since the power was insufficient.

Post-reading Exercises

1. The mean diastolic blood pressure (SD) is observed to be 113 (12) mm Hg in pre-eclamptic pregnant women. A study is to be carried out to determine whether calcium supplementation would decrease the blood pressure. It is planned to include two groups of pregnant woman - one without supplementation (control group) and the other with supplementation (test group). Calculate the size of each group.
2. When an oral hypoglycemic agent is administered to patients with diabetes mellitus 20% are well controlled. A clinical trial is to be conducted to compare the extract of *Pterocarpus marsupium* which is claimed to be better than the hypoglycemic agent. It is decided that a 10% increase in control rate would be clinically important. The alpha and beta are set at 0.02 and 0.1 respectively. The results will be analysed using Chi Square test. How many patients would be required for the trial?
3. The hypotensive effect of a compound is to be studied in dogs. It was decided to administer the compound *i.v.* and measure the blood pressure before and 5 minutes after the administration. How many dogs are required?

Chapter 8

Statistical Tests of Significance and Choosing a Test

The ten commandments of statistical inference

1. Thou shalt not hunt statistical inference with a shotgun.
2. Thou shalt not enter the valley of the methods of inference without an experimental design.
3. Thou shalt not make statistical inference in the absence of a model.
4. Thou shalt honour the assumptions of thy model.
5. Thy shalt not adulterate thy model to obtain significant results.
6. Thy shalt not covet thy colleagues' data.
7. Thy shalt not bear false witness against thy control group.
8. Thou shalt not worship the 0.05 significance level.
9. Thy shalt not apply large sample approximation in vain.
10. Thou shalt not infer causal relationships from statistical significance

From http://www.xs4all.nl/~jcdverha/scijokes/8_1.html#subindex

8. Statistical tests of significance and choosing a test

Use of significance tests

Types of tests

Selection of a test

Null hypothesis

Degrees of freedom

Tests of significance

When a study designed to test a hypothesis is completed, the data are subjected to 'statistical procedures' to see whether the difference between groups is significant or not. These procedures are called statistical tests of significance and many such tests are available. Though the actual analysis is conducted later, the test(s) to be used should be identified at the planning stage and mentioned in the protocol. This requires knowledge of different types of tests and criteria for their usage. This chapter considers the commonly used statistical tests and illustrates on what basis a particular test is chosen for analysis. The philosophy behind significance testing is dealt later.

Why use significance tests?

Why should we subject the results of an experiment (data) to a statistical test? For example *it would be obvious that a student who scored above 90% marks is better than the other who scored less than 30% in all six tests.* In this case no statistical test is needed to decide who is better. But in research the difference between two (or more) groups is almost never that obvious. A biological experiment is subject to many variations and errors. As we are aware the quality of an effect of a drug may be same in all/most of the subjects but not the quantity. Consider the following hypothetical data :

Table 8.1 **The diastolic blood pressure before and after administration of a drug (HYPOTEN) in normal adult volunteers**

No.	Before drug (mm of Hg)	After drug (mm of Hg)
1	82	84
2	76	64
3	80	84
4	78	78
5	86	72
6	84	84
7	76	62
8	80	80
9	80	74
10	78	66

It is clear from Table 8.1 that in five subjects there is an obvious decrease in the BP, whereas in two subjects there is an increase and no change could be observed in the other three. In the light of the above data, is it possible to conclude that the drug "Hypoten" decreases BP? Is it possible to answer the question just by looking at the data? No, it is not, because it is not obvious. However, this is the type of data we are likely to obtain from an experiment.

In this type of situation one may suggest that means for both groups may be calculated to conclude whether the drug has a beneficial effect or not. This cannot solve the problem because it is necessary to draw a conclusion about the population from which the sample was drawn and not just the individuals (sample) who participated in the study. Since there are five cases which have not positively responded to the drug one may not be sure whether similar results will be obtained if the study is repeated i.e., *will the difference between groups and the proportion of non-responders be the same if another set of volunteers (from the same population) is tested?* Could it be possible that the drug is no better than placebo but because of mere chance there was a difference between the means of both groups? In simple terms, one has to know whether the difference obtained in the present study is real, or just due to chance and chance alone. To rule out (or prove it sometimes) the chance factor, the data have to be analyzed statistically before declaring that a drug or treatment is effective for the population concerned.

An analogy might help those find the above explanation difficult to understand. No statistics is required to conclude that a lion is different from a cow. Suppose you want to compare two trees in a forest, again no statistics is required to conclude which of the individual trees is taller. If two groups of trees are to be compared, calculation of mean heights may be sufficient to draw conclusions provided (a) the conclusion is limited to the groups (samples) only and not the populations of trees or (b) it is practically possible to measure the heights of all the trees in two populations. When two samples (groups) of trees (representing two populations of trees) where 'all' trees in one group (sample) are distinctly taller than 'all' trees in the other group are compared, statistics may not be needed/ may not be of much help to conclude which group is taller provided each group (i.e., *sample representing a population*) has adequate numbers. But if some trees in one group are taller than some in the other, some are equal in height and the remaining are shorter than the other, then there is a considerable overlap between groups. In this situation, use of statistics is necessary to conclude which group on the whole is taller than the other and this conclusion holds good to the entire population of trees to which the group belongs.

Why are there many tests?

Life would have been much simpler for many if only there is only one statistical test that can analyse data from any study. In fact there was a time either Student's 't' test or Wilcoxon test was used indiscriminately. But why do we need more than one test? An analogy would explain better. We use many measuring devices such as weighing balance, thermometer, measuring jar and measuring tape. Each of these devices measures a different characteristic. A thermometer can measure only the temperature, a weighing balance the weight and not *vice versa*. We have already seen data fall into different types – nominal, ordinal, continuous, and discrete. Studies use different experimental designs and they will have a varying number of groups – one, two, three and so on. So the characteristics are different for different studies and hence a single test is just not sufficient/appropriate for analyzing data from these studies.

What are the tests available?

The tests can be broadly classified into 'parametric' and 'non-parametric'. Parametric tests use parameters such as mean and SD/SEM for analysis and non-parametric tests do not. Box 8.1 lists some of the commonly used tests under each category.

Box 8.1 **Tests of significance**

Parametric	Non-parametric
1. Paired t test	1. Wilcoxon signed rank test
2. Student's t test (unpaired)	2. Wilcoxon rank sum test (Mann-Whitney Test)
3. One-way ANOVA	3. Kruskal-Wallis test
4. Repeated measures ANOVA	4. Friedman two-way test
5. Two-way ANOVA	5. Spearman's rank correlation
6. Correlation analysis	6. Chi-square test
7. Regression analysis	

She has used every available statistical test on her data but she is not getting the much wanted P<0.05. Either she has to throw her study into the dustbin or repeat it on us. I hope she does not choose the later.

Parametric tests

When a parametric test is used the variable under investigation (e.g., *heart rate*) must be normally distributed (most of the times it is assumed). If the data are skewed, transformation techniques can be used so that the data would be suitable for parametric tests. Alternatively non-parametric tests can be used for skewed or non-normally distributed data. When a variable is normally distributed a suitable parametric test is preferred because the parametric tests are much more robust than their non-parametric equivalents.

1. Student's `t' test (Unpaired `t' test)

   This test is a parametric test described by W.S.Gossett whose pen name was 'Student'. It is used for small samples i.e., *less than 30.* There are different formulae for paired and unpaired samples called paired `t' test and unpaired `t' test. Paired `t' is used for a group which is its own control (e.g., *blood pressure measured before and after a drug in a sample*) and unpaired `t' for comparing two different groups one of which may be control and the other test group.

   This test is used when:

   - the data are quantitative,
   - it is needed to compare <u>NOT</u> more than two means,
   - the sample size is small (ideally < 30),
   - the data are distributed normally,
   - the standard deviations (SD) of both the means are almost same or the SD of one group is not twice greater or lesser than that of another.

2. Analysis of variance (ANOVA)

   This test is to compare the means of three or more groups together. For example *the mean haemoglobin levels of Indians living in different regions of India (North, South, East and West) are to be compared. Samples from states belonging to the four regions are taken and the mean haemoglobin level for each region is determined. These means are compared together to ascertain any difference between them.* One should not (or need not) individually compare each mean with the remaining means (e.g., *north vs south, north vs east, north vs west and so on*). One-way analysis of variance is used to compare all the means together to find out whether there is any statistically significant regional difference in mean haemoglobin levels. Two-way analysis can be used in the above situation if the influence of gender (apart from the region) is also to be taken into consideration. In this case the data are classified by two factors i.e., *region and gender.*

   This test is used when the :

   - groups to be compared are defined by just one factor-region in the above example (use one-way analysis of variance),
   - groups are based on two factors-region and gender in the above example (use two-way analysis of variance). In this

case the objectives are to find out whether the haemoglobin levels are influenced by (a) region, (b) gender and (c) interaction of region and gender,

- data are normally distributed.

As said above, ANOVA will show whether the means are significantly different between groups but does not indicate which group is significantly different from which one. For example *when three means (A, B, C) are to be compared :*

- It is wrong to make comparisons individually using a 't' test (A *vs* B, A *vs* C, B *vs* C).
- Use one-way ANOVA and find out the P value.
- If $P < 0.05$, then individual comparisons can be made using a suitable post-hoc test to determine which pairs are significantly different.
- There are many post-hoc tests such as Bonferroni, Tukey, Dunnett and Student-Newman-Keul. A suitable test should be used.

3. Correlation Coefficient (r)

Correlation coefficient is calculated to find out the degree of linear (straight line) association between two variables. For example, *to find out whether there is a correlation between blood insulin levels and the blood sugar in type 2 diabetes mellitus patients, data on blood sugar level and insulin level from 20 or more patients can be collected and the correlation coefficient may be calculated.* If the correlation is good and statistically significant it can be concluded that two variables tested have good linear association. The correlation may be positive (i.e., *when one variable increases, the other also increases correspondingly*) or negative (i.e., *when one variable increases, the other decreases correspondingly*)

This test should be used when:

- the association between 'two' variables is to be determined (Remember: t test deals with a single variable i.e., *difference between two groups with regard to a single variable*),
- both the variables are continuous and distributed normally.

One has to look at a scatter plot of the data before placing any importance on the magnitude of correlation. Association does not mean causation. This test determines the association between two variables but does not indicate whether the variables are causally related.

4. Regression

   The dependence of one variable on the other is described mathematically using this test. It is used to estimate a dependence relationship so that one variable can be predicted from the other. For example, *in a concentration verses time plot of a drug, we can predict the concentration at a given time*. Correlation coefficient cannot be used for such predictions as it indicates just the strength of association. Normally the 'predictor' or 'explanatory' variable is plotted on the X axis (time in the above example) and the 'response' or 'dependent' variable 'concentration' on the Y axis.

   To use regression analysis:

   - the dependent variable must be normally distributed,
   - the relationship should be linear,
   - the variability (SD) of dependent variable (Y) should be same for each explanatory variable (in the example above, the mean concentrations for each time point should have more or less same SD values).

Non-parametric tests

These tests do not make any assumptions about the distribution. They are preferred when the data are not normally distributed.

1. Wilcoxon rank tests (signed rank and rank sum tests):

   These tests are non-parametric equivalents of `t' tests. Wilcoxon signed rank is used for paired data and Wilcoxon rank sum is used in case of unpaired data.

2. Analysis of variance (Kruskal-Wallis and Friedman):

   These are similar to parametric ANOVA tests. Kruskal-Wallis test is used for one-way analysis of variance and Friedman test is for two-way analysis of variance by ranks. The latter is also said to be equivalent of parametric repeated measures ANOVA.

3. Correlation:

   Spearman's rank correlation and Kendall's rank correlation are the non-parametric equivalents of correlation coefficient test.

4. Chi square test (χ^2 test):

   Chi refers to a Greek letter (pronounced as 'kai' not 'chai/chee'). This test is a goodness of fit test and can be used to find out the association between variables, e.g., *whether smoking is associated with lung cancer.* This test is useful in various situations where proportions or percentages of two groups are compared. e.g., *proportions of died and survived in treated and untreated children with diarrhea can be compared.* There is no parametric equivalent for the test.

Parametric or non-parametric test?

Which test to use? It is advisable to use a parametric test wherever possible. If the data are skewed, a suitable transformation method may be applied and the transformed data may be subjected to a parametric test. Only when this is not possible, a non-parametric test may be used.

How to choose a test?

A test is chosen based on the characteristics of the data and the study design. The following characteristics influence the choice of a test:

1. *Type (expression) of data:* Nominal (proportion), Ordinal(Scores/Ranks), Interval/Ratio (Continuous/Discrete).
2. *Distribution of data:* Normal or non-normal.
3. *No. of groups or data sets:* 1, 2 or more (some studies will have only one group of volunteers but each one will be measured repeatedly over a period of time. In this case the no. of group will be 1 but the no. of data sets which will be 2 or more will dictate the choice of the test e.g., *blood pressure measured in 10 volunteers daily for one week*).
4. *Study design:* paired, unpaired.
5. *Type of analysis:* comparison (of means/medians) or association (correlation between two variables) or regression (to predict one variable from the other).

Having decided the above, one can find out the test to be used from Table 8.2. A row must be chosen based on the type of data and its distribution (no. 1 & 2- see above). A column must be chosen based on the number of groups/data sets, design, type of analysis (no. 3-5 above). The cell where the chosen column and the row meet indicates the test to be used.

Worked out example

A study was planned to compare the pain scores of three drugs in three different groups of patients. What test should be used for significance testing?

With above information the following could be identified:

1. *Type of data – Scores summarized as median*
2. *Distribution of data - Non-normal*
3. *No. of groups – 3*
4. *Study design – unpaired*
5. *Type of analysis – comparison*

Looking at Table 8.2, the row that matches criteria 1 and 2 above is row no. R2 and the column that matches the criteria 3, 4 and 5 is column no. C1d. The cell where C1d and R2 meet indicates "Kruskal-Wallis test".

Please note that the list of tests in Table 8.2 is not exhaustive. The table is simplified and it lists only a few tests. It is given here to demonstrate how to select a test for statistical analysis of data.

Table 8.2 **How to choose a statistical test?**

		C1				**C2**	**C3**
		Comparison				**Association of two variables**	**Regression analysis of two variables**
		of 2 data sets		**of >2 data sets**			
		Paired	**Unpaired**	**Paired**	**Unpaired**		
		C1a	**C1b**	**C1c**	**C1d**		
R1	**Normally distributed continuous data (summarised as means)**	Paired t test	Unpaired t test	Repeated Measures ANOVA	One-way ANOVA	Pearson correlation	Linear regression
R2	**Scores, ranks and non-normally distributed continuous data (summarised as medians)**	Wilcoxon singed rank test	Wilcoxon rank sum test (Mann-whitney test)	Friedman test	Kruskal-Wallis test	Spearman's rank correlation	Nonparametric regression
R3	**Dichotomous data (summarised as proportions)**	Mc Nemar's test	Fisher's test or Chi square test	Cochrane Q	Chi square test	Contingency coefficients	Logistic regression

Readers are asked to refer to text books of statistics on how to apply a test. Many books explain in detail with worked out examples. Statistics software packages can also be tried. It is advised to consult a statistician or someone experienced in statistical methods to choose a test.

What do these tests do?

Statistical tests, in general, use the data to calculate the probability of getting a difference between groups by chance or luck (when the real difference does not exist). If the probability is "low" (what can be considered "low" is to be decided by the investigator - this is discussed later) the difference obtained is taken to be "statistically" significant. The statistical tests use certain formulae/procedures based on certain concepts/assumptions to calculate the P (Probability) values, which reveal whether a difference is statistically significant or not (real or false). A significant difference is the one which is unlikely to have occurred by chance.

Null hypothesis

We have already discussed what a research hypothesis is and how to formulate one. There is another type of hypothesis which is called null hypothesis. Research hypothesis leads to null hypothesis which is also called statistical hypothesis. Research hypothesis states that there is a difference between groups. But null hypothesis states the opposite i.e., *there is no difference between groups.* Null hypothesis (which assumes that there is no difference between groups) is the one that is tested by the significance tests and is either rejected or not rejected. This hypothesis, if not rejected concludes the observed difference between the groups could be due to chance alone and not due to a systematic cause. On the other hand its rejection signifies that the observed difference between groups is statistically significant indeed. How and when you will reject or not reject the null hypothesis is discussed here.

Here is an example of null hypothesis

> *Erythromycin does NOT relieve gastric stasis occurring due to complete vagotomy.*

This is called statistical hypothesis because the statistical tests of significance begin by hypothesizing that there is no real difference between groups and the observed difference is due to chance alone. These tests then calculate the probability of obtaining the observed value (difference) due to chance (spurious result). This is called P value. The idea is to reject the null hypothesis if the probability (of observing a difference when there is no real difference) is small and thereby accept the research hypothesis (or reject the null hypothesis).

A significance test can be equated to a judge in the court of law. At the beginning of the trial, the accused is 'not' guilty (no difference) until proved otherwise (null hypothesis). If the prosecution (researcher) presents a strong evidence (data) against the accused, the judge (statistical test) rejects the null hypothesis and pronounces the accused guilty (significant difference). If the prosecution fails, the null hypothesis is 'not' rejected which means the accused is 'not' guilty (no difference).

P values

On applying the tests described above, one will end up with a value that may be called t, F, r and χ^2 depending upon the test used. For example *'t' (t statistic) is the value obtained at the end of a 't' test.* After obtaining this value refer to a table (given in almost all books on statistics) showing critical values for 't distribution' to find out the P (probability) value using the 'degrees of freedom' and 't' value. At this juncture it is appropriate to explain the concept of the degrees of freedom.

Degrees of freedom (d.f.)

Degrees of freedom can be calculated by subtracting 1 from number of subjects (n–1) for each group when 't' test is applied. For example *the degrees of freedom for a study consisting of two different groups of ten animals each is 10+10–2=18 (n=10 in each group).* For a single group (paired sample) it will be 10–1=9 (n=10). The rationale of calculating the degrees of freedom is based on a concept that one could not have exercised his freedom to select all the elements (animals in the above case) in a sample. The number of elements that can be chosen freely is called the degrees of freedom.

For example *if x in the following equation is 4 then y must be 6.*

$$x + y = 10$$

One has freedom to choose x but not y or *vice versa*. When one element is chosen, the other is automatically determined. So the degree of freedom in this case is one. In the following example, however there is freedom to choose two say x and y but not z if values 2 and 5 are allotted for x and y respectively.

$$x + y + z = 10$$

The degrees of freedom in this case is two since the third value is fixed when two values can be freely chosen. The third value is dependent on the other two and not freely available. So for n numbers, the degrees of freedom will be n–1. The readers must note that the method of calculating the degrees of freedom varies with the statistical test used. Books on statistics must be consulted for the exact calculation.

How does a P value help us?

P value lets us conclude the study – whether the groups are significantly different or not. Remember the conclusions drawn are about the population i.e., *they are applicable to populations from which the samples were drawn*. The obtained P value which ranges from 0-1 is compared with the significance level set at the beginning of the study (alpha or type I error). If P is less than the significance level (used as a cut-off), the groups are considered to be different. More details about P value and its interpretation are dealt later.

Other than the tests of significance (where one ends up with a P value), there are some statistical procedures or methods which readers will come across very often. These procedures do not calculate P values but yield some measures that will be useful for clinical decision making. The following is the brief account of a few important methods (summarized in Box 8.2)

Risk and odds

These are measures of association determined in cohort and case-control studies. Suppose one thousand heavy smokers and one thousand non-smokers are followed up for 20 years and the occurrence of lung cancer is recorded. One hundred smokers and 10 non-smokers develop cancer. The absolute risk in each group is calculated as follows :

Absolute risk (over 20 years) =

no. of subjects who develop disease during follow-up /
no. of subjects free of disease at the start

In the above example the absolute risks in each group are

Smokers 100/1000 = 10%
Non-smokers 10/1000 = 1%

The risk is expressed as percentage. It is the probability of an event occurring over a specific period of time.

With the above measures, one can calculate the relative risk (10/1 =10) which means the risk of developing cancer is 10 times for smokers when compared to non-smokers. It may be noted that relative risk not expressed as % as in the case of risk.

The odds is calculated by dividing number of occurrences by the number of non-occurrences.

Odds of disease (over 20 years) =

no. of subjects who develop disease during follow-up /
no. of subjects who do NOT develop disease during follow-up

Smokers = 100/900 = 0.11

Non-smokers = 10/990 = 0.01

Odds has no units. The odds ratio is calculated by dividing odds of smokers by that of non-smokers (0.11/0.01 = 11). The odds ratio and relative risk would be very close if the risk is low. Though in cohort studies (prospective studies) both the measures can be calculated, generally relative risk is preferred.

For case-control studies (retrospective studies) only odds ratio can be determined but not relative risk since the patients cannot be followed forward in time and the absolute risk cannot be calculated. The odds ratio in a case-control study is calculated as follows :

$$OR = \frac{\text{No. of cases exposed / no. of controls exposed}}{\text{No. of cases not exposed / no. of controls not exposed}}$$

Many case-control studies reported in journals mention relative risk rather than odds ratio. Since these studies deal with rare cases and the odds ratio is in close approximation to relative risk where the risk is low, it may be justified to mention odds ratio as relative risk for the sake of convenience and better understanding. (Daly LE, Bourke GJ. Interpretation and uses of medical statistics. 5th ed. Oxford, U.K.: Blackwell Science, 2000:167)

Agreement and validity

In studies where methods are compared and we need to find out whether two quantitative tests agree (with each other) or not, correlation coefficient cannot be used as the test of significance. Correlation tests can determine whether the values correlate or not i.e., *when one parameter increases, the other correspondingly increases or decreases.* For example, *values (of a drug level in blood) obtained by RIA method agrees with a HPLC method or not, cannot be found out by determining how well the measurements from two instruments correlate.* Only if the readings from two instruments are the same (or almost same) for blood samples, we can call the method/instruments agree. This cannot be tested by the conventional correlation tests. To find out the agreement one has to calculate the difference between two readings for each blood sample and mean and SD should be calculated for the difference obtained. If this mean difference is very small or negligible, we can say the methods agree very well on average. Further 95% limits of agreement can be calculated by mean $\pm$ 2 SD. However there is no predefined acceptable level of agreement. It all depends on the clinical situation and the decision of the researcher.

If two qualitative tests agree or not can be found out by calculating k (Kappa) value. For example *if the diagnoses of two physicians agree or not can be determined by calculating k.* The method of calculating k is not described here and the readers are advised to consult a statistics book.

Box 8.2 **Some common statistical procedures**

Parameter	Purpose	Situation
Absolute risk Relative risk	To find out the risk of developing a disease upon exposure to a factor (e.g., *cancer and smoking*)	Prospective study (Cohort study) where exposed group and control group are followed forward in time
Odds ratio	To find out the ratio of the odds of a disease subsequent to exposure to a factor (e.g., *foetal malformations detected at delivery and drug intake in the first trimester*)	Retrospective study (Case-control study) where cases (patients) and control subjects are followed backwards in time
Agreement (95% agreement limits; Kappa)	To find out whether two methods/tests agree or not	Method comparison studies involving (a) two quantitative tests (e.g., *whether two glucometer readings agree or not*) (b) two qualitative tests (e.g., *whether diagnoses by two physicians agree or not*)
Validity (Sensitivity, Specificity)	To find out whether a test is valid by comparing it with a gold standard (e.g., *Diagnosis based on CT scan results is compared with autopsy findings*)	Validity based on a gold standard

The validity of a test can be determined by comparing it with a gold standard. For example, *a new diagnostic test is developed for a disease and it has to be validated. The gold standard available is clinical diagnosis or autopsy finding. Patients undergo the diagnostic test as well as clinical/autopsy examination. The diagnostic test may be positive for some and negative for the rest. Similar results could be obtained with autopsy examination. With these results, we can calculate the sensitivity, specificity, false positive rate and false negative rate.* Whether the test is valid or not should be decided by the researcher depending on the values of above measurements, clinical condition and how much false positive/negative rates can be tolerated. There are no predefined acceptable levels of validity.

Post-reading Exercises

Choose an appropriate statistical test for the following studies :

1. 10,000 smokers and 10,000 non-smokers were followed for 10 years. During this period 1221 smokers and 213 non-smokers developed IHD.
2. The antihypertensive effect of a new drug was measured in 20 hypertensive patients. Baseline diastolic BP was measured on day 0 (109 $\pm$ 11 mm Hg). The drug was given daily for 6 months and the blood pressure was measured at the end of each month (105 $\pm$ 9, 101 $\pm$ 12, 98 $\pm$ 8, 92 $\pm$ 11, 90 $\pm$ 7, 84 $\pm$ 10 mm Hg).
3. Yanomami Indians do not seem to develop hypertension and there is not even an age related increase in BP (**INTERSALT Study, 2003**). Do their blood pressure vary with bodyweight? To find out this, BP and weight of 1000 Indians aged between 40-60 years of age were measured. The mean diastolic BP was 84.24 $\pm$ 2.8 mm Hg and the mean body weight was 62.43 $\pm$ 15.23 kg.
4. Four weight loss programmes were compared with control in 5 groups of 10 patients each. At the end of 6 months the fall in cholesterol levels (mmol/l) was as follows: 0.29 $\pm$ 0.8 (control), 0.55 $\pm$ 0.7 (prog-1), 0.35 $\pm$ 0.6 (prog-2), 0.5 $\pm$ 0.5(prog-3), 0.5 $\pm$ 0.18(prog-4).
5. Hepatic damage was scored (1 to 6) using histopathology of liver in 2 groups of 10 patients each. The median damage was 4.0 in test group and 2.5 in control.
6. The wound healing effects of three drugs (topical creams) were tested in patients with diabetic foot ulcer. Three groups of patients (10 each) were administered either one of the drugs and the effect was measured in scores(0-5; 0 -No healing; 5- Complete healing)

Worked Example – *Task:* Food intake in 2 groups of adult, healthy subjects after administration of an antiobesic drug HMR1426 in one group and placebo in other was measured. The mean intake for twenty four hours was 0.8 $\pm$ 0.2 kg and 1.34 $\pm$ 0.24 kg.

Aim - *To see whether the drug alters food intake.*

Analysis type - *Comparison of means*

Parameter to be analysed - *food intake*

No. & Name of the groups / data sets to be analysed - *2; saline & HMR1426*

Distribution of data (Normal or Non-normal) - *Normal*

Design (Paired or Unpaired) - *Unpaired*

STATISTICAL TEST TO BE USED - ***Unpaired t*** (to be chosen from Table 8.2)

Chapter 9

Protocol Writing

Why God failed to get a grant from the NIH?

Once God submitted a proposal/protocol for funds to create another world. His protocol was rejected for the following reasons :

1. He had only one major publication which was in Hebrew and Greek.
2. His last publication was way too far back in the past and it had no references.
3. It wasn't published in a refereed, indexed journal.
4. Nobody has ever been able to replicate his experiment.
5. He never got permission from the ethics board to use human subjects.
6. When subjects didn't behave as predicted, he deleted them from the sample.
7. The proposal/protocol does not explain the problem, the justification and the objectives clearly.
8. The utility of the expected outcome of the proposal is doubtful

From http://www.xs4all.nl/~jcdverha/scijokes/8_11.html#1226_4

9. Protocol writing

What is a research protocol?

A research protocol is a well organized framework of instructions and procedures to be implemented in a systematic manner for the conduct of research. A research protocol by convention means a preliminary draft in which the information and/or knowledge needed for the actual conduct of an experiment is compiled briefly to outline the execution of the study.

What is the need for a protocol?

A clear and concise protocol guides the researcher step by step throughout the study and also provides solutions to problems that may arise during the course of the research project. Ideally the protocol should be prepared in consultation with the guide to incorporate his/her suggestions or modifications. This helps in plugging loopholes in the plan of study.

A good protocol can serve as a framework when writing the manuscript after completing the research. It keeps the researcher on track by efficient management of time and resources. It also allows the institute research council (IRC), institute ethics committee (IEC) and funding agencies to judge the proposed research work.

Hence a protocol is an essential prerequisite for any scientific research and no research work should be conducted before finalizing the protocol.

Elements of a research protocol:

The components of a protocol can be summarized as follows

1. Title
2. Names and affiliations of all investigators with contact details (phone numbers, email ID)
3. Introduction – the actual research problem and justification
4. Aims and objectives
5. Hypothesis

6. Review of literature
7. Methodology *(Mnemonic : PICO)*

    Study design

    Population – inclusion & exclusion criteria

    Intervention – details of intervention/drug (formulation, dose, frequency of administration), duration of intervention and the no. of follow up visits

    Comparator – no. of groups, control (standard drug/placebo) and size of the sample in each group

    Outcome – primary (efficacy), secondary (safety, ADRs) parameters to be measured

8. Brief procedure
9. Statistics

    Sample size calculation

    Statistical test for each parameter

    Level of significance

    Method of analysis

10. Ethical issues
11. References
12. Signature of the investigator, guide, co-guide & Head of the department

Great. I have all the results with me. All you have to do is to write a protocol for these data, submit it to the research committee and ethics committee and get the approval to do the study.

How to write?

1. *Title:* It should be short, clear and concise. It should describe the purpose of the study and incorporate the study design.
2. *Names and affiliations of all investigators with contact details:* Take care to mention the name of the guide and co-guide(s) correctly without spelling mistakes. Contact information should be accurate, with mobile number and email ID.
3. *Introduction:* It should include the background of the study and clearly state the lacunae and the researchable problem. This section should also mention the justification for the study.
4. *Aims and objectives:* Aims should describe the broad goals of the study. The specific objectives can be divided into primary and secondary ones. A dissertation/thesis usually has only one primary objective. The objectives should be specific, measurable, attainable, relevant and time bound.
5. *Hypothesis:* Hypothesis is a research question in statement form. The readers are advised not to confuse the research hypothesis with the null hypothesis tested during statistical analysis.
6. *Review of literature:* It is a very short summary of current knowledge in the topic. It should explain the limitations encountered till date and the controversies with evidence. Concentrate on the best studies that are closest to yours.
7. *Methodology:*

   Study design: State the design of the study – descriptive, cross sectional, observational (prospective/retrospective), experimental (animal), clinical trial.

   Population and sample: Clearly mention population to be studied, the subject selection (inclusion and exclusion) criteria and setting of the study.

   Intervention: The nature of intervention (drug therapy/surgical procedure) should be mentioned. If it is drug therapy, the name of the drug, dose, formulation, route and frequency of administration, duration of therapy should be clearly specified. If it is an animal study and the control group gets the solvent, the name of the solvent should be given.

   Comparator: The number of groups in the study, sample size of each group, the details of control group (healthy volunteers/patients) including the intervention (standard drug/placebo) should be given in this section.

Outcome: The outcomes of the study should be clearly defined. Efficacy of the intervention is usually kept as the primary outcome and the safety parameters and adverse drug reactions form the secondary outcome. The end point of the study should also be written. The end point can be clinical (relief of pain), surrogate (serum liver enzyme levels) or composite, in which the participant may experience any one of the events (e.g., *An end point may be defined if any one of the following occurs – ST-T segment elevation in ECG or hypokinesia of ventricles in echocardiogram or elevation of AST, ALT and LDH in serum*). The parameters to be measured should also be listed.

My boss has submitted to ICMR a 162 paged protocol to measure 258 parameters from 20,583 patients with common cold to be studied over a period of 99 years.

8. *Brief procedure:* Describe the procedure of the study/data collection methods in clear and simple words. It should explain the sequence of events like baseline investigations that will be carried out on the participants, the interventions made, timing of sample collection/measurement and follow up visits.

9. *Statistics:* The method of sample size calculation (minimum expected difference, standard deviation, power, drop out percentage, software used) should be mentioned. The statistical test to be used for each parameter should be specified clearly. It is common practice to write 'appropriate statistical tests will be used'. This is strongly discouraged. The level of significance and the method of analysis should be written.

10. *Ethics:* The risks and benefits of the study and ethical issues (if any) should be described. The incentives, remuneration, compensation given to the subject/patient (if any) should also be mentioned.
11. *Reference:* The references should be current and relevant. It is advisable to follow the Vancouver style of referencing which is used by many journals.

What next?

1. *Getting signatures:* Signatures of the guide and co-guide(s) should be taken. It is better to affix the seal for each one. The date the protocol is signed should be mentioned.
2. *Approval from IRC and IEC:* A copy of the protocol should be submitted for approval from IRC and IEC. Informed consent document (ICD) written in English and in the vernacular (local) language should accompany the application.
3. *Data handling and record keeping:* Case record form (CRF) should be made incorporating all the demographic details and parameters measured. Master chart using a spread sheet software (e.g., *Microsoft Excel*) should be prepared with all relevant data and should be updated regularly.
4. *Clinical trials registration:* All clinical trials should be registered in the clinical trials registry of India (CTRI). Most of the journals have now made it mandatory for clinical trials to be registered for them to be published.

Post-reading Exercises

Comment on the protocol given below :

Protocol

(to be submitted to the Institute Research Committee for approval)

Title : Role of Yoga in Modifying Certain Functions in Diabetic Patients

Principal Investigator :	Supandi M
Co-Investigator :	Muniandi S
Address :	CIMRI, New Nagar, Newcherry
Phone & Fax numbers	0473-2271969
Email ID :	supa@supa.com

Background & justification for the study :

It is known that patients with Type II diabetes mellitus (Type II DM) have a high mortality rate. Most of them die due to diseases such as myocardial infarction, heart failure, or stroke[1]. Scientists have linked QT lengthening to an increased risk of unexpected deaths in Type 2 DM patients with severe autonomic neuropathy[2-4]. This lengthening is associated with high insulin levels (Metabolic Syndrome) that cause Na reabsorption, and enhance smooth muscle contractility. This results in hypertension. Hypertension in diabetic patients aggravates both macro and microvascular disease, especially nephropathy. It is essential to lower blood pressure to below 135/85 mm Hg in diabetic patients. This may be done with medicines alone, nonpharmacological means alone or in combination of both in mild cases.

Yoga has been applied in the field of therapeutics in modern times. Yoga has given the patient hope to reduce medication and slow the progress of disease. *Yoga* employs stable postures or asanas and breath control or pranayama. Through regular practice of these, the autonomic equilibrium shifts towards a relative parasympathetic dominance. Parasympathetic balance is essentially concerned with conserving and restoring bodily resources and energies. This is achieved by inhibiting the heart and alimentary activity, promoting secretion. The possible role of yoga in reducing the blood pressure in Type 2 DM patients has been established in south, east and west Indian populations[5,6,7]. Hence we set out to study the same in the north Indian population.

Objective(s) :

1. To study the effect of forty days of Yogic exercises on blood pressure and cardiac functions in Type II
2. To study the effect of 3 weaks of Yogic exercises on blood glucose level, glycosylated hemoglobin.

Work done already on the subject of research :

Sampath et. al. conducted a large scale, randomized controlled trial of Yoga in modifying blood pressure and other cardiovascular parameters in patients with hypertension[5] and established its role in reducing the blood pressure. Gupta et. al. studied the beneficial effects of yoga in diabetes in a few hospitals in Mumbai and Kolkata[6-7]. We conducted a pilot study in normal adult healthy volunteers and it was found that there was no effect of Yoga on blood pressure[unpublished data].

Method(s) :

Selection of subjects

Patients of type 2 diabetes mellitus of 30-60 years with history of diabetes of 1-10 years will be selected. Patients of nephropathy, retinopathy (proliferative) and coronary artery disease will be excluded.

Design & Procedure

The patients will be recommended on diet and oral hypoglycemic drugs as per standard clinical practice. They will be assessed before and after 40 days of Yoga asanas for biochemical and autonomic parameters.

Biochemical parameters

Plasma glucose levels will be estimated[9]. Plasma glycosylated hemoglobin (GHb) will be estimated by fast ion-exchange resin separation method using human GmbH kit[10].

Autonomic parameters

The pulse rate will be recorded. Blood pressure will be measured using mercury sphygmo-manometer. QT interval will also be measured in lead II ECG. QT interval was measured from the onset of QRS to the end of T wave. Since ventricular depolarization (diastole) is affected by change in heart rate, QT interval is standardized for rate using corrected QT interval Bazett formula QTc = QT /√RR interval.

Analysis

The data will be analysed using suitable statistical tests.

Expected outcome :

The study will establish the influence of Yoga on cardiovascular parameters and diabetic patients may be treated with yoga for hypertension rather than drugs.

References :

1. Mortality and survival diabetes mellitus. Wikepedia. Accessed on 12-10-2007
2. Sawicki PT, R Dahne, Bender R, Berger M. Prolonged QT interval as a predictor of mortality in diabetic neuropathy. NEJM 1996;39:77-81.
3. Ewing, Boland, Neilson. Autonomic neuropathy QT interval lengthening and unexpected deaths in male diabetic patients. BMJ 2007; 204-209

4. Corrected QT interval in relation to severity of diabetic autonomic neuropathy. Ind J Pharm 1997;39:51-6.
5. JC Sampath, G Williams. Text Book of Diabetes, 1997;2:(Second Edition).
6. Gupta DD, Khardori R. Diabetes Control Care 1978.
7. P Trinder. Determination of glucose in blood using glucose oxidase with an alternative oxygen receptor. Ann Clin Biochem 1969;6:24.
8. Swamy Vyas Dev Ji Translated by Bala-Brahmachari Dr. Ram Pyari Shastri. First Steps to Higher Yoga. Yoga Niketan Trust, Gangotri, Uttar-Kashi, Rishikesh (Uttarakhand). The Raisana

Chapter 10

Pilot Study

An unwritten footnote in a paper

We ran 12 pilot studies and finally got the design to work after threatening the subjects with bodily harm.

Edwin A. Locke, Ronan M Conroy and others

From http://www.xs4all.nl/~jcdverha/scijokes/8_2.html

10. Pilot study

Definition
Problems in a study
Advantages
Utilisation
Limitations

Definition

"A small experiment designed to test logistics and gather information prior to a larger study, in order to improve the latter's quality and efficiency" (Altman et al., Why do a pilot study?, http:// www. nc3rs.org.uk/downloaddoc.asp?id = 400). This definition succinctly explains everything about a pilot study. It is smaller than the main experiment/study and is done prior to the main study. It is designed to test the logistics and collect data to improve the quality and efficiency of the main study.

Problems faced in a study

It may not be possible to anticipate all the difficulties encountered in a main study. Having faced the problems, the investigator may be able to overcome some, but not all. Or he may not be prepared to handle them at that stage. Sometimes the problems may necessitate the investigator to modify the technique or the methodology. If a problem is serious enough to affect the outcome of the study and cannot be solved, the investigator may have to abandon the study. That is why a pilot study is carried out to predict/avoid such problems in the larger/main study or even if the problems cannot be avoided, the investigator will at least be better equipped to handle them appropriately.

Problems may arise if the

1. subjects/materials are not available in adequate quantities,
2. instructions to investigators are not given properly,
3. variability in the results are very wide,
4. tools and the instruments are not working properly,
5. cost involved is more than anticipated and hence not affordable,

6. total time taken for collection of data from each volunteer is longer than expected,
7. methodology is not suitable for volunteers,
8. investigators and technicians are not experienced/skilled enough to carry out the procedures,
9. animal does not perform the task as trained,
10. dose of the drug is inadequate or too high,
11. adverse effects which occur are likely to be severe,
12. procedure is too inconvenient to the patient/subject,
13. animals experience extreme distress.

Why conduct a pilot study?

Assessing the practicability of the study and its outcome is one of the purposes of a pilot study. It is also called feasibility study and can check whether above problems are encountered or not in a study. Remedial measures can be instituted for the problems faced. If the pilot study is encouraging and the problems, if any are sorted out one can proceed with the main study. On the other hand if a serious problem such as a severe/fatal adverse effect cannot be solved, the investigator may not have any option other than canceling the study.

Types of pilot studies

External: External pilot study is independent of main study. The participants are different from those that take part in the main study and they will not be included in the main study.

Internal: Internal pilot study involves first pre-specified number of subjects participating in a trial (main study). Using the data from pilot phase, sample size is recalculated and if the result is more than the size calculated initially, more number of subjects are recruited and experimented on. However if the new figure is less than the initial estimate, no adjustments in size are made but the original size is retained. Hence internal pilot study is not independent of main study.

When they said they were going to do a pilot study, I thought it was something to do with pilots. I never thought we would be......

Advantages of a pilot study

The defects in the design can be exposed by a pilot study and investigator may be able to rectify them. This can help the investigator avoid the loss of resources such as time and money.

Sometimes pilot studies are used to generate preliminary data which can be used to plan a larger study. For example *one can use the mean and SD values generated in a pilot study to calculate sample size for the main study*. These estimates may not be valid if the size is small; a slightly larger pilot study may be required.

Pilot studies can be useful for the investigators to solidify or fine tune their techniques. Surgical intervention in animals may need some practice and the investigators' capability may be assessed before the main study starts. Sometimes only a single animal is used to test the logistics.

Pilot studies can be used to find out the likely response of a compound and determine whether the proposed parameters can be quantified with expected precision under different experimental settings.

Pilot studies are useful for testing new drugs or procedures. The results of a pilot study may be used as evidence to support a proposal to be submitted for funding. The pilot study data, if convincing will increase the chances of the proposal being funded.

How to utilise the data/information obtained in a pilot study?

Information on logistical issues should be used to modify the study design. The data may not be useful if a serious methodological flaw is detected in the pilot phase; else the same data if suitable may be included in the main study. The data as well as information from a pilot study may be published along with the main study. Slightly larger pilot studies may be published independently but reporting should be mainly descriptive. If a hypothesis testing is done, not much importance can be attached to the results since such results are considered preliminary and require careful interpretation.

Limitations

Pilot studies are generally small and the data generated in the pilot phase cannot be heavily relied upon. Being small, the pilot studies may not reveal all the problems some of which might show up during the main study only. Such problems will be mainly logistical and the investigator should be prepared to handle them. Sometimes it is necessary to do a second pilot study to evaluate the modified design.

Chapter 11

Screening of Volunteers and Animals

Excerpts of a warning letter from the US FDA

WARNING LETTER

Linzer, Dov M.D. 6/12/09 09-HFD-45-06-01

Dov Linzer, M.D.

302 NW 179th Avenue, Suite 102

Healthworx, Pembroke Pines, FL 33029

Dear Dr. Linzer

Between December 3 and 15, 2008, CDR Ileana Barreto-Pettit, representing the Food and Drug Administration (FDA), conducted an investigation and met with you, to review your conduct of a clinical investigation (Protocol (b) (4) entitled (b) (4) of the investigational drug (b) (4) performed for (b) (4).

From our review of the establishment inspection report, the documents submitted with that report, and your written response dated December 29, 2008, we conclude that you did not adhere to the applicable statutory requirements and FDA regulations governing the conduct of clinical investigations. We wish to emphasize the following:

....

3. You failed to conduct the studies or ensure they were conducted according to the investigational plan [21 CFR 312.60].

....

Source documents showed that Subjects #003 and #015 did not meet this inclusion criterion, but were randomized into the study and dispensed study drug.

....

B. The protocol specified that subjects with severe renal impairment (estimated creatinine clearance < 30 mL/min) were to be excluded from the study. Lab results identified that Subject #003's screening creatinine clearance was 21 mL/min and thus met this exclusionary criterion. We note, however, that your site randomized this subject into the study.

....

2. Your site failed to perform hepatitis screening tests on Subjects #033, #042, and #056 to ensure that these subjects did not meet this exclusion criterion prior to randomization of the subjects into the study.

....

D. The protocol stated that subjects with contraindications to (b) (4) treatment were to be excluded from the study. Records indicate that Subject #062 had been hospitalized for (b) (4) toxicity with (b) (6) on (b) (6), prior to enrollment into the study, and thus met this exclusion criterion. Your site, however, randomized this subject into the study on September 7, 2006.

....

Within fifteen (15) working days of your receipt of this letter, you should notify this office in writing of the actions you have taken or will be taking to prevent similar violations in the future. Failure to adequately and promptly explain the violations noted above may result in regulatory action without further notice.

Tejashri Purohit-Sheth, M.D.
Food and Drug Administration

(those who wish to read the entire content of the letter may visit http://www.fda.gov/ICECI/EnforcementActions/WarningLetters/2009/ucm174744.htm)

11. Screening of volunteers and animals

What is screening of volunteers?

Screening of volunteers is examination (both clinical and investigational) of willing subjects to find out their suitability to take part in a study. All volunteers - patients as well as normal subjects, must be screened before being included in a study in the best interests of volunteers and researchers.

How to screen?

Once the proposal is cleared by the ethics committee, the next step is to recruit or select the subjects for the study. When an apparently suitable patient or a normal volunteer is identified, tell him/her about what is proposed to be done and get his/her consent. Fill in the consent form and get the signatures.

Data sheet

Before the volunteers are recruited, data sheets must be prepared. This is a proforma in which details like age, gender and weight of the volunteers and results of the study can be noted down. There is no standard format and one can design a data sheet that suits his study. Include provisions for noting all data /information pertaining to the study. A sample format is given below :

Title: **Difference in protein binding of propranolol in South Indians and North East Indians**

Investigator(s):	Dr.R.S.CHANDRA	Supervisor: Prof.K.VITTAL
	Dept of Pharmacology	Dept of Pharmacology
	CIMS & RI	CIMS & RI
	Newcherry - 606 006	Newcherry - 606 006

VOLUNTEER DETAILS

Name : Mr.G.S.REDDY Age : 25 yr Gender : Female

Weight : 65 Kg Height : 165 cm

Volunteer number: SI-3 (SI - South Indian group)

Volunteer code: PBP-3 (to be marked on the test tubes for sample identification)

Address : 111, Rue de laporte
Orion salai
Armagedam - 607001
Tel : 0413-233453, 09993155067
Email : gsrpondy@gmail.com

SCREENING Date: 10-7-2010

Clinical Examination:

General Health : GOOD Pulse : 80/min BP : 124/82 mm Hg
Respiratory rate : 15 / min

History of illness (past and recent past) : NIL

Is the volunteer anemic? NO

Is he/she jaundiced? NO

If the volunteer is a female, is she pregnant? NO

Is he/she taking any medications including contraceptive pills? NO

(if YES details must be given)

Cardio vascular system :	NAD (no abnormality detected)
Nervous system (CNS & PNS) :	NAD
Respiratory System :	NAD
Abdomen :	NAD
Genitals :	NAD
Skin :	NAD
Oral cavity, ENT and Eye :	NAD

Investigations :

Hemogram :	(results awaited)
TC	
DC	
ESR	
Blood urea:	(repeat sample sent; results awaited)
Blood sugar :	104 mg% (Random)
Urine albumin :	(results awaited)
Urine sugar :	Nil
Stool :	NAD
Liver function tests :	(results awaited)
SGOT	
SGPT	
Serum Bilirubin	
X-ray Chest (if required) :	NAD
ECG :	NAD

Tests for detection of commonly abused drugs (if possible) : (not done)

HABITS

Vegetarian or Non-Vegetarian: Vegetarian

Intake of Alcoholic beverages :	Amount	120 ml
	Frequency	Daily
YES ~~or NO~~	Addiction (yes or no)	No
	Duration (years)	4 yr
Smoking :	Cigars / Beedi / Cigarettes	
	Duration (years)	
~~YES or~~ NO	Number per day	
Drug abuse :	Name of drug	
	Duration (years)	
~~YES OR~~ NO	Amount	

Any other (i.e. *Betel nut chewing, pan/beeda usage*) : Nil

SAMPLE

Tissue / Fluid : Blood Date of Collection : 14/7/2010

Amount Collected : 10 ml

ANALYSIS

Date	Measurement	Result
15-7-2010	Alpha-1 AGP	824 mg/l
15-7-2010	Protein Binding	91%

What next?

The steps to be followed are given below.

1. Fill in the personal details like name, age, gender, weight and address.
2. Take a complete history of past and present illnesses and current drug intake, if any. It may be a herbal preparation or homeopathic drug but do not omit the details at this stage.
3. Ask about his personal habits like smoking, drinking and drug addiction.
4. Then do a general clinical examination to find out if he is suffering from diseases like anaemia or jaundice. Examine each system. Fill in the details like heart rate and respiratory rate.
5. Withdraw adequate blood to do blood total count (TC), differential count (DC), erythrocyte sedimentation rate (ESR), sugar and urea. Collect urine to find out the presence of albumin and sugar.
6. If possible, an ECG may be taken to rule out any cardiac abnormalities. Laboratory tests for common drugs abused may be carried out if facilities are available.
7. If the volunteer is a female ask her (a) whether she is pregnant and (b) whether she is using contraceptive pills. Elicit menstrual history, if the study requires such information.

Inclusion and exclusion criteria

The inclusion and exclusion criteria must have been defined before submitting a proposal to ethics committee. Once the screening is over and the laboratory results are received, make sure the inclusion criteria are met. If a volunteer meets any criteria that is defined under exclusion criteria, he must be dropped from the study.

One must be careful when drawing inclusion and exclusion criteria :

1. Each criterion must be justified i.e., *if males only are included there must be valid reasons for the same.*
2. Definition should be precise as far as possible and not vague i.e., *instead of just saying adults, define the age range for adults also - "adults between 25 to 40 years of age".*
3. When defining cut off, give a sufficient buffer zone e.g., *A study on anemic and non-anemic patients defined a cut off of 10 g% of Hb. Those who had Hb of 10 g% or above were considered normal and those with <10 g% Hb were defined as anemic. Using this definition, those with 9.9 mg% of Hb will be considered anemic but practically there will not be any difference between one with 9.9 g% and another with 10 g%. Further, because of error in measurement even if it is minor, the patients with borderline levels are likely to be placed wrongly on either side. Hence it is better to include patients with >10 g% in normal group and <8 g% in anemic group.*
4. Too many criteria will restrict the number of patients eligible to participate in a study. It might appear there are many patients before starting the study but once the study is started suddenly one would realize the number of patients eligible are very little. The inclusion and exclusion criteria must be realistically drawn.
5. Mutually exclusive criteria need not be mentioned under both inclusion and exclusion sections i.e., *'males only' under inclusion criteria automatically excludes 'females' and hence 'females' need not be mentioned under exclusion criteria.*
6. Volunteers should fulfill all the inclusion criteria (unless otherwise choices are given) and none of the exclusion criteria. Even a single criteria met (in case of exclusion criteria) or not met (in case of inclusion criteria) can exclude volunteers from the study.

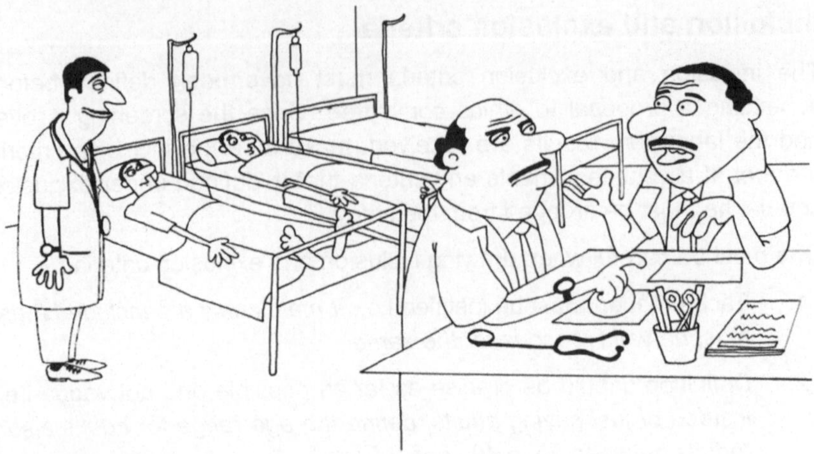

He is a stickler for details. His inclusion and exclusion criteria are so detailed and so strict that he could find only 2 eligible patients for his study in the last 4 years and 11 months.

Run-in period

Run-in period is the period before the commencement of a study during which neither group receives intervention. This period helps the participants to adapt to the study. If any subject finds it difficult to satisfy the demands of the study, they can drop out from the study. Hence run-in period can help in the screening of non-compliant participants.

Run-in period is also called lead-in period. It is usually 2-3 weeks. Baseline data is collected at the end of run-in period and randomization should be done once the run-in period is over, so that drop outs during the run-in period subvert randomization. The advantage of run-in period is that it acts as a screening method to increase internal validity and reduce heterogeneity of subjects. Its disadvantage is the increase in duration and cost of the study.

Why to screen?

Screening is needed for the following reasons :

1. To strictly adhere to the inclusion and exclusion criteria. This will protect the investigators in the event of a serious adverse event occurring to the subject during the study.
2. To do ethically acceptable research. It is unethical to include an already anaemic patient in a study which requires taking 10 ml blood daily for 10 days. In such studies, one must make sure the volunteer has a normal haemogram.

3. To minimize the variation among volunteers by excluding those who have extreme or abnormal values. This will help reducing the variation in the data.
4. If the patients or volunteers have a history of hepatitis/HIV positivity, the investigating team involved in the study can handle the blood samples carefully so as to protect themselves (if they are included in the study for some reason).
5. The volunteer may be taking some drug which may interfere with the study or interact with the drug the investigator intends to give.
6. To interpret the results in the light of conflicting characteristics of volunteers (if they happen to participate in the study).
7. To give allowance while interpreting the results of volunteers who have larger variation of one or more characteristics.

So one should never forget to screen a volunteer and record the details before proceeding further.

Screening of animals

General condition of the animals: If the study requires animals make sure the animals are healthy and free of disease. Even if the animals are bought from a reliable source or from the central animal house in the institute, it is better to personally check whether the animals are healthy before starting the study. The data collected from unhealthy animals will be of poor quality and hence unreliable.

Acclimatization: All animals should be allowed to undergo a period of acclimatization in the laboratory where the experiments are to be conducted. During this time, sick animals will usually die or exhibit obvious signs of illness like decreased locomotor activity, refusal to feed, abnormal movements and skin disease. Such animals should be identified and isolated. Acclimatization also helps animals to adapt to changes that are needed to be enforced for experimentation e.g., *changing to experimental diet, changes in housing conditions such as subjecting the animals to dark-light cycles, single housing, pairing with same gender, adapting to instruments such as restrainer and some procedures such as gavage.*

Selection: Select animals in the average weight range. Discard animals which are over or under weight for the age. Studies on reproduction may require animals of only a particular gender. Most studies are conducted on young adult animals. If the protocol requires younger or older animals, make sure the age of the animals has been recorded correctly. If in doubt as to the age of the animals, wait for a fresh litter and carefully record the date of birth and choose accordingly. Animals may be selected based on age, gender, species/strain, experimental history (carriers of virus/bacteria), social experience (mother reared) and training experience.

Training/conditioning the animals: Some experiments may require animals to be trained for certain procedures or conditioned to do certain things. Only those animals which do the tasks/are conditioned satisfactorily should be selected for the study e.g., *sling-trained dogs for ECG studies.*

Post-reading Exercises

Prepare a data sheet for the following hypothetical study :

Title : Comparison of efficacy of different weight loss programmes currently practised in teaching hospitals

Methods : The obese subjects will be allotted to anyone of the following groups and undergo treatment accordingly :

Group No.	Group name	Intervention
1	Control 1	No intervention
2	Control 2	Exercise (no diet control)
3	Programme 1	Diet type 1 + Exercise
4	Programme 2	Diet type 2 + Exercise
5	Programme 3	Diet type 3 + Exercise

The subjects will be recruited after screening. They will be administered treatment accordingly. Subjects who are allotted to groups 3-5 will be given diet as previously defined. Groups 2-5 will be asked to walk for 30 min every day for at least 5 days in a week. The treatment will last for 6 months and weight and biochemical parameters will be measured before, during and after the treatment.

Chapter 12

Data Quality, Collection and Management

Rules of the lab

1. When you don't know what you're doing, do it neatly.
2. Experiments must be reproducible; they should fail the same way each time.
3. First draw your curves, then plot your data.
4. Experience is directly proportional to equipment ruined.
5. If you can't get the answer in the usual manner, start at the answer and derive the question.
6. Do not believe in miracles - rely on them.
7. Team work is essential. It allows you to blame someone else.
8. Any delicate and expensive piece of glassware will break before any use can be made of it (Law of Spontaneous Fission).

From http://www.xs4all.nl/~jcdverha/scijokes/8_1.html#subindex

12. Data Quality, Collection and Management

Data quality

Errors in measurement

Coefficient of variation

Estimating error

Data collection

Data storage and retrieval

Data management

GCP and GLP

Data Quality

Research revolves around data. If the data collected are not of good quality, the entire study will be a waste of time and resources. But what exactly is quality data and what characteristics determine it? The extent to which the data depicts the actual phenomena can be considered as its quality which is determined by accuracy, precision and completeness. High quality data will lead to correct decisions, good planning and serves the purposes for which it is collected.

Precision: Precision is freedom from variation. When a sample from a source (e.g. *blood sugar level of patient from a single sample of blood*) is measured again and again, the individual values need not be identical; rather there will be variation each time. The variation may be slight or large depending on many factors. If the variation between individual values is wide, the precision is less and *vice versa*.

Accuracy: Accuracy is freedom from error. Data are said to be more accurate if they are closer to truth (actual value).

For example, *if a 1.00 gram coin is weighed six times, one of the four situations described in Box 12.1 can emerge.*

Box 12.1 **Precision and accuracy**

Sr. no.	Measurements (6 times)	Result	Explanation
1	1.01, 1.00, 0.99, 1.01, 1.01, 0.99	Each time the value is closer to 1 g	The data are precise as well as accurate.
2	0.61, 0.59, 0.62, 0.57, 0.60, 0.60	The values are closer to 0.6 g	The data are precise (because the range is narrow) but not accurate (because the actual weight of the coin is 1 g).
3	0.32, 1.53, 1.84, 0.45, 1.13, 0.88	The range of values is very wide	The data are neither precise nor accurate.
4	1.05, 0.96, 0.97, 1.03, 0.95, 1.04	The values are close to 1 g but variation is relatively large	The data are relatively accurate but at the same time they are relatively less precise.

Errors in measurement:

Lack of accuracy and precision indicate errors in measurement. Such errors may be either 'random' or 'systematic' in nature. A random error, as the name suggests occurs randomly with respect to frequency and extent. The readings cannot be repeated exactly and no two readings will be identical. But the random error can be reduced by taking several observations and finding the mean of the observed values. The situation no. 1 in Box no. 12.1 exemplifies this, whereas a systematic error is likely to occur with every measurement with the same degree and finding the mean of observations will not affect the error. This is demonstrated with situation 2 (Box 12.1) which could be the result of a 'zero error' in the weighing machine. Random errors reduce 'precision' and systematic errors affect 'accuracy'. Systematic errors must be eliminated and the random errors must be reduced as far as possible.

There are three important sources of errors. They are :

1. Investigator
   due to ignorance (lack of knowledge), incompetence (lack of skill/training) and bias.
2. Instrument
   due to variability, calibration problems and malfunctioning.

3. Sample (subject/animal)
   due to biological variation in response, non-compliance and bias.

A researcher must know the sources of error and has to take every effort to reduce/eliminate them. Strategies for eliminating errors/bias have already been discussed in chapter 4.

Non-compliance of subjects to the instructions and/or the treatment prescribed is one of the major sources of error. The investigators should make sure that the subjects follow the instructions given and take the drugs if any prescribed as a part of the experiment. Non-compliance to drug intake is often a problem in studies involving patients on long term treatment. One can check the compliance by asking the patients to bring the drugs they have not used and counting them or estimating the blood levels of a drug under investigation. Checking the compliance is not an easy task.

How to estimate error?

The extent of random error can be estimated using a measure called co-efficient of variation (CV). One must always calculate the CV to make sure the error in the instrument or procedure does not exceed the acceptable level. It is better to mention the CV under materials and methods when writing the dissertation.

Coefficient of variation

It is nothing but the standard deviation expressed as percentage of the mean. Standard deviation (SD) is one of the measures of variability of data about the mean. The CV can be calculated as follows :

$$CV = (SD/mean) \times 100\%$$

The CV can be determined in a pilot study. For example *the blood histamine levels are estimated using a spectrofluorimeter available in the department/institute. Six to eight identical samples from a single source are prepared by taking adequate blood from a single volunteer. A uniform procedure applied to process the samples and the blood histamine levels are estimated.* From the data one can calculate the mean, the standard deviation and the CV. Since all samples are from a single source and treated uniformly one should expect very little variation and low CV. On the contrary if the CV is large, there is some serious problem. The instrument may be malfunctioning or the investigator/technician is making some error in processing the samples. Each step followed must be carefully checked and the procedure must be standardized. A high degree of random error could be due to a wrong procedure or a faulty instrument.

Data collection

How to collect good quality data? This requires some preparations and precautions to be taken. Since completeness is one of the important characteristics of good quality data, every care must be taken not to miss out any data.

Preparing to collect data

1. Data sheet: It is important to prepare a data sheet (proforma) in which all data collected will be entered. It should be designed to include boxes/spaces/tables for entering all the necessary data/information which the investigator may require for his study. A data sheet normally has three major parts:
   (a) ID of patient/subject/animal: record all necessary information including phone numbers. For animal work record the strain, cage number, animal number, the place where the animals were procured.
   (b) Data related to one time measurement: the history, presenting symptoms and signs and in some cases number of children.
   (c) Data requiring more than one entry: like blood pressure over several weeks – for this, it is better to construct a table and record date, time, reading and if necessary who did the recording (which will help the investigator do an inter-rater check later).
2. Device a storage/filing system to transfer and store the data from data sheets. If a database software and a computer to store the data are used, construct the structure of the database and design the lay out. Make arrangements for backing up data regularly.
3. If codes (for animals, tissue blocks, slides, test-tubes) are given, make sure they are short and legibly written using appropriate ink/glass marking pencil. Avoid using I, 1 and l as codes since use of these numerals/letters as codes may cause confusion. The key to the code should be clear and unambiguous. It would be prudent to keep the keys (to codes) in two places.
4. Train the field workers/technicians or other staff. If the work involves questionnaires, field-test questionnaires and make modifications if required.
5. Standardise the techniques (staining, cell culture, assay), experimental procedure/surgical methods. Calibrate the instruments and check their precision and accuracy.
6. Conduct a pilot-study.

During data collection

1. Check the equipment from time to time. Some equipments need periodic calibration and testing for accuracy and precision. If so, this must be carried out without fail.
2. Supervise data collection. If others are involved in data collection (e.g., *technician*), check the technique and the procedure followed. Sort out any difficulties in data collection reported by them.
3. Run validity checks. Check the results with a known sample.
4. Monitor data entry into log books.
5. Check dosage of medication, batch number, expiry date of drugs/kits.
6. Take good care of animals if used. The data from poorly maintained animals will not be reliable.

Data storage and retrieval

Data storage plays a crucial role. An ideal storage system should be easy to transfer data to and from the system, easy to update and edit and easy to back-up. Set up an electronic database system on a PC using a spread sheet or a database software (e.g., *MS Excel or MS Access*). Transfer data from the source documents such as log books, lab reports and pathology reports to the storage system. Save the data in a file and place the file on the hard disk where one can easily locate. Do not forget to back up the data periodically on different media i.e., CD, pen drive.

Data Management

When the collection is over, data should be prepared for analysis.

Preparing to analyse data

1. Data checking or data cleaning: This is done mainly to find out the errors occurred
   - (a) when taking down from the case notes or log book,
   - (b) when entered into the computer and
   - (c) due to a mistake in the units of measurement and typographical errors.

   When checking the data, pay special attention to:

   - (i) Categorical data: e.g., *blood groups. There cannot be group C.*

(ii) Continuous data: e.g., *range checking (study on pregnancy; the maternal age may be 14-45). If the age is 55 or 65, it could be a data entry mistake.*

(iii) Logical checks: e.g., *if the patient is admitted for delivery, check whether gender of the patient is mentioned as female and not male.*

(iv) Dates: e.g., *correction is needed if an entry mentions 30 days in February or 31 days in April. Pay attention to correct sequence of dates; e.g., 'date died' cannot precede 'date of surgery'.*

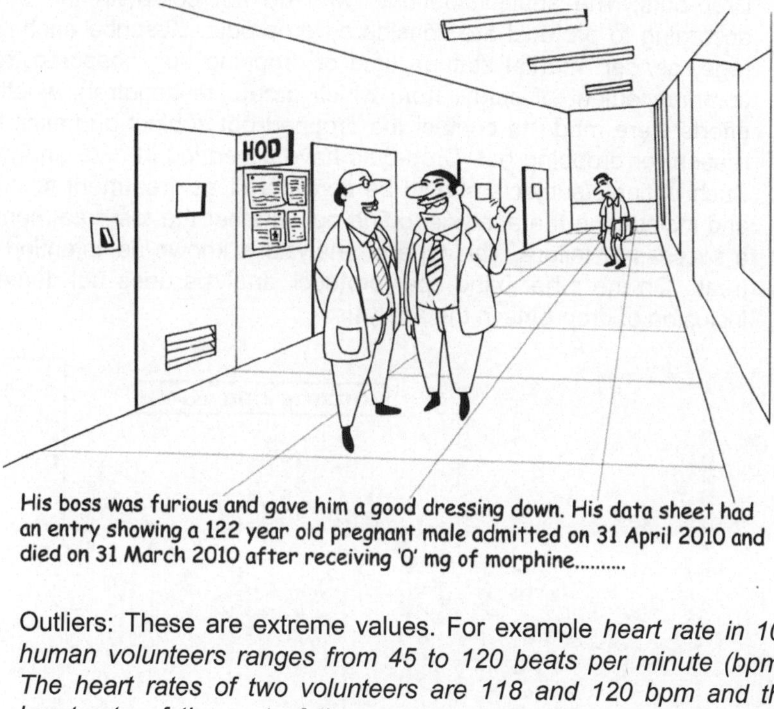

His boss was furious and gave him a good dressing down. His data sheet had an entry showing a 122 year old pregnant male admitted on 31 April 2010 and died on 31 March 2010 after receiving '0' mg of morphine..........

2. Outliers: These are extreme values. For example *heart rate in 100 human volunteers ranges from 45 to 120 beats per minute (bpm). The heart rates of two volunteers are 118 and 120 bpm and the heart rate of the rest of them ranges from 45 to 85 bpm.* In this dataset, 118 and 120 bpm are considered outliers. Why are they so? Are the values mistakenly transcribed or recorded or are they at the outer limits of normality? What should be done about them? The implication of extreme values in a dataset is they might lead to inappropriate conclusions if they are included in the analysis. Outliers can be removed from the dataset using the established statistical methods. Before doing so the researcher should try his best to find an explanation for such extreme values. Assuming them

mistaken entries and removing them without any concern is not desirable since these values are not implausible.

3. Missing data: Every effort should be made to retrieve the missing data. If not, the reason for missing the data should be recorded (e.g., *lost to follow up, lack of samples, sudden power failure during the analytical procedure*). If data are missing, it must be indicated so in the database. This can lead to problems during statistical analysis and the software may demand the user to indicate the missing data in a particular way i.e., some software packages demand the missing data to be indicated with letter 'M'.

4. Drop-outs: The subjects/patients who do not complete the study according to protocol are considered drop-outs. Describe each one (age, gender, marital status), time of dropping out measured from commencement of study, from which group (test/control), whether efforts were made to contact the dropped out subject and elicit the reason for dropping out. Drop-outs have a bearing in data analysis. Such patients/subjects should be considered as 'treatment failures' and included in the analysis to find out whether the test treatment is a success or failure. This type of analysis is known as 'intention-to-treat'. On the other hand, 'per protocol' analysis does not demand inclusion of drop-outs in the analysis.

I am reporting for the first time in the world a unique study which has a maximum drop-out rate. All patients - 133 out of 133 and 6 out of 7 investigators dropped out of the study.

5. Censored data: Values that cannot be measured (below the sensitivity of the test or assay or equipment) or when waiting for an event to occur (death / survival data) and the experiment is terminated before data for all subjects are collected. (e.g., *survival time > 5 years; concentration of paracetamol < 1 mg/litre*). This data should be included in the final analysis and not treated as missing data.
6. Derived data: Sometimes the data obtained are not used as such for analysis. Calculations may have to be carried out and the resulting data are used for final analysis. For example *in a pharmacokinetic study, the drug levels in blood obtained during data collection are used for calculating pharmacokinetic parameters such as half-life, volume of distribution and clearance.* These calculated parameters are used for analysis. Similarly the body surface area calculated from weight and height of subjects may be used for analysis. In some studies, calculated values of percentage change rather than original values will be used for analysis.
7. Transforming data: Changing data from one scale of measurement to another is called transformation of data. Parametric tests make assumptions on normal distribution of data. If the data are not normally distributed or skewed, it may be necessary to transform data so that this requirement can be met. The logarithmic transformation of data (the individual values are converted to the corresponding log values such as CD4 cell counts, biochemical values of tests, dose-response curve of drugs) is the best example of data transformation. It takes care of skewness and the data which previously looked bizarre may appear quite reasonable. Ease of analysis and valid statistical interpretation are the two main advantages of data transformation. Different types of transformation and when they are applied are given in Box no. 12.2.

Box 12.2 **Data transformation**

Type of transformation recommended	Skewness that can be corrected
Square root	Positive, low
Log	Positive, medium
Reciprocal	Positive, high
Square	Negative, low
Cubic	Negative, high

8. Exclusion of data: Decision on which data will be included or excluded should be made ***before*** beginning the analysis. e.g. *exclude data obtained from patients >60 years*. This kind of exclusion is not normally allowed. If done, there must be valid reason(s) and the decision should be taken before starting the analysis of data. Implications such as subversion of randomization and validity of conclusions must be considered.
9. Sub grouping of data: It should be planned *a priori* i.e. sub groups should have been planned at the design stage. One cannot attach much importance to results obtained from post-hoc sub group analysis. The results of such analysis can, of course form the basis for further research.

Good Clinical Practice (GCP) and Good Laboratory Practice (GLP)

These are standards set for obtaining high quality data.

GCP encompasses a set of defined procedures called 'standard operating procedures' (SOP) for each aspect of a clinical trial such as design, conduct, monitoring, auditing, recording and analyses and reporting. SOPs ensure that the data, results and conclusions are trustworthy and accurate. GCP also addresses ethical aspects (quality data + ethics = GCP)

GLP is no different from GCP in principle but it addresses laboratory experiments. "*It is a quality system concerned with the organizational process and the conditions under which non-clinical health and environmental safety studies are planned, performed, monitored, recorded, archived and reported*" (OECD Principles on Good Laboratory Practice, 1997; OECD – Organisation for Economic Co-operation and Development).

"Standard Operating Procedures (SOPs) means documented procedures which describe how to perform tests or activities normally not specified in detail in study plans or test guidelines" (OECD Principles on Good Laboratory Practice, 1997).

If a study complies with GCP/GLP standards, its results and conclusions are considered reliable (because of the high quality of data) and hence acceptable to laboratories/institutes/countries other than where the study is conducted. It avoids doubts being raised about data quality and repeating the same study everywhere.

It is out of scope of the book to describe GCP and GLP in detail. Nevertheless, the readers are advised to go through the material available on the internet.

Post-reading exercises

Situation: *A commonly prescribed new antibiotic is reported to produce oral ulcers resembling aphthous ulcers. The ADR monitoring centre of a large teaching hospital undertook a study to find out the incidence and severity of the ADR. The data collected are given in the tabular form below.*

Task : *Find out if there are*

(a) Errors in the data entry (perform a thorough data checking)

(b) missing values.

Results as entered in the log book:

Patients who developed oral ulcers during treatment with a new antibiotic. Total number of patients screened = 1854

Ulcer score 1-5 based on pain, discharge, number of ulcers and location.

Pt. Sr. No.	*Age (yr)*	*Gender (M/F)*	*Wt (kg)*	*Dosage (mg)*	*Severity of pain*	*Any discharge from ulcer*	Ulcer score	*No. of drugs co-prescribed*
4	45	Male	67	500 bd / 5days	Severe	Y	1	2
37	56	Female	65	250 tid/ 7days	Mild	N	5	3
98	32	Female	68	500 bd / 5days	Severe	Y	2	1
123	67	Male	89	250 bd/ 7days	Moderate	Y	5	0
134	890	Female	98	250 tid/ 7days	Mild	N	5	3
156	12	Female	147	500 bd / 5days	Severe	N	4	4
278	34	Male	46	250 cid/ 7days	Mild	N	3	-1
290	54	Female	76	250 tid/ 7days	Moderate	Y	4	4
297	32	Female	72	250 tid/ 7days	Mild	N	2	7
355	56	Male	74	500 bd / 5days	Severe	Y	3	3
377	78	Male	58	250 tid/ 7days	Mild	Y	1	2
399	54	Male	43	500 bd / 7days	Severe	Y	2	4
402	32	Female	37	250 tid/ 7days	Moderate	Y	3	5
456	45	Female	81	250 tid/ 7days	Moderate	N	4	2
478	65	Female	73	300 tid/ 7days	Moderate	Y	5	1
484	12	Female	63	500 bd / 5days	Severe	Y	4	3
511	23	Female	46	250 tid/ 7days	Mild-Moderate	Y	3	
576	45	Female	41	250 tid/ 7days	Moderate	N	2	3
624	65	Mafemale	43	500 tid / 5days	Mild	Y	2	4
634	168	Female	56	500 bd / 5days	Mild	Y	3	3
689	46	Female	53	250 tid/ 7days	Mild	Y	4	2
699	24	Female	87	500 bd / 5days	Severe	Y	5	1
700	58	Male	43	2500 bd/ 7days	Mild	Y	6	3
712	90	Female	56	250 tid/ 7days	Mild	N	3	3
714	36	Female	78	500 bd / 5days	Severe	Y	4	3
788	62	Female	-	500 bd / 5days	Moderate	N	3	9
823	61	Female	83	500 bd / 5days	Severe	N	2	3
879	34	Female	51	500 bd / 5days	Moderate	Y	3	4
910	57	Female	73	250 tid/ 7days	Moderate	Y	4	5
1010	35	Male	54	250 tid/ 7days	Mild	Y	5	3
1059	36	Female	41	500 bd / 5days	Severe	Y	4	0
1111	38	Female	183	500 bd / 5days	Severe	G	4	3

Pt. Sr. No.	Age (yr)	Gender (M/F)	Wt (kg)	Dosage (mg)	Severity of pain	Any discharge from ulcer	Ulcer score	No. of drugs co-prescribed
1245	32	Female	12	250 tid/ 7days	Mild	Y	4	4
1276	39	Female	51	250 tid/ 7days	Mild	N	5	5
1367	34	Male	72	500 bd / 5days	Severe	N	4	4
1389	23	Male	52	500 bd / 5days	Moderate	N	3	3
1418	25	Male	53	250 tid/ 7days	Mild	Y	2	3
1435	28	Female	48	250 tid/ 7days	Moderate	N	4	2
1478	28	Male	161	250 tid/ 7days	Mild	N	3	3
1587	20	Female	53	250 bd/ 7days	Moderate	N	2	4
1698	34	Female	84	250 tid/ 7days	Moderate	Y	1	5
1745	56	Female	54	250 tid/ 7days	Moderate	Y	3	0
1918	12	Male	541	250 tid/ 7days	Mild	Y	4	3

Chapter 13

Data Analysis

> **An unwritten footnote in a paper**
>
> We tried 37 different analytic techniques, some invented in ancient China, including Optician's c-test, Hate's d-test, the Lastwill n-test, Pretty's q-test, the Van Gough r-test, Washes' y-test, followed by the Wineman post-hock test. The one reported here (The Kawasaki Inverted-Listerine Analysis) was the only one that got significant results.
>
> Edwin A. Locke, Ronan M Conroy and others
>
> From http://www.xs4all.nl/~jcdverha/scijokes/8_2.html

13. Data Analysis

Calculation of mean, SD and SEM

Application of significance tests

Confidence intervals

Once the data are collected and organised, analysis must follow. Sometimes the data may not be subjected to statistical analysis as such. One may have to calculate a parameter or two from the collected data using a formula and the calculated parameter (derived data) may be the one which needs statistical analysis e.g., *half-life calculated from drug concentration data*. If required, the derived data should be calculated and tabulated for all groups before proceeding with statistical analysis. If it is needed to derive data from the collected data, then remember :

1. The required formulae or procedure for analysis must have been worked out at the time of planning itself.
2. One must have read the formula and the relevant text and understood it completely or at least the principle involved in the calculation.
3. The analysis can be done manually or using a computer. But never forget to use a sample data which has already been worked out (in a book may be) to find out whether the manual method or computer yields the identical result. Do not take it for granted whatever the computer displays is true. Validate it manually at least once if possible.

Statistical consideration

Statistical analysis of data can be broadly classified into summary statistics and inferential statistics. Summary statistics, as the name suggests, is used to summarise the data from a group e.g., *Mean, Median, standard deviation (SD) and standard error of the mean (SEM).* Central tendency (mean and median), variation (SD and SEM) and range are the common derivatives to depict summary data. Final stage in data analysis is inferential statistical analysis which helps us make inferences from data. Significance testing and estimating confidence intervals fall under this category.

By the time the data are ready for analysis, one must have clearly identified which data or parameters are subjected to analysis. This decision (of what to analyse) should be made by the investigator and not the statistician or the computer. A lot of parameters may have been estimated and documented but it does not mean all need to be analysed. The parameters which are likely to answer the research question(s) raised in the beginning must be analysed. Having decided the parameters, calculate the mean/median, the standard deviation and/or the standard error before going in for significance testing.

Calculation of Mean, SD, SEM

Mean: This is otherwise called arithmetic mean. (There are other types of mean also). It is obtained by adding up the individual values and dividing the sum by the number of observations. Calculating mean is appropriate if the data are normally distributed e.g., *heart rate, blood pressure*. Mode or median is estimated if the data are skewed or non-normal e.g., *pain scores*. Generally mean is calculated for interval data (such as continuous and discrete data), mode for nominal data and median for ordinal data. If data are normally distributed assuming a perfect bell-shaped curve on a frequency distribution plot, then mean, median and mode will be identical i.e., *all three measures will be located at the centre*. If the data are largely skewed, mean does not represent the central point of the data.

Standard deviation (SD): Identical means may be obtained from two sets of data. For example see Table 13.1. In both sets the mean is 25 but in data set I, the individual data do not vary from mean much. The same is not true with set II. This indicates mean does not give an idea of how the individual values vary. But the standard deviation does. It describes the variability of the observations about the mean. It can be calculated as follows :

(a) determination of the sum of squares of deviations of each unit from the mean.

(b) determination of variance.

(c) determination of standard deviation.

Example of calculation of SD : See Table 13.1

Table 13.1 **Calculation of Mean, SD and SEM**

No.	SET I	square of set I	SET II	square of set II
1	28	784	48	2304
2	23	529	12	144
3	25	625	23	529
4	21	441	27	729
5	26	676	31	961
6	27	729	09	81
total	150	3784	150	4748
mean	25		25	
SD	2.60		14.13	
SE	1.06		5.76	

	SET I	SET II
n (no. of observations)	6	6
mean	25	25
total	150	150
Square of total	22500	22500
Sum of Squares	3784	4748
sum of squares of deviations (sum of squares-(square of total/n))	34	998
variance (sum of squares of deviations/n–1)	6.80	199.60
standard deviation (square root of variance)	2.60	14.13
standard error of mean (standard deviation/square root of n)	1.06	5.76

Standard deviation must be expressed as positive numbers. There need not be ± sign when SD is expressed alone. The sign ± is required only when expressed along with mean (see Box 13.1).

Box 13.1 **Correct and incorrect expressions of SD**

Correct	Incorrect
SD = 2.51	SD = ± 2.51
Mean ± SD = 25 ± 2.51	Mean = 25 (SD ± 2.51)
Mean(SD) = 25(2.51)	Mean(SD) = 25(± 2.51)

As already said, SD indicates the variability of observations in a sample studied. The mean ± 1 SD gives an indication how 68% of subjects in that sample vary. The mean ± 2 SD includes 95% of the sample.

For example *the mean (SD) systolic blood pressure of 25 randomly selected adult Indians was found to be 120 (20) mm of Hg.*

One can deduce that:

1. approximately 68% of the subjects in the sample have a systolic blood pressure ranging from 120 – 20 to 120 + 20 mm of Hg. (i.e., *100 to 140*),
2. approximately 95% of the subjects in the sample have a systolic blood pressure ranging from 120 – (2 × 20) to 120 + (2 × 20) mm of Hg. (i.e., *80 to 160*)

The above interpretations are true only if the distribution of variable under investigation is normal. The 95% range (mean ± 2SD) is also called 'reference range or reference interval' and is used for calculating the normal range (reference range) for biochemical and other laboratory parameters.

Well.....the experiment is over and all the data are ready for analysis. Let us give it to 3 or 4 statisticians for analysis and use the most favorable report for publication.........

Standard error (SE): It is also called standard error of the mean (SEM) and is calculated by dividing SD by square root of n (number of subjects). See Table 13.1 for a worked out example of calculation of SE.

The mean obtained from a sample (group) may not be the same as that of another sample from the same population studied. If the whole population is studied by dividing them into small samples of equal size, the means obtained from each group will differ slightly. This variation in means is accounted by SE. In other words SE or SEM is nothing but standard deviation of means of different samples from a single population. It is not practicable to study the entire population. Hence we study only one sample and calculate the variation in means using statistical methods. If it were possible to study the entire population there would no longer be any need for statistical methods which are used to draw conclusions about populations from limited samples. When SEM is expressed it indicates how means (of different samples) in a population vary and NOT how observations in a sample vary.

SD is used to summarise a set of data because it indicates the variability in the sample (data). Hence SD is used as a measure of variation whenever samples are described e.g., *tabulating patient characteristics in a study report*. SE is used when inferences about population are drawn.

Confidence interval of a mean, confidence limits, confidence levels

If the sample mean in the above example is 120 mm Hg, what is the population mean? The exact figure cannot be arrived at but a range of values within which the true population mean lies can be calculated with a degree of certainty. This range called confidence interval is calculated using the sample mean and the SE. The mean ± 1SE and mean ± 2SE will give approximately 68% and 95% confidence intervals respectively. In the above example, the 68% and 95% confidence intervals are given by (120 – 4) to (120 + 4) and 112 to 128 respectively. The end points of the confidence interval i.e., *lower value and upper value* are known as confidence limits or fiducial limits. Confidence interval is always mentioned with a particular degree of certainty e.g., *95%*. This is called confidence level and is expressed as a percentage. The confidence level which is commonly used is 95% but confidence interval for 90% and 99% confidence levels can also be calculated and presented if the situation warrants.

The 95% confidence limits in the above example is 112-128. What does it mean?

(a) we are 95% confident that the true population mean lies between 112-128,

(b) there is a 5% chance that the range given by 112-128 does not include the true population mean,

(c) the above limits include the true population mean with a probability of 95%,

(d) if the 95% confidence intervals for each of the 100 means (of the random samples from the same population) are worked out, 95 of the 100 confidence intervals will include the true population mean.

All the above are true and they mean the same. Higher the confidence, broader will be the range. The 95% confidence interval is narrower than that of the 99%. If someone asks you for the exact time when you do not have a clock/watch, you will be less confident to tell him the exact time. You are probably 50% confident. You can say with more confidence (say 70%), if you are allowed to give a range i.e., *2:00 - 2:15 PM*. If the range is wider (1:45-2:30 PM), your confidence is higher, say 95%. If you want to be much more confident (99.99%), the range should be still wider (1:00-3:00 PM).

Application of significance tests

The tests of significance have been described in some detail in chapter 8. When planning a study, the test to be used and the level of significance (at what level P values are considered significant i.e., *10%, 5% or 1%.*) must have been decided. The criteria for selecting a test have also been discussed in chapter 8. Use the chosen test to find out whether the data of test group is significantly different from that of control. The steps are :

1. Decide upon the parameter to be tested (e.g., *blood sugar level*).
2. Isolate two (or more) sets of data (one may be control and the other test) to be compared.
3. Apply the test and obtain the value it yields (it may be t, F or CHI statistic depending upon the test used).
4. Refer to the appropriate table of critical values (usually given in statistics books) and find out the P value.

Refer to statistics books for the exact method of doing each test. If the P value is < 0.05 and the error you have decided to allow is 5% (significance level) then the groups are significantly different for the parameter concerned. The software packages can calculate the exact P value which if less than the level of significance indicates a statistically significant difference.

Confidence interval for the difference between means

Nowadays many journals insist that confidence interval must be mentioned especially when a non-significant result is presented. Quoting P values alone is not enough. As discussed earlier confidence intervals indicate the range of likely values of sample means in a population. When two groups are compared the likely values of difference in means of two populations under study can be calculated. For example *the difference in the weights of two groups (say Europeans and Indians) can be found out and confidence interval for the difference in weights can be calculated.* The 95% confidence interval for the 'difference' can be calculated using the following formula if t test has been chosen to analyse the data :

Upper limit = mean + ($t_{0.05} \times SE_{diff}$)   Lower limit = mean – ($t_{0.05} \times SE_{diff}$)

It should be noted that the above formula is used to calculate the confidence interval for the 'difference' between group means and not for the individual group means. $t_{0.05}$ refers to the t value for a probability 0.05 for the degrees of freedom calculated and SE_{diff} refers to SE of difference between means (SE of individual group means should not be used). Many statistical software packages can calculate and display the confidence limits.

If 95% confidence interval includes a 0 value, the difference is not statistically significant at 5% significance level. Look at the following example for a better understanding :

Example: *The means of heart rate of 10 volunteers before and after giving a drug were 72.4 and 60.3 beats/min. The paired t test was carried out and the difference was found to be significant. The df were 9 (10 – 1). The confidence intervals were calculated as follows :*

The mean difference is 12.1 (72.4-60.3)

The SE of difference is 3.4 (the difference between 'before and after' was obtained for all the volunteers and the SD and the SE values were calculated for the difference).

The t value corresponding to 0.05 probability for 9 df is 2.26 (obtained from the t distribution table).

Upper limit = 12.1 + (2.26 × 3.4)   *Lower limit = 12.1 – (2.26 × 3.4)*

= 12.1 + 7.7 = 19.8   *= 12.1 – 7.7 = 4.4*

The confidence interval is 4.4-19.8 which does not include a 0 value since both the limits are on the positive side. Suppose the SE of difference is 6.5 (due to a large variation in the results), the confidence interval will be – 2.6 (12.1 – 14.7) – 26.8 (12.1 + 14.7). This interval does include a 0 since lower limit is 'minus 2.6' and upper limit is 'plus 26.8'. The former indicates the difference is statistically significant and latter does not as the confidence interval includes a 0 in between.

Whether a difference is statistically significant or not can be found out by P value. Then why should we calculate confidence intervals? - because the confidence intervals can reveal the precision of the estimate as indicated by its narrowness or broadness. The interval between 4.2 – 19.8 is narrower than that between 1.2 – 25.3. The former is more precise because the population mean value lies within a narrow range. If the range instead is 1.2 – 25.3, it is relatively less precise than the former because the population mean can lie anywhere in the range that is broad. One can infer from confidence intervals how precise the results are.

An analogy might be of help. Suppose two persons are asked the price of a Maruti car model Zen LX. Both do not know the exact price but they can give you a range within which the price is likely to fall. One says "Rupees 2.2 to 6.4 lakhs" and the other "Rupees 3.7 to 4.3 lakhs". Both of them are 95% confident that the exact price falls within the range they have given. If you were to use the above information to make a decision on buying a new car, which one would you prefer? The answer and the justification for the same are too obvious to waste a few lines on them. In science too, precise results are desirable as they have more practical utility.

Post-reading Exercises

I. Find out the suitable measure of central tendency and variation for the following sets of data. Find out the confidence interval :

1. The heights (cm) of 10 patients with hypopituitarism are given below :

   152, 141, 138, 139, 140, 128, 110, 111, 121, 108

2. An antiepileptic drug was tested in rats. Control group received saline and the duration of clonic convulsion (millisecond) was measured :

   Control : 600, 610, 622, 595, 601, 599, 611, 596

   Test : 574, 521, 533, 555, 553, 538

3. An antidiabetic was tested in diabetic patients. The fasting blood sugar values (mg%) before and after the drug are given for 6 patients :

   Before : 120, 122, 134, 128, 131, 125

   After : 110, 87, 111, 116, 93, 87

4. The histopathological scores for severity of ulcer (no ulcer, mild, moderate, severe, very severe) in 12 samples are given below :

   0, 4, 3, 3, 4, 1, 0, 2, 4, 3, 2, 1.

II. Analyse the data using the suggested statistical test :

t test – unpaired

1. In an experiment, 2 groups of 6 rats were injected with amphetamine and saline respectively and food intake was measured for 2 hrs. The initial weight of rat food was 10 g for each rat. At the end of 2 hrs, the remaining food was weighed and the following data were obtained:

   Group I - Amphetamine - 8.21, 5.3, 6.4, 7.5, 6.1, 7.2 g

   Group II - Saline - 9.5, 9.4, 9.2, 8.9, 9.9, 9.2 g

2. The analgesic effect of morphine (3 mg/kg; sc) and aspirin (10 mg/kg; sc) were compared using 0.6% acetic acid writhing. The data are as follows.

   Aspirin (n=7) : 15, 18, 18, 20, 22, 17, 16 writhings (in 15 min)

   Morphine (n=6) : 5, 8,11, 2, 10, 4 writhings (in 15 min)

t test - paired

1. The effects of atropine (1.0 % solution) on the pupil size was studied in 6 rabbits. The pupil size was measured before and after administration of saline in one eye and atropine in the other. The data obtained were as follows:

   Right eye

   Saline(1drop) before 5, 6, 3, 4, 7, 5 mm

   after 6, 5, 4, 4, 6, 6 mm Difference : 1, -1, 1, 0, -1, 1

   Left eye

   Atropine(1 drop) before 6, 4, 7, 3, 5, 6 mm

   After 7, 8, 9, 6, 8, 9, mm Difference : 1, 4, 2, 3, 3, 3

2. The cardiostimulant activity of a plant extract (2 μg) was tested on 6 isolated frog heart preparations and the following data were obtained :

   Basal heart rate - 75, 70, 61, 52, 73, 75 bpm

   Plant extract - 91, 89, 83, 59, 81, 87 bpm

Wilcoxon test

Wilcoxon – paired

1. The severity of pain was scored using a 10 point scale (0 – no pain, 10 – intolerable pain) before and after giving an analgesic in 6 subjects :

   Before – 8, 6, 8, 9, 7, 8, 7, 8, 7, 9 After – 1, 5, 2, 3, 5, 5, 0, 2, 3, 4

2. The number of stools passed per day in 10 children suffering from acute gastroenteritis is given as follows :

   Before treatment – 6, 4, 5, 6, 6, 8, 7, 5, 9, 9

   After treatment – 6, 8, 5, 2, 2, 3, 4, 4, 5, 6

Wilcoxon – unpaired

1. The wound healing effect of a traditional drug was tested in rats. Two groups of rats (6 each) were administered either saline or test drug and the effect was measured in scores (0-5; 0 – No healing; 5 – Complete healing)

   Saline – 0, 1, 3, 2, 1, 0 Drug – 2, 1, 3, 4, 5, 2

2. The effect of atropine on physostigmine induced salivary secretion was studied in 2 groups of dogs. Salivation was scored (0 - no salivation; 1 - mild; 2 - moderate; 3 - high; 4 - frothing) after physostigmine administration. One group was pretreated with atropine :

   Saline pretreatment – 4, 3, 4, 2, 4, 4, 3, 4, 3, 4

   Atropine pretreatment – 1, 0, 0, 2, 2, 1, 1, 2, 2, 1

Chi Squared Test

Task: Compute a 2×2 contingency table for the following and answer the questions.

1. Out of 25 women who had uterine cancer, 20 claimed to have used estrogens. Out of 30 women without uterine cancer 5 claimed to have used estrogens. Is there an association between uterine cancer and estrogen use?

2. In a clinical trial of a new antiepileptic drug "epistil", 1540 patients received the test drug and 1603 received the control drug (phenytoin). 152 patients in the test group and 214 in the control group developed nystagmus.

   Is there an association between nystagmus and epistil?

Correlation and Regression

1. In a pharmacokinetic study the plasma drug levels at different time points were estimated in a volunteer. Carry out the regression analysis:

Time	4	8	12	16	24	48	h	8
Conc.	121	65	30	17	4	01	µg/ml	176

2. In diabetic rats the blood sugar and endogenous insulin levels were estimated. Find out if there a correlation between these two parameters:

Rat no	1	2	3	4	5	6	7	8	
Blood sugar	156	102	134	184	198	203	123	176	mg%
Insulin	16	21	18	11	10	8	20	11	IU

3. The blood levels of a drug were measured by two different methods using the HPLC. One method is the gold standard used routinely. The other one is newly developed. Find out whether the new one "agrees" with the standard?

Sample no	1	2	3	4	5	6	7	8	
GS	12	23	43	14	15	17	16	19	µg.ml
New	14	22	48	17	16	19	16	24	µg/ml

ANOVA

1. The % change in blood sugar level after administration of three doses of a plant product was compared with that in vehicle treated (control) animals (n=6 in each group). The data are given below :

Groups	% change in blood sugar (mean ± SEM)
Control	12.21 ± 2.81
Plant (10 mg/kg)	18.43 ± 3.12
Plant (30 mg/kg)	26.33 ± 2.96
Plant (100 mg/kg)	28.78 ± 3.02

Find out whether the plant product exhibits a dose dependent effect.

2. Tail flick latency observed for three different plant based drugs are given below:

Groups	n	Latency in sec (mean ± SEM)
Control	8	13.2 ± 0.8
Plant 1	8	18.43 ± 1.2
Plant 2	8	20.33 ± 1.3
Plant 3	8	19.78 ± 0.9

Analyse whether the plants exhibit analgesic action or not.

Chapter 14

How to Interpret P?

Statistical significance *Vs* practical significance

A beautiful young woman invited a brilliant statistician friend to her company dinner-dance.

The invitation stated that she could either bring her spouse or her 'significant other' as a guest. Having just met this chap and being unmarried, she felt certain that he would be more than suitable since all statisticians are by definition 'statistically significant'.

When they arrived at the door, the maitre d' inquired as to the status of her escort. She smiled and promptly introduced him as an up-and-coming statistician that was her 'significant other' for the evening.

The maitre d' was stunned and his face grew red. He finally stammered in an embarrassed tone of voice, "I am so sorry madam, we cannot admit your friend. 'STATISTICAL SIGNIFICANCE' DOES NOT IMPLY 'PRACTICAL SIGNIFICANCE'!"

From Gary C. Ramseyer's first internet gallery of statistics jokes

my.ilstu.edu/~gcramsey/HypTest.html

14. How to Interpret P?

P value and its interpretation

Misuse of statistics

Statistics and decision making

Understanding P

The results given by the statistical test of significance will be valid provided the selection of subjects, methodology and data collection are perfect and the conditions for the test chosen are met. For example *the use of t tests for highly skewed data tends to give invalid results*. Why should a t test provide a correct result when the data do not suit it? Statistical tests are only tools in the hands of the investigator and they never bother (because they cannot) to detect or point out the non-normality/skewness of data or the mistakes made in the design or the execution of the study. They simply analyse the given data to yield a statistic such as t, F, or Chi value leading us to find out the P value. So if the design of the study or data collection is imperfect and the conditions specific to each test are not met, the statistical analysis – even if it is done correctly – gives an unreliable result. If the data are garbage, the results are garbage too irrespective of obtaining a P value < 0.05 or > 0.05.

Significant and highly significant results

When a P value is less than 0.01, the difference (between groups) is dubbed as `highly significant' and when it is less than 0.05 but > 0.01 then the difference is considered `just significant'. Many believe that lesser the P value, greater is the difference between the actual values (means) of two groups. This need not be so. Consider the data in Table 14.7.

Table 14.7 **Effect of two drugs on the mean blood pressure (mm of Hg) of dog**

	DRUG I BP		DRUG II BP	
	Before	After	Before	After
Mean	149.90	151.50	152.20	193.00
S.D.	0.65	0.53	31.56	25.92
n	8		8	
Difference in means	1.63		41.75	
P values	0.0005		0.048	

(calculated using the paired `t' test)

The P value for the first drug is smaller than that of the second because the variation in the data of both groups (drug I) is very small. That is why the P value (< 0.01) is small and it indicates a highly significant difference between the groups. This does not mean the difference between means is large but the evidence for the difference (either small or large) being a true one is strong. The chances of concluding that there is a difference, (when the real difference does not exist between the groups) is < 1% (i.e., *the false positive error is < 1% and the investigator is ready to tolerate it*). Similarly if a P value is < 0.05, then the chances of finding a difference (when it does not exist in reality) is less than 5% (i.e., *the false positive error is < 5% and the investigator is ready to tolerate it*). Both the sets of data for the second drug in the example vary widely. That is why the P value is 0.048 even though the difference between means is much higher than that obtained with the first drug. Hence the P values cannot indicate the magnitude of the difference between groups.

P values and confidence intervals

Let us consider two situations. In one the P value is 0.49 (P < 0.05) and in the other it is 0.51 (p > 0.05). Since the latter is more than the 5% significance level, the difference is not considered significant whereas we happily declare the former statistically significant. This is something like declaring a pass for the student who has scored 50% and a fail for the one who has scored 49%. We know very well there will not be any difference in the levels of knowledge or performance of these two students and we assume that one is just lucky and the other is not. Yet we do accept such results in our day to day life and the 50% cut-off which we very well know is arbitrary (what is the rationale for the 50% cut-off and who fixed it?).Remember that 5% (0.05) level used for significance testing is also an arbitrary value (like 50% cut off for passing the examination) and it was originally introduced as a guideline rather than a cut-off. Hence it is more appropriate to look at the confidence intervals to find out how precise the results are. This is another reason why confidence intervals are given more importance than P values and many journals insist that along with P values confidence limits should be given for significant results. The reader will then have an idea how precise the results of the study are.

Should it be 0.05 always?

It is not a rule (by the Gods of significance!) from heaven that a difference between two groups will be considered statistically significant only if $P < 0.05$. This 5% level is arbitrary and it is conventionally followed. It can be fixed at 10%, 2%, or 1% depending on the study conditions such as inherent wide variation in the data to be collected and too small a sample size due to rarity of the condition under study. It is recommended that the level of significance may be fixed at 5% unless advised otherwise by the statistician or the guide.

Interpretation of P value

Suppose an otherwise flawless study was completed, the results were statistically analysed.and the P was reported to be < 0.05. What does it mean? It means the difference between the groups compared is STATISTICALLY significant i.e., *the chances of observing a difference (when it does not exist) is less than 5%.* The investigator is allowed to conclude that there is a difference between groups provided he realizes that there is a 5% uncertainty which he can afford to ignore.

Is it not possible to get a result which is 100% certain? Impossible, according to statisticians! The P value will always be between 1 and 0 but never 1 or 0. Think of the experiment as a diagnostic kit. The clinicians are always reminded of the false positive rate and the false negative rate when a patient is declared positive or negative for a disease using the kit. When the result is positive, the chances of it being false positive is equal to or less than the rate mentioned in the brochure. There is no kit which is 100% specific and/or 100% sensitive. We are aware of the errors that can occur, are willing accept the same and declare the test positive (and land up in court when the patient finds out later he actually does not have the disease). The statistical analysis puts us in a similar situation except that there is no one to sue us for the results we declare.

What if the P > 0.05? How to interpret it? Before declaring in haste the groups are NOT significant, one should try to find out the power. The power of a study is its ability to pick up the difference when it exists. Though the level of power to be achieved is set at the beginning, the actual power achieved may not be same and hence power should be calculated especially when P > 0.05 to see whether the study is really equipped with enough power to pick up the difference. The power may be low due to various reasons; the sample size may be smaller than expected; the actual drop-out rate may be more; non-compliance may be more than anticipated. Hence when P > 0.05, one should carry out *posteriori* power calculation. Many statistical packages will be able to estimate power.

If power is < 80% (0.8) and P > 0.05, it is prudent to conclude that the study did not have enough power to detect the difference. Avoid stating that the groups are not significantly different. If power is 80% or more, the conclusion would be the study did not find any difference between groups. In either case it is better to avoid categorically declaring that there is no difference between groups.

Statistics and decision making

Suppose an antihypertensive drug which lowers the blood pressure by 2 mm of Hg (mean reduction) is tested and the statistical test concludes the results are highly significant ($P < 0.01$). This raises an interesting question. Will you recommend this drug for clinical use if the maximum tolerable dose produces only this much (2 mm of Hg) reduction? Here comes the CLINICAL significance of data. It is true the difference between groups is STATISTICALLY significant. But this does not in any way justify the use of this drug in therapeutics since the actual difference or effect obtained is not at all significant CLINICALLY. Since the drug is useless from a practical point of view, it would not be recommended for clinical use though statistics clearly yields a positive result. Therefore the final conclusion or decision making should be based on the knowledge of therapeutics/practicality and not on statistics alone. Statistics is only a tool and it illuminates whether the data in both the groups are different or not. But it never understands the real meaning of these numbers and it does not take the meaning into account during analysis. So it is the investigator who should take the final decision and this decision should be based on the professional knowledge and experience.

Suppose a statistical test shows that the groups are not statistically different. Does it really mean the groups are not different? No. Not necessarily. As discussed earlier the study may not have enough power to detect the difference. The variation of individual values from mean may be more and hence the overlapping between groups. Or the sample size may be too small to detect the difference which actually may be small. In such a case if the number of subjects is increased the test may produce a significant result. That means the study is now equipped to detect a small difference that exists between groups. A word of caution though – the aim of the study should never be to find out a statistically significant difference only. That may be meaningless if the detected difference is not clinically significant as we have seen already. While planning a study one must decide the 'practically important minimum difference' expected to be detected. Whether it is large or small, it must be meaningful and the sample size must be decided accordingly. One should not decide upon a large difference with the sole aim of reducing the sample size. In such a case the investigator may not detect the difference if it is actually small but still meaningful. So when a negative result – non-significant result - is obtained it may be that the sample size in the study is not adequate to detect the difference which is small.

Can we reject a non-significant result and accept that the difference is clinically significant? i.e., *accepting a statistically non-significant result as clinically important and applying the findings in clinical setting or going ahead with further research*. Consider the following hypothetical situation:

> A herbal product was tried as a cure for rabies. A group of 10 patients with confirmed rabies were administered the herbal product and another group of same size was given the existing treatment. Three patients who received the herbal product survived but none in the other group. The Chi Square test showed the difference was not significant.

What would you do in the above situation? Will you dump the study since the statistical analysis says the difference is not statistically significant? We know that rabies is a 100% fatal disease and if a drug can even save one patient, it is a miracle and clinically most significant. May be that the dose was not adequate for other patients who did not survive or the drug worked only in a few patients due to some factors. Whatever it may be but rejecting the finding as non-significant is most unwise in this hypothetical situation. There are situations where clinical significance overrides statistical non-significance. One such a situation is drug adverse effects. A fatal adverse effect of a drug is 1 in 100 i.e., *for every 100 patients who get the drug one is lost*. Again statistical analysis not showing a significant result is not a good reason for ignoring the deaths. Clinicians at times ignore a statistically non-significant result in situations where the life saving drugs such as anticancer agents are tried; because a large inherent variation in patient data may mask the effect of the drug.

When collection of data is over, prepare a master chart of parameters studied and the data. Before proceeding to do a statistical test, take a close look at the data focussing on anything obvious or striking. The investigator may be able to make out an obvious difference between two groups just by viewing them (That does not give him an excuse for not doing statistical analysis though). More than that one should look for anything unusual and any pattern or trend emerging out of the data.

Don't get dejected if the statistical test yields a non-significant result when a significant result is expected. As we have already seen the number of observations may not be adequate to pick up a real difference which may be small. Take a good look at the data to see anything that gives a clue for having ended up with a non-significant result. Try to find out whether there are any reasons for getting such a result.

William Whithering (1785 AD) who gave us digitalis for congestive cardiac failure might have concluded that digitalis was ineffective if he blindly used statistics (if he had used one at that time) to analyse the results of his study on digitalis. He found out that digitalis was effective only in a few cases and not all. This was because in his time all edema patients were grouped together as suffering from 'dropsy' and the physicians at that time did not know this group of patients actually comprised of cases of renal failure as well as cardiac failure. That was why digitalis was effective only in certain patients and Withering was alert enough to observe this important finding and note it. Had he had blindly used statistics he would have concluded digitalis was ineffective and who knows...we might not have had a chance to use digitalis all these years. Can we say with confidence that such errors cannot occur today since the medical field is so much advanced now? No. Take hypertension for example. When a cause is not known, we group it as essential hypertension. Actual cause in this group need not be limited to one. It may be one or more than one. If the causes are more than one, a sample of patients with essential hypertension need not be homogeneous, since the patients with similar disease process but with different causes might be included in the study. If a drug which is to be tested on these patients, is effective only in those with a certain cause and such patients are only a few in the sample selected, the results may not be significantly different and the drug will be considered ineffective.

Take a look at the data to see whether you can infer anything from it. It is always a good practice to visually inspect the data to see anything eye-catching. Consider the following hypothetical situation. A study on the effect of a new drug on hypertension is conducted and the data obtained are given below (Table 14.8):

Table 14.8 **Effect of a new drug on diastolic blood pressure in patients with essential hypertension**

Patient No.		BP before drug (mm of Hg)	BP after drug (mm of Hg)
1		116	120
2		110	100
3		108	116
4		100	80
5		106	78
6		108	116
7		104	92
8		98	110
	mean	106.60	101.50
	S.D.	5.70	16.66
	P value (Paired t test) = 0.395		

It is obvious that the drug is effective only in a few patients and in fact it appears to increase the diastolic blood pressure in some. If a significance test is applied straight away, what one would get is P>0.05 i.e., *no significant difference between groups and the conclusion will be the drug is ineffective.* Now look at the master chart (Table 14.9) and see whether there is anything apparent.

Table 14.9 **Effect of a new drug on diastolic blood pressure in patients with essential hypertension**

Patient No.	Age yr	Body wt Kg	Gender M/F	BP before drug mm of Hg	BP after drug mm of Hg
1	47	56	F	116	120
2	57	75	M	110	100
3	61	68	F	108	116
4	42	90	M	100	80
5	51	76	M	106	78
6	59	60	F	108	116
7	62	82	M	104	92
8	4	64	F	98	110

It is obvious that the drug has decreased blood pressure in all male patients and it appears to increase it in all female patients. This may mean that the particular drug may have a peculiar property or mechanism of action. It could also mean that the pathogenesis of essential hypertension could be different in different genders. However one cannot draw a conclusion at this stage since the number in each gender is small. Further such sub group analyses should not be done unless these sub groups are defined at the time of planning. The difference between the sub groups could easily be due to chance and hence little importance is attached even if the results of a retrospective sub group analysis is statistically significant. The results of such sub group analysis may form the basis for future studies but should not be used to draw conclusions in the current study. All one can do is to form a hypothesis and plan a separate study where one can include one group for each gender and execute the study to prove the hypothesis. The hypothetical situation given here is very simple (for illustrative purposes) and in practice it would not be that easy to stumble upon such exciting findings. The point is that one has a chance to find something earth shattering only when he is alert enough to look for it. The data may narrate a number of stories which will be missed if he does not look for them. One should visually inspect the data before trying statistical tests on it.

Alert readers may have noticed one flaw in the statistical analysis of the above data. The standard deviation of one mean (after drug) is thrice greater than the other. As we have already pointed out, `t' test can be used only if the standard deviations of means of two groups are equal or not very different in size. One has to use alternative tests in situations like the above one.

Misuse of statistics

Andrew Lang said *"An unsophisticated forecaster uses statistics as a drunken man uses lamp-posts - for support rather than for illumination".* One should use statistics to illuminate the data/study rather than for support. Statistics is only a tool and not a substitute for a good experiment. Like any tool, statistics must also be appropriately used and its appropriateness must be judged by the investigator. As someone said *`men have become the tool of their tools'*. It is especially true when it comes to statistical analysis of data. Many students make no attempt to understand the principles involved in statistical analyses but believe that research is all but finding out a P value and concluding whether the groups are significantly different or not. Some are bent upon arriving at a P value less than 0.05 so that they have a positive finding (they don't fancy a negative one) and misuse statistics to meet their objectives. Such misuses should be avoided at any cost. There is a saying that *'torture the data long enough and it will confess to anything'*.

The biggest myth about statistics is that the poor quality data can be salvaged using statistical methods later. Truth is that statistics can be used to rectify certain deficiencies but a badly planned or conducted study can never be salvaged by statistics.

Chapter 15

Drawing Conclusions

Conclusion

A scientist was interested in studying how far bullfrogs can jump. He brought a bullfrog into his laboratory, set it down, and commanded, "Jump, frog, jump!"

The frog jumped across the room.

The scientist measured the distance, then noted in his journal, "Frog with four legs - jumped eight feet."

Then he cut the frog's front legs off. Again he ordered, "Jump, frog, jump!"

The frog struggled a moment, then jumped a few feet.

After measuring the distance, the scientist noted in his journal, "Frog with two legs - jumped three feet."

Next, the scientist cut off the frog's back legs. Once more, he shouted, "Jump, frog, jump!"

The frog just lay there.

"Jump, frog, jump!" the scientist repeated. Nothing.

The scientist wrote the conclusion in his report, "When all legs are cut, frog loses its hearing".

From http://hiox.org/6544-frog-scientist.php

15. Drawing Conclusions

Inference

Interpretation

Conclusion

Limitation / weakness of the study

Having analysed the data statistically, write down the inferences. It will be clear from the data and results of analysis whether the test group and control group are significantly different and if so how much difference exists between them. The reliability of inference depends on the correctness of the study design and the accuracy of data collection.

Drawing inferences may be a straightforward process but interpretation need not be. As we have already discussed, statistical significance does not guarantee clinical significance. Another point to remember is limitations of the study. No study is perfect and every study is bound to have some pitfalls. The design may not be the most appropriate one for the study. The criteria for the chosen statistical method might not be completely fulfilled. The control and test groups may not match in all respects. Sample may not be homogeneous though it appears so. The study might end up with a smaller sample size in spite of all the precautions taken. The drawbacks of the study may be well known to the investigator from the beginning and maybe they are beyond his control to rectify. For example *an investigator may be using a diagnostic test/procedure which can detect only 85 out of 100 patients suffering from a disease*. There may be a better procedure which has 95% success rate but he could not use it due to non-availability of the same in his country. In such a situation one must keep in mind that the success rate of the procedure used is only 85% and interpret the results taking this fact into consideration. Interpretation must be made in the light of drawbacks. Sometimes a single result is not interpreted in isolation but by taking other findings also into consideration.

Final conclusions must be drawn on the basis of interpretations. An example of inferring, interpreting and drawing conclusions from a set of hypothetical data given in Table 16.1 is illustrated below.

Table 15.1 **Effect of ethanol and drug X in methanol poisoning**

Outcome in methanol poisoning	**Treatment**	
	Ethanol (*p.o.*)	**Drug X (*i.v.*)**
Treated	32	31
Survived	16	18
Dead	16	13
Hypoglycemia	22	3*
Intoxication	26	1*
Other adverse effects	6	3

*P<0.01 when compared to control (Fisher's test); the values represent the number of patients.

From the data available in Table 15.1 one can

(a) Observe :

1. Sixteen out of 32 in the ethanol group and 18 out 31 in the drug X group survived.
2. Hypoglycemia occurred in 13 and 16 patients in the ethanol and drug X groups respectively.

Observation is factual description of data.

Right..you may be her husband but the baby is not yours.

(b) Infer :

1. Ethanol and drug X are equally effective.
2. Significantly more number of patients had intoxication and hypoglycemia due to ethanol.

Inference is an act of deriving logical facts based on observation.

(c) Interpret :

1. The treatments are not administered by the same route. Ethanol was given through a nasogastric tube and drug X intravenously. Hence the route of administration does not match (*if it was possible to give ethanol intravenously, could the results be different?*).
2. Though the efficacy of both the treatments is same, drug X is better than ethanol since the occurrence of adverse effects is much less and the desired plasma level could be achieved and maintained easily as the drug is given *i.v.*

Interpretation is the explanation or analysis of what the inference means.

(d) Conclude :

1. Drug X is as effective as ethanol and can be used in the treatment of methanol poisoning.
2. Because of lesser instances of adverse effects compared to ethanol and easy administration and maintenance of plasma levels, drug X can replace ethanol in the treatment of methanol poisoning.
3. Methanol poisoning occurs due to consumption of hooch (illegally brewed alcohol mixed with methanol) very often leading to mass casualties and hence drug X may be more suitable than ethanol in such situations.

Judging or making decisions after considering the inference and the interpretation can be called conclusion which should match the objective and be supported by the data collected. However it is not incorrect or inappropriate to stretch a conclusion or two a bit beyond data e.g., *the third conclusion does not match any objective of the study and there is no hard data that supports it.* It is more of a speculation and it is perfectly alright to make one like this.

Chapter 16

Preparing a Dissertation

Dissertation

Hubert Humphrey was asked to be an advisor on a university student's dissertation. A request he accepted with delight. All proceeded well and on the date the paper was due the student delivered a nicely bound copy. Two months went by and the student hadn't heard a word. So, he went to Mr. Humphrey's office and asked him what he thought of the paper.

"Well," said Mr. Humphrey, "I think it needs to be redone."

Although dejected, the student decided to take another crack at the project.

And two months later, the student delivered the new version to Mr. Humphrey, and another month went by without hearing a word. So, again, the student went to see Mr. Humphrey, and again was told the paper had to be redone.

Totally beside himself, the student went back to the drawing board and rewrote the paper for a third time. Two months later he returned to Mr. Humphrey's office with the new term paper in hand and said to him, "I've re-researched and rewritten to the extent that I've left no stone unturned and no thought unanalysed. There is just nothing more I can do."

"OK," said Mr. Humphrey, "I guess I will read this one."

Cerberus Jokes -- From The Gates To Hades
www.xs4all.nl/~jcdverha/scijokes/8.html

16. Preparing a dissertation

As someone said "*good writing is difficult to define. It is easier to say what it is not, than what it is.*" It is not difficult to prepare a good dissertation; neither is it easy. One has to pay attention to the guidelines, norms and etiquette of scientific writing. This chapter deals with general considerations on preparing a dissertation. It is a good idea to start early, so that you can take your time and complete it by the deadline for submission. In fact one can start writing the review of literature and methodology sections soon after starting the project, provided literature search has been done and references collected and methods are finalized. Trying to write dissertation within two or three weeks (as is the case with many postgraduates) is not a good idea, since scientific writing requires time.

Formatting guidelines

Check with the university whether there are any guidelines regarding the number of pages, font size, line spacing, pagination, binding and so on. If there are guidelines, get a copy of the latest one and then follow it. If there are none, ask the guide and find out whether there are any departmental guidelines or preferences. If there are none one can follow the formatting guidelines given below (Table 16.1).

Table 16.1 **Formatting guidelines**

Characteristic	Format
Length	approximately 50-60 pages
Font	Arial/Times New Roman
Size of font	11/12
Spacing	1.5 to 2
Lines/page	25-30
Words/page	400-450
Margins	Left 1.5", Right 1", Top 1", Bottom 1"
Pagination	Continuous – number all pages

IMRAD and other sections

The dissertation is usually written in the IMRAD format, with the sections 'Introduction' (*Why did I do it?*), 'Methodology' (*What/how did I do?*), 'Results' (*What did I find?*) and 'Discussion' (*What do my findings mean?; what might be the implications?*) forming the main template (the questions were originally posed by Sir Bradford Hill, an English epidemiologist). However some additional sections are also a part of it and are usually arranged in the following order (Table 16.2).

Table 16.2. **Sections in the order of appearance in a dissertation**

Section	Approximate number of pages
Title page	1
Certificate	1
Acknowledgement	1-2
Table of contents	1
Introduction	2-3
Aims and Objectives	1
Review of literature	10-12
Methods	4-5
Results	10
Discussion	4-5
Conclusion	1
References (bibliography)	5-6
Summary	1-2
Annexures:	
List of tables, figures, photographs	1-2
Data sheets	2-3
Informed consent form	2-3
Definitions	1-2
Abbreviations	1-2
Questionnaire(s)	1-2
Master Chart	2-3

There is no consensus regarding the arrangement of sections. Some teachers will insist that the review of literature should precede the aims and objectives while some, with equally persuasive arguments will say it should be placed after. Our advice is to follow what the guide wants. If the choice is given to you, place the objectives section after the review, since it would be more logical.

The terminology for some of the sections is a matter of preference. The methods section can also be called methodology, materials and methods, patients and methods, subjects and methods and so on. Again our advice is to give in to guide's choice. The list of references are also called bibliography, though in the strict sense of the term you will only be listing the cited references and it would be appropriate to call it "list of references" or "reference list" or "references".

Raw data

There is a difference of opinion as to whether the master chart should be included in the dissertation or not. It is common practice to find that clinical disciplines include the master chart while non-clinical disciplines do not. One of the common arguments for inclusion is that the examiner gets to see the raw data and can check the conclusions. It also serves to prove the authenticity of the work to some degree. The argument against it is that, with the numerous instances of copying that have come to light, postgraduates can easily copy a dissertation and submit. As before, we would advise the students to ask their guides.

The question is whether to include the raw data or not in the dissertation.
My co-guide says I should and my guide says I shouldn't. What should I do now?

Tips for a good dissertation book

Paper quality: Use good quality paper for the final printing, either executive bond or copier paper which should be very white and thick enough so that printing or photocopying does not imprint on the other side. Choose A4 size paper which will give sufficient length for trimming prior to binding.

Binding: Do not get spiral binding done. This does not last long and gets damaged during transport, so that by the time the dissertation reaches the examiners it may not be in good shape. Use hard cover binding. The cover of the dissertation can be made to your taste if the university does not prescribe one.

Printing: Use a good quality laser printer to print the first copy and the subsequent copies can be photocopied. Make sure that the quality of photocopies is good. It is a good idea to check the copies while it is being photocopied so that one can ensure that the centering is good and the quality is acceptable. When printing the graphs and figures in colour, a good quality colour laser printer should be used. Depending on the cost one may go in for colour photocopying or printing. If the figures such as graphs drawn in MS-Excel are imported into a word document, one may not get an exact reproduction of what is seen on the monitor when printed. It is better to print the graphs from the MS-Excel itself. Photographs may be printed on whatever paper is being used for the dissertation with the proper legends. They can also be printed on photographic paper and inserted. The older practice of pasting photographs on Bristol board or thin cardboard and inserting them into the bound copy is no longer practiced.

Pagination: Pagination should be continuous throughout. Many times the pages on which photographs and figures are printed are not included in the pagination. This is not an acceptable practice. Make sure that all pages carry the correct number. The page number should be preferably placed in the bottom right corner though any other placement will also be acceptable to most examiners.

Spelling mistakes: One of the common mistakes found in the dissertation is misspelling the guide's/co-guide's and dean's names and getting the year of submission and the specialty wrong. This happens because these certificates are usually copy-pasted from other dissertations done in the previous years and not enough care is taken to alter them.

Chapter 17

Title

Signboard

A fisherman was designing a signboard for his shop and it read "Fresh Fish Sold Here Today". His friend who came to see him read it and asked "What is the need to write 'Today'? You sell fish every day. The fisherman agreed with him and struck off the word 'Today'. The friend read it again and said "You never sell stale fish. So the word 'Fresh' is redundant". The fisherman said that was right and removed the word 'Fresh'. "You sell fish here only and not anywhere else. If I were you, I would erase the word 'Here'" so said the friend. The fisherman thought for a moment and erased the word "Here". The friend read the signboard now "Fish Sold". He warned that the word "Sold" may possibly be interpreted by the customers that fish were sold out. He told the fisherman "Everyone knows you sell fish and not give it free. The word 'Sold' is not really necessary". The fisherman reluctantly wiped out the word. The friend was still not satisfied with the single word left out on the signboard - "Fish". He concluded that "Even this word 'Fish' is not required. Anyone can smell your shop miles away and find out that you are selling fish and fish only". The fisherman deleted that last word and threw the signboard into the dustbin. He vowed never to have a signboard for his shop.

- Adopted from a old joke

(dissertation titles should not end up this way)

17. Title

The importance of a title

The title is the one part of the dissertation that everyone will read. It serves as a signboard, directing the readers to the topic, study design and at times results (in case of a paper). In the case of a dissertation, the title has to be submitted to the university before the end of the first year of post-graduation, which is usually before one would have finished (or at times even started) data collection. Once the title is submitted, it is better not to change it, since any change in the title has to be intimated to the university in writing. Therefore it is in your interest to select the most appropriate title for the work proposed.

What are the characteristics of a good title?

A good title should be informative without being too long, stimulate interest without being ambiguous, should be precise without being too pedantic. It should not be in the form of a question or contain any puns. It is a good idea to insert the keywords of the dissertation into the title since many universities put the titles of the dissertations (and at times the full text) on their websites. This will help someone searching for the particular topic to find your work.

Forming a title

The title should suggest the topic, the purpose of the study and its utility. e.g., Effect of music on the quality of nocturnal sleep. At times, journals expect the major conclusions to be reflected in the title e.g., Music improves the quality of nocturnal sleep. However, since a title for a dissertation is given long before the work is started, this is not possible for a dissertation. The title should also state the study design when possible, as this would increase the chances of your work being searched for inclusion into a meta analysis (if your study is a clinical trial). Hence, specific designs such as meta analysis, randomized controlled clinical trial, case-control study etc., should be included into the title. If it is a clinical trial, it would be also prudent to add whether it is open labeled or single/ double blind study.

We would suggest that one should make four or five titles and then ask peers, guide or other senior faculty to choose, deleting those titles that are not suitable. Never select the first and only title that comes to your head. There will always be room for improving on a title.

How to write a title?

Having chosen a title one should follow the rules of writing a title. The following rules will be of help:

1. All the first letters of each word should be a capital unless the words are prepositions, adverbs or connecting words. Remember Microsoft Word has an option called "title case". This capitalizes each and every word of the title and it is incorrect. Similarly typing the title with all the letters of all the words in capitals is also incorrect.
2. If the scientific name of a bacterium or animal is used, capitalize the first letter of the genus but not the species, and the whole name must be in italics.
3. If numbers are used, and the number is a single digit then write it in words. If more than that, it should be in figures.
   e.g., Antibiotic sensitivity testing of *Streptococcus faecalis*: A study of 2018 samples from healthy young adults in four health care facilities.
4. Never use abbreviations in the title, unless the abbreviation is very well known. e.g., HIV or AIDS.
5. Preferably avoid using symbols in the titles, unless you are sure the correct symbol will appear when finally printing. Microgram when written as µg gets converted to mg if the text is copied/exported from one software to another (MS Word to Pagemaker). Beta blockers, if written as β-blockers may get converted to another meaningless symbol.

Some examples of bad titles

A descriptive study of the medical and social indicators of poor compliance to medications in diseases requiring life-long therapy with drugs in patients belonging to the lower socio-economic groups

Comment: *Too long. The word compliance is no longer preferred.*

Medical and social factors affecting adherence to drug therapy in chronic diseases

Comment: The above title may be one way of modifying it. Note that this new title does not draw attention to the poor socio-economic status of the patients.

Medical and social factors which prevent adherence to drug therapy in chronic diseases in patients from poor socio-economic group

Comment: *This is a better way of stating the title. There may still be better ideas.*

Keep off grass

Comment: *The paper was on the adverse effects of drug abuse. It is unsuitable for a scientific paper but most apt for an article in a magazine or newspaper.*

Will the pill make you ill?

Comment: *This was a paper on the possible adverse effects of the oral contraceptive pill. It is not suitable for a dissertation or thesis.*

On the effects of passive smoking in pregnancy and its effects on the growth and development of the foetus.

Comment: *This was an experimental study on rats. The title misleads the reader to think it is a study on human foetus. Starting the title with the words such as "on," "a discourse on," "an account of" sound pompous and are not in vogue anymore.*

Some more tips...

Check the title for spelling mistakes and grammatical errors. If you are not familiar with punctuation, check it with someone who knows. Use British English rather than American English for spelling of words such as colour, diarrhoea and for drug names such as adrenaline, paracetamol. However, if you choose to use the American English/spelling, stick with it throughout the dissertation for the sake of uniformity. Remember this is not a mistake; only a preference.

Chapter 18

Introduction

Friend or foe

One way of dealing with errors is to have friends who are willing to spend the time necessary to carry out a critical examination of the experimental design beforehand and the results after the experiments have been completed. An even better way is to have an enemy. An enemy is willing to devote a vast amount of time and brain power to ferreting out errors both large and small, and this without any compensation. The trouble is that really capable enemies are scarce; most of them are only ordinary. Another trouble with enemies is that they sometimes develop into friends and lose a great deal of their zeal. It was in this way the writer lost his three best enemies. Everyone, not just scientists, needs a good few enemies.

-- Georg von Békésy (Hungarian-born American physicist and psychologist, 1899-1972), quoted in George A. Olah, "A Life of Magic Chemistry" (2001),146

18. Introduction

Purpose of introduction
Approaches for introduction
Elements of introduction
Number of references

The purpose of introduction

The introduction of the dissertation is meant to

(a) introduce the reader to the topic of the dissertation,
(b) describe in general terms what was undertaken and why, and
(c) state the justification for the study. It is meant to whet the appetite of the reader. Usually this section is no longer than 2-3 pages. Remember, it is not a summary of the study, nor should you give a detailed review of literature. It is much easier to write the introduction towards the end, after finishing the other sections.

How to write the introduction?

Commonly two approaches may be followed:

1. Inverted pyramid approach: This is the style used in newspaper reporting, wherein the very first sentence states the problem e.g., *the opening sentence of a newspaper report on a robbery may be as follows "In the early hours of Monday morning, two armed men entered the house of Mr. ABC, owner of KLM steel mills, which is situated in Temptation Gardens, the posh residential area of Mumbai and got away with three lakh rupees in cash and some gold ornaments worth 2 lakh rupees after tying up the security guard while the occupants were asleep in the third floor of the house"*. As is evident, the very first sentence states (a) the time of the robbery (b) how many men were involved (c) whether they were armed or unarmed (d) whose house was robbed (e) where the house is situated (f) how much was robbed and (g) whether they escaped or not. The continuation of the paragraph will usually explain in detail the whole episode. Translating this approach in scientific writing would mean describing the problem, what needs to be done and stating the aim of the study in the very first sentence of the introduction.

e.g.

It is well known that adherence rates are low in patients with Type 1 diabetes mellitus mainly due to the pain of the injection and the difficulty they face in injecting themselves many times a day with insulin, leading to improper glycemic control and the development of complications which can be addressed by an educational programme to improve their knowledge, attitude and practice.

2. The "build up" approach: Here the problem is described gently and is revealed slowly (like a suspense thriller). It is customary to begin by stating why the topic is relevant in medicine. Give current, authentic statistics from your own country and if possible your region to explain the dimensions of the problem being investigated. Next, narrow down the topic to the problem which is intended to be studied. Describe some of the work already done and the lacunae which you hope to fill. In a nutshell the reader will be taken from a general account of the topic to more specific areas. In the process, the research question will slowly develop and evolve as a logical, formal summary of the line of reasoning.

I like your dissertation because I did not have to exert myself to read beyond 'Introduction'. I gave my verdict "not approved".

Three elements in the introduction

1. Statement of the problem and its description
2. What has been done about it or the lacunae in previous work
3. What the researcher intended to do (research question) and why (justification)

In dissertations, the aims and objectives form a separate section. Hence it would be appropriate to stop the introduction with the justification of the study. However, some guides would advise the students to write the aims in the introduction section. If you are writing a scientific paper, the introduction should end with the objectives of the study.

What an introduction should not have

There is no need to give a detailed review of the literature, since there is another section for it. Similarly, results, methodology should not figure in this section. Generally this section need not contain figures or photographs.

How many references?

There is no magic number as to how many references should figure in this section. Usually about 6-7 or less than 10. All must be related to describing the problem.

Chapter 19

Review of Literature

Plagiarists beware

One of the authors (of this book) was asked to evaluate an MD dissertation from a reputed institute in India. It was found that a major portion of the literature review section was plagiarized. The candidate copied paragraphs from various articles available on the internet and pasted the same. An online plagiarism detecting tool revealed the sources. The original articles were downloaded and the plagiarism was confirmed. The registrar of the institute was informed and it was recommended that the student should rewrite the section on review of literature and resubmit the dissertation. The examination was withheld and the student was asked to resubmit. The revised version came for scrutiny again and finally the dissertation was approved. The examination was conducted after a delay of couple of months. It is not known what other punitive measures were taken against the student at the other end.

The morals of the story: (a) the examiners do read your dissertation and they do have enough patience and time to go through the literature review section also. (b) they do take pains to log on to the internet to check and detect plagiarism in your dissertation, (c) if you are caught, you are likely to miss your examinations since you cannot appear for the examination without the dissertation being approved.

19. Review of literature

Purpose of review

Preparing to write

An easy method

References

Why review literature for a dissertation?

The review of literature is one of the longest portions of the dissertation (usually 10-12 pages in length). It is that part of the dissertation which proves that the student has achieved some amount of proficiency in scientific writing. It also permits the examiner to assess whether the student has understood his topic, searched the relevant literature adequately and is able to provide a fairly comprehensive write-up on the subject in his own words. The review sets the stage for the rest of the write-up. What is expected is a coherent critique of previous work done on the topic, outlining the strengths and limitations of such work. Since the justification would already have been stated in the introduction section, this section serves to reinforce the arguments for the need to conduct the study.

Preparing to write

Collect all relevant literature, make hard copies and file them. Then start reading all the papers/materials that are important to get a good grasp of the subject. Remember to make notes by writing a précis of each article in, say 100 words. Write this in a card and staple it with the original article. Then, further condense what has been written to about 30-50 words, using yet another colour to differentiate. This second précis is probably what you can use when writing the literature review.

An easy method

Write down the dissertation title on a sheet of paper. Underline the key words. Write each key word one below the other leaving some space between them. For each keyword write some subheadings, usually four or five. Now write two to three paragraphs for each of these subheadings. Ensure that there is a link between these paragraphs. Your review of literature is ready!

To illustrate how it is done:

The title of a dissertation is: *Medical and social factors affecting adherence in elderly patients with rheumatoid arthritis.*

The key words would be:

1. Adherence
2. Medical and social factors (affecting drug therapy)
3. Rheumatoid arthritis
4. Geriatric patients

The sub-headings for **adherence** could be:

1. Definition of adherence
2. Factors improving adherence
3. Factors causing poor adherence
4. Consequences of poor adherence in rheumatoid arthritis

I agree tuberculosis was identified in Egyptian mummies but don't you think it is a bit too much to say that dinosaurs which lived more than 100 million years ago suffered from tuberculosis...

Similarly the sub-headings for **rheumatoid arthritis** could be:

1. Description of the disease – prevalence (give figures from India), description of the disease, pathophysiology, disease burden, complications
2. Management – non-pharmacological management and pharmacological management, cost of therapy

By following this simple method you will avoid getting stuck wondering how to start. Add or delete paragraphs later on, but this method will ensure that all aspects will be covered. Do not hesitate to use illustrations or flow-charts to explain difficult concepts, tables to expand on classifications, photographs to show organisms or certain signs.

How many references should figure in this section?

Use as many as needed. About two thirds of the total references would normally figure in this section.

Chapter 20

Methodology

Language used by thesis guides

What your guide says	What your guide means
Look at this as a learning experience	You're going to suffer
I would like to have had more time to study this.	I didn't read it.
There are some aspects of the study that I would like to hear more about.	I read it but I just don't remember anything about it.
You have failed to take into account some of the more relevant literature.	You failed to cite me.
I would like you to explain...	I don't know anything about this stuff so you'll have to explain it to me.
Your statistical results don't seem to support your hypothesis.	I don't understand statistics.
You will be ready to write up soon, but need to do just one more experiment/program/chip.	You have now become a useful slave, and I am not about to let you graduate without doing more footwork for me.
Think of this as an investment in skills that will be useful to you in your later career.	We're going to exploit you to the gills.
Don't listen to XYZ, just listen to me.	Both XYZ and I are fools, but I'm funding you.
Let me explain the format of the defense.	Let me make you even more nervous.
I'm here to lend you support.	I'm here to destroy you so you won't look smarter than me.

What your guide says	What your guide means
I found the overall concept interesting.	This is my token compliment before ripping your idea to shreds.
Your hypotheses are not linked strongly enough to the existing literature.	You came up with an innovative idea and I want to make sure you never do it again.
Your research is an interesting extension of my own work.	Why didn't I think of this before you did?
Your selection of statistical tests is rather simplistic.	I'm the only one here who understands statistics and I wanted to rub it in.
How did you ensure that you had drawn a random sample?	I had to come up with at least one question and this one always works.
Let's wrap this up.	I'm hungry.

http://www.molecularstation.com/forum/science-lab-jokes/1683-thesis-supervisor-advisor-meanings-joke.html

20. Methodology

Purpose

Detail

References

Checklists

This section is commonly called by different terms – methods, material and methods, methodology, patients and methods or subjects and methods. Depending on the study design one could choose any one of the terms e.g., *in case of a phase III clinical trial, it would be apt to call the section 'patients and methods'.* Beginners to writing should start writing this section first since it is easy to write as it describes what was done and does not require much language or writing skills.

What is the purpose of this section?

The purpose of this section is to permit any person who wants to duplicate the study to do so. It should be written like a recipe, carefully, with attention to detail giving all the specifics of the drugs given, instruments used, experiments or interventions done and the statistical analysis. Use subheadings wherever needed, for clarity.

How much details should be given?

Provide as much details as necessary for a person to read what is written and conduct the study without seeking any clarification. However, if in the course of the study, you have performed standard procedures (such as measuring blood pressure using a mercury sphygmomanometer) and well established laboratory tests, for example, *like the glucose oxidase method for estimating blood sugar,* there is no need to describe the method in detail. It is enough to give the reference for this method. However, if this method was modified and the modified version was used in the work, then describe the whole method. If, as a part of the study, serum melatonin has been estimated by the RIA method as one of the parameters, in the methodology section give only details such as type of assay (RIA), the source of RIA kits (company, with country) and whether analysis was done in duplicates or triplicates. In the annexure section, one can include a detailed methodology or even give (copy) the procedure verbatim from the company's insert which comes with the kit. However, it must be clearly written that what is being reproduced is indeed the information given in the insert.

Do we need to cite references?

Give references for all uncommon and relatively new methods (including modified standard methods) which were used. If the standard treatment for rabies is used no reference is needed; if Milwaukee protocol is used, reference should be given since it is a rare method as on date. There is no hard and fast rule about what needs a reference and it is something one will learn by practice. If in doubt, ask your guide.

The following checklists are meant to act as a guide for some of the common types of dissertations. The term qualifying the various types are chosen purely on a descriptive basis and do not reflect the study design terminology.

The information under Materials & Methods is so cryptic that when I tried to replicate the study I ended up removing the rat liver rather than the heart you have managed to remove.

Checklist for methodology

Checklists can be very useful when writing the methodology section. It helps us by ensuring that all relevant details of the methodology are given and no important point is missed. Checklists for a few types of studies are given below to help the readers write this section. However, a word of caution: these are generic check-lists only, and do not cover each and every aspect of the methodology of all studies. Specific protocols may require more details to be added to describe the study.

1. **Animal study:** studies which use animals and are usually of experimental in nature.
    1. Animals – species, strain, number, age, gender, special types (pregnant/ weanling), weight, rationale for selection.
    2. Housing conditions – single/group, if group how many to a cage, light/dark cycle, food and water, temperature, acclimatization (if done – how long).
    3. Groups – name the group, how many to a group, what drugs/interventions done to each group.
    4. Drugs – name (generic), dose per kg body weight , number of doses per day, route, timing of dose
        - name of the company where drug was produced, how the solution was prepared. (fresh/stock solution), vehicle for dissolving, storage conditions of stock, drug
        - if plant extract was used – give full name of plant, which part of the plant was used, when collection was made, how was it extracted, which extract was used for study.
    5. Surgical procedure – method, anaesthesia, mortality, sham operation for controls.
    6. Tests: Describe method completely (if well established method, give reference e.g., *testing for analgesia using tail flick assay in rats*).
    7. Instrument – name, company, software (name, version, company).
    8. Ethics clearance – animal ethics committee clearance obtained or not.
    9. Statistical analysis – tests used, if more than one test say which test was used for which parameter, level of significance.
2. **Laboratory based study:** Those studies which are mainly done using samples of body fluids, tissues etc., (biochemical, microbiological, pharmacokinetic studies).
    1. Specimens collected from whom, what time, how many samples, method of collection, how were they stored (or analyzed immediately).
    2. Method of analysis – name, instrument for measurement, company.

3. Describe method of analysis – if kits were used give details of name of kit, company, sensitivity, whether duplicate or triplicate samples were used.
4. If other parameters were calculated using the plasma levels or serum levels mention which formulae were used. If dedicated software was used give the name/version/company.
5. Statistical analysis - tests used, if more than one test say which test was used for which parameter, level of significance

3. **Descriptive study:** Clinical studies which involve a description of the clinical presentation and laboratory findings in a series of cases. Sometimes referred as clinico-pathological descriptive studies.
    1. Setting – hospital OPD/in-patients, primary health centre, subcentre etc.,
    2. Time during which data collection was done (give months and years of the starting and stopping time), was it prospective or retrospective
    3. Ethics clearance
    4. Description of cases selected, diagnostic criteria, inclusion criteria, exclusion criteria, whether cases were divided into groups – if so what was the criteria used for the grouping
    5. What was done – tests performed, normal/abnormal values, treatment – medical/ surgical procedure
    6. How was outcome measured – criteria, measured after how long, who assessed outcomes
    7. Statistical analysis – were all cases included, if any were not included give reason, tests used, compared which group with what, level of significance, confidence intervals

4. **Epidemiology study:** Community based studies, pharmao-epidemiological studies, surveys as well as other designs.
    1. Detailed study design; prospective/retrospective, survey/case control/cohort
    2. Description of the population studied : Catchment area
    3. Sampling frame
    4. Sample size (how obtained)
    5. Method of sampling : Describe the method used - random, snow-ball, purposive, cluster, stratified random etc.
    6. Ethics clearance, informed consent, was community clearance obtained?
    7. Instrument or tool used -Questionnaire – If previously published scale/questionnaire used give reference, was a

translation used? Was it pre-tested? Was the questionnaire validated? Give full questionnaire. Who administered the questionnaire? Were they trained? Where was it administered (in the houses/school/community room)

- If any measurement was done using an instrument(s) (e.g., *measuring blood pressure with sphygmomanometer – how frequently were the instruments calibrated, was there a difference between the instruments used (if more than one instrument was used*), inter-rater variability (interindividual), intraindividual variability, mention whether these were checked.

8. Statistical analysis – Spread sheet used for data entry, was data entry checked?, software used for analysis, tests used, if more than one test, say which test was used for which parameter, level of significance.

5. **Clinical trial**

1. Setting: Place, level of care
2. Planned study population
3. Inclusion criteria – define terms e.g., *hypertension (in the study what did you consider as hypertension)*
4. Exclusion criteria
5. Planned interventions and their timing
6. Ethics clearance/informed consent
7. Sample size - how calculated/how target sample size was protected
8. Sampling procedure - random allocation (simple/ stratified/ block/geographical?) done or not, if so how was it done – computerized/tables, controlled by whom
9. Method of allocation concealment and timing of assignment, method to separate the generator from the executor of assignment
10. Masking (Blinding): Describe mechanism (e.g., *capsules, tablets*), similarity of treatment characteristics (appearance/taste), allocation schedule control (location of code during trial and when broken); evidence for successful blinding among participants, person doing intervention, outcome assessors and data analysis
11. Outcome measures - primary and secondary outcome measures and the minimum important differences

12. Dropouts – number, causes, at which stage
13. Analysis – Rationale and methods for statistical analysis? How many were subjected to final analysis? Was intention-to-treat analysis done or was it analysed on a per-protocol basis? Interim analysis, prospectively designed stopping rules if warranted.

The readers should note that item numbers (under the various types of studies) are given for convenience only and does not necessarily mean they have to be written in this order while writing the dissertation.

Chapter 21

Results

How not to write the results section

A Shortcut to Rejection: How Not to Write the Results Section of a Paper

David L Streiner, PhD

Can J Psychiatry 2007;52:385–9

http://publications.cpa-apc.org/media.php?mid=413

How you report your results reflects how well you understand statistics and, by implication, whether you are aware of the possible limitations of your results. If you commit any of these, or other, errors, you will be signaling to the reviewer that something is amiss—that you simply pressed the compute button without being fully aware of what you were doing or what the results may mean. In *The Doctor's Dilemma*, Shaw had the crusty physician say, "I tell you, Cholly, chloroform has done a lot of mischief. It's enabled any fool to be a surgeon." In the same way, desktop computers and the ready availability of statistical packages have enabled anyone to be a statistician. Nevertheless, just as chloroform doesn't take the place of training in surgery, so computers don't obviate the need for knowledge of statistics. If you don't have it, find someone who does. Don't be afraid to ask—most statisticians are (relatively) tame and friendly.

21. Results

Preparation

Text

Tables

Types of figures

Master chart

Statistical information

The results section of the dissertation is the segment which bears testimony to all the hard work. It is one of the parts which can be creatively written.

Before writing the results

1. Prepare a list of the data to be presented. During data collection one may have collected a lot of irrelevant data which may not have any bearing to the study and need not be displayed e.g., *in a pharmacokinetic study on healthy volunteers the investigator would have carried out the liver and kidney function tests to prove the subjects are normal. There may be no need to present this data.*
2. Select the most important finding(s) which you want to present.
3. Prepare the tables with summary data i.e., *mean values and dispersion (S.D. or S.E.) which will aid in the final write-up.*
4. Keep all the statistical data such as p values, degrees of freedom, F values ready before starting to write.
5. Read similar papers in journals to see how other authors have presented similar data.
6. Prepare the tables in the final format. If any table appears too complicated, try and make it into a figure. If any of the tables or figures conveys trivial information, write that information in text form.

How to begin

Having done the steps given above, begin writing the results. The first statement should describe the experimental subjects. It is good to start with the baseline characteristics of patients/volunteers. This can be given as a table. If there are two or more groups and only a few parameters, then a single table can list all the characteristics. If the baseline characteristics compare twenty or more parameters, think of splitting the table into two or more. In case only one or two characteristics are significantly different between the groups, then place an asterisk on the value which is different from the control or the other group and mention it in the footnote. If the group(s) differ significantly for each or majority of the items, one can make a separate column listing the p values.

The next set of results should describe the primary outcome measure. This can be followed by the secondary outcome measures. After this is done, give any unexpected results or surprising findings. In case there were negative findings, one should mention them too.

You probably have stumbled on a really wonder drug. Otherwise how would rats under 'Materials & Methods' section get transformed into mice under 'Results' section!!!!

Text, table or figure, how to choose?

Data with little amount of information can be given in a text form e.g., *if the sample had 40% men and 60% women it can be described in a single* *sentence as text rather than using a pie chart.*Tables are best used when important numerical data are being described,or when many variables are being compared at once. If a table is rather complex, it is better to device a way of splitting it into two. If the table is too simple with only two rows and two columns one may think of a way to combine the data from two or more tables. Figures are best chosen for data where the exact values do not add to the overall understanding of the paper/dissertation. It also is effective in giving a visual appeal to the results and may be the best way to present the primary results. To describe multiple observations on patients or groups, graphs may be the most suitable type of figure. However, whether tables or figures, remember they must stand alone, that is, they must be comprehensible to the reader without him having to revert to the text of the paper for any clarification - which means that the methods such as dose of drug and route should also be given along with the tables/figures to some degree.

A set of results can be described by running text, a table or a figure (Box 21.1). The only rule is never describe the same set of results using more than one method. The commonest mistake seen in dissertations in this section is that each set of results will be described in three different ways i.e., *first as text, then as a table and a figure*. Perhaps this is done with the aim of increasing the number of pages. However, this should not be done.

Box21.1 **Common methods of presenting data**

Text
Tables
Line graphs
Scatter plots
Bar diagram
Histogram
Pie-chart
Leaf and Stem plot
Pictogram
Photographs
Line-drawings

Tables

Tables are the commonest way of presenting data. Variables are arranged in either columns, rows or both depending upon the complexity of the data. A table must be simple, self explanatory, compact and readily understandable. Tables generally form the primary presentation since it can include all details and be more precise. Each row should have a heading, and so should every column (Box 21.2). Always place the control group column or row first and the experimental group(s) next. Comparison should be between groups placed side by side (preferably) and not above and below.

Box 21.2 **Format of a table**

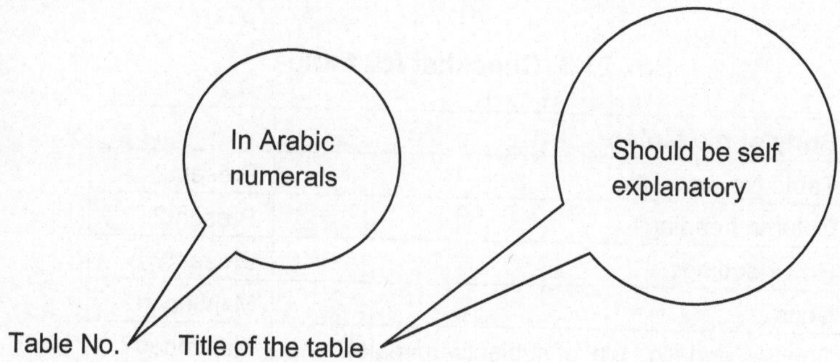

Stub	Column A heading	Column B heading	Column C heading	
			Column C1 subheading	ColumnC2 subheading
Row 1 descriptor				
Row 2 descriptor				
Row 3 descriptor				

Footnote and explanatory notes

Each table should have a number in Arabic numerals based on the order of appearance in the text. The title of the table should be self explanatory. Do not give titles such as "Clinical parameters" or "Systolic blood pressure". These are not complete titles. Footnotes and explanatory notes should be placed below the table. Check whether units for each column or row have been given. After filling up the cells make sure that the numbers add up to the total number of animals/subjects in the study.

Formatting the table: It is easy to format a table using MS Word. Each cell should be left justified (vertically) and centred (horizontally). Do not have the gridlines of each cell. It is conventional for only the top line of the table and the bottom line to be visible. In addition, the line under the column headings should also be visible. Box 21.2 illustrates the format of a table. A checklist for tables is given below in Box 21.3. It is a good idea to check the tables with a checklist to make sure they are complete in all respects.

Box 21.3 **Checklist for tables**

Body of the table :	
Table No. and Title	Present?
Column headings	Present?
Row headings	Present?
Units	Mentioned?
Species and No. ('n' of subjects/animals)	Mentioned?
Drugs name and doses, route if any	Mentioned?
Asterisks to indicate significance	Given?
Foot notes:	
The central tendency and dispersion of values (Mean/Median; SD/SEM)	Indicated?
P values /df (degrees of freedom)	Mentioned?
Expansion of abbreviations if any	Given?
The details of important derived data.	Mentioned?
Characteristics :	
Lines drawn	Appropriate?
Alignment - horizontal and vertical	Proper?
Uniformity	Achieved?
Precision	Appropriate?
Simplicity	Built in?
Clarity	Achieved?

Figures

Figures can be used to highlight important data. A list of figures is given in Box 21.1.Selection of a figure depends on the type of data. If the data is voluminous and highly complex, use more than one way of presentation. You can get tips on how to present the data from published literature which is similar to your work.

Types of figures

There are many types of figures. One should choose a figure that is appropriate for displaying the data to be presented. Box 21.4 gives a few types of figures and a rough guideline for using the same.

Box 21.4 **Types of figures**

Type	Purpose
Line graph	To show the time course of an event
Scattergram	To point out the relationship/ association between two variables
Bar diagram	To illustrate the comparative data
Histogram	To present the frequency distribution of quantitative data
Pie chart	To display the division of the whole into segments i.e. the proportions of the different components

Line graphs and scatter plots

Data can be presented very effectively using line graphs and scatter plots. The relationship or association between variables can be displayed and they can illustrate how one variable affects the other or the change in a variable over time. Y axis may increase or decrease for a corresponding change in the X axis variable. The association or lack of it between two quantitative variables may be shown using scatter plots. It is also called scattergram. Figure 21.1 depicts concentration versus time plot for a single patient. If multiple patients are involved, the mean concentration values should be plotted against time. Error bars (SEM) for each mean should also be displayed. (see Figure 21.6)

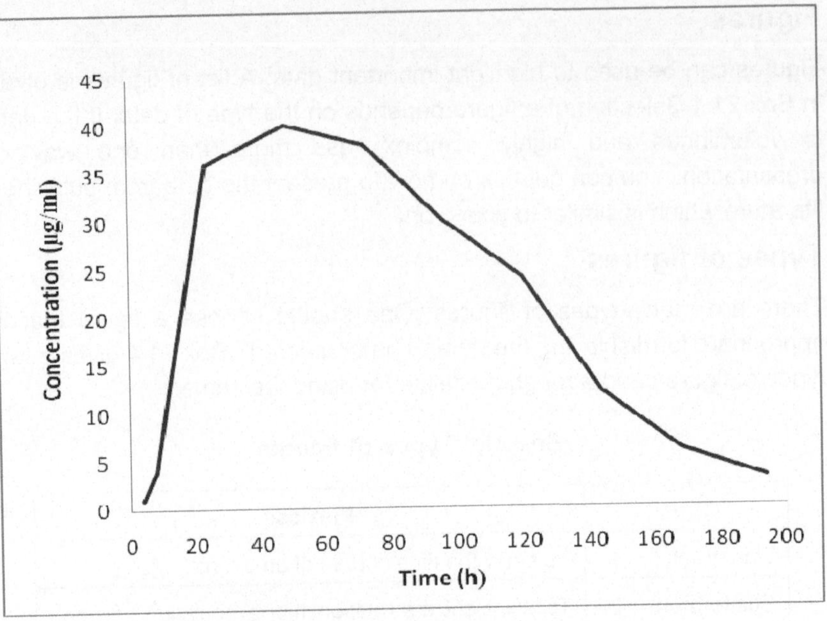

Figure 21.1 **Line graph showing concentration *Vs* time profile of a drug after oral administration in a patient**

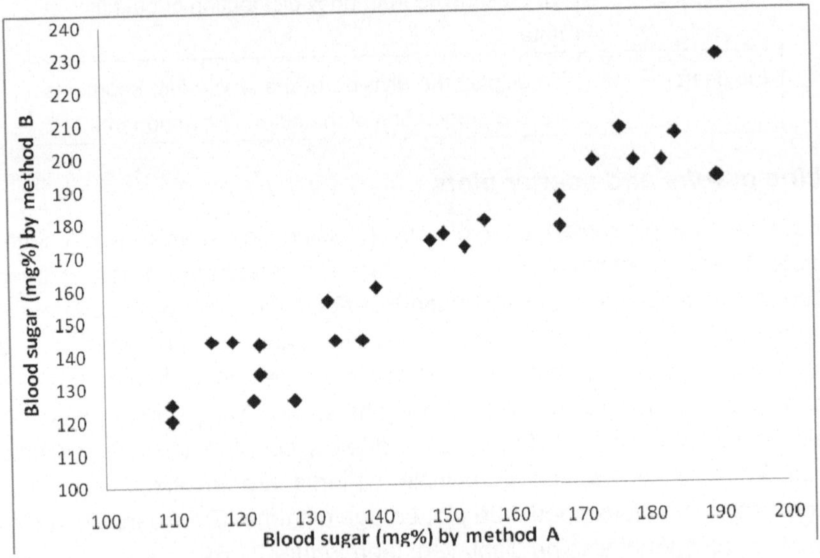

Figure 21.2 **Scatter plot of blood sugar levels measured by two methods in patients with diabetes mellitus (n=25)**

Bar diagram

Qualitative data can be presented using bars. Variables are displayed in the horizontal axis and frequency in the vertical axis. Frequency of each group is shown by the height of the bars and width is kept equal. The scale should start at zero. Note that Figure 21.3 shows error bars (SEM) for each bar (mean value)

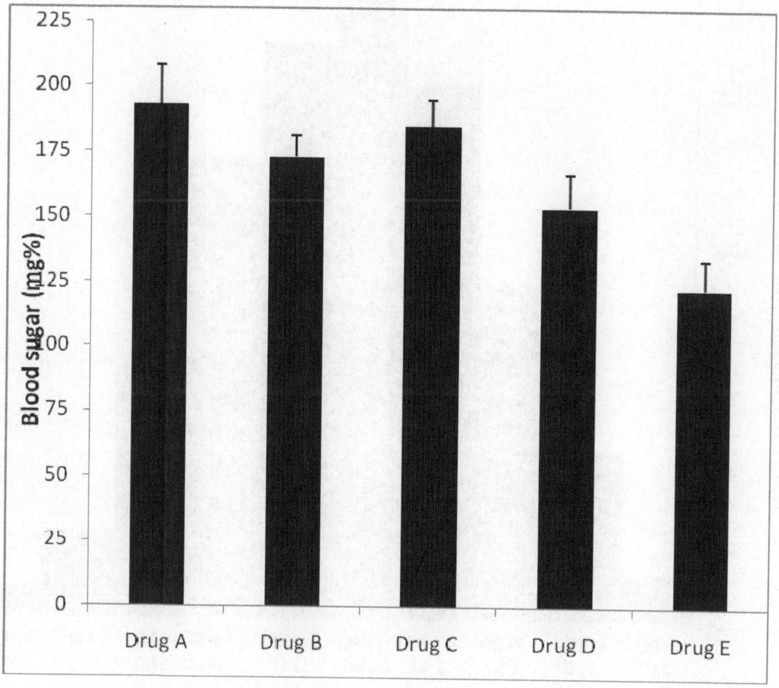

Figure 21.3 **Bar diagram showing the effect of five drugs on the mean blood sugar level in patients**

Histogram

A histogram can be considered as a bar chart for quantitative data. It is similar to bar chart but the main difference between the two is the type of data they represent. In a bar chart the order in which variables in horizontal axis are displayed is irrelevant. But in a histogram the order is maintained. Histograms are used to depict the trend in a population e.g., *for plotting the heights of adults in a population of 500 adults, first divide the population based on height in cm or in feet into various groups. Now plot the height in the X-axis and the number of persons in the Y-axis.* Generally there are no spaces between the bars and all bars are of equal width.

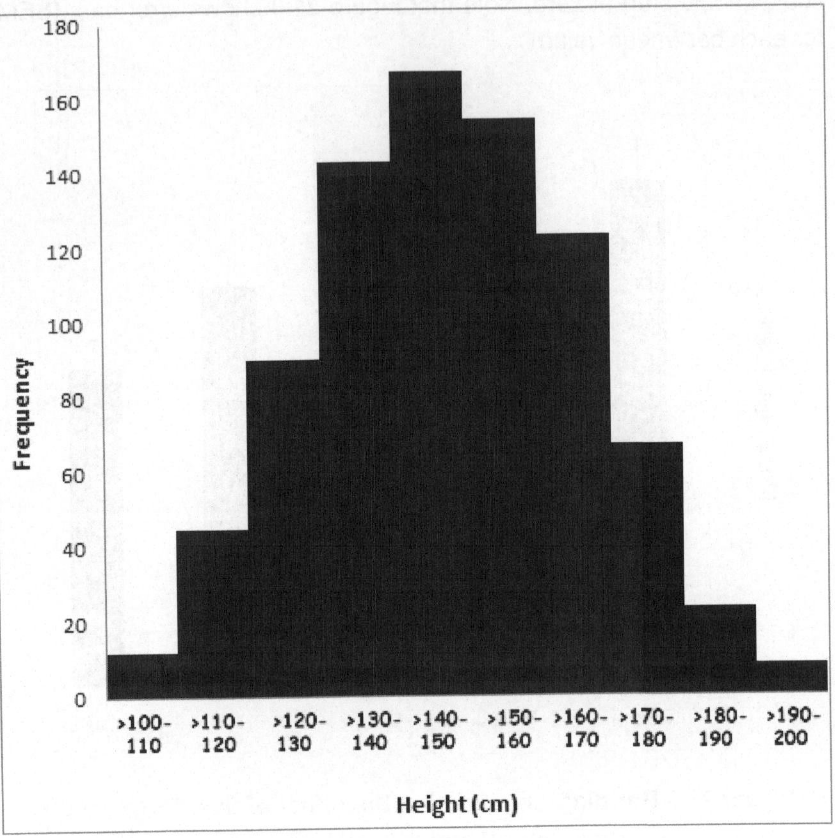

Figure 21.4 **Histogram of the height of 832 adult males in a town**

Pie chart

This is useful to display the frequencies in qualitative data. Total frequency of all variables is represented by a circle which is divided into segments like the slices of a pie (Fig 21.5). The area of each segment is proportional to the frequency observed in each category of the variable.

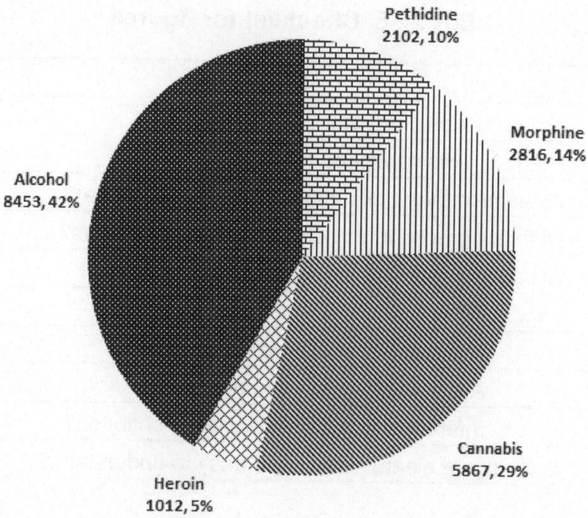

Figure 21.5 **Pie chart showing the number of addicts in a town**

Two or three dimensional figures?

Always choose a two dimensional chart for presenting data. The reason is that the variations in heights of the bars, or the visual assessment of the surfaces of a pie chart is far easier to gauge in a two dimensional figure.

Colour or black and white?

Colour printing has become so cheap that almost all students go for colour printing of the figures. Take a single colour laser print out and have the others colour photocopied or take colour laser prints of all the copies depending on the cost and how much one is willing to spend. Use primary colours for the fills. Ensure there is enough contrast between colours which are placed next to each other on the figure. If you choose to use black and white, make sure the contrast used for the fills is sufficiently bright to make it stand out.

If the figures prepared in MS Excel are imported into a word documentand printed (as a word document), the contrasts chosen may not print as seen on the monitor. Hence it is advisable to print the figures from MS Excel.

Checklist for figures

Use a checklist to verify the figures. One such checklist is given in Box 21.5. A model figure is given in Box 21.6

Box 21.5 **Checklist for figures**

Figure no. and caption (title) given?
X and Y axes graduated?
X and Y axes captioned (titled)?
Axes have their units mentioned (if appropriate)?
Different groups indicated with different markers?
SD or SE represented (graphically)?
Legend given?
`n' – number of subjects?
Are the values mean/median?
Inferential statistics (p value) mentioned?
Is the figure clean, simple and easy to understand?

Box 21.6 **A model figure**

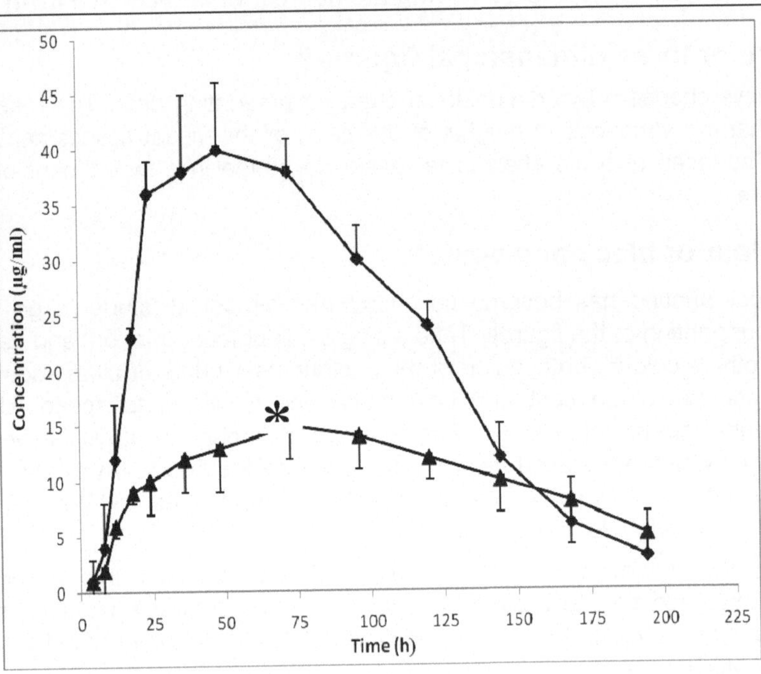

Fig 1. Mean concentration *Vs* time profile of phenytoin sodium in patients (n=12 in each group) taking(-♦-)and not taking(-▲-) cimetidine. The values are mean and the error bars represent SEM. *P<0.001; significantly lower when the area under the curves (AUC) are compared.

Placing the tables and figures

Do not present all tables and figures together at one place. Since dissertations are prepared using a word processor, it is not difficult to place the tables/figures along with the running text at an appropriate place. One has to decide the right place for a table/figure so that the reader/examiner can read the text and the table/figure without having to sift through too many pages.

Master chart

A master chart is nothing but a table which contains each and every item of data collected. Such a chart will be useful as a reference and source for overall information. It can give some idea about how to make smaller tables containing data of one or two related parameters.

Units of the parameters should be given. If using abbreviations such as h for hour and kg for kilogram, make sure the internationally accepted abbreviations are used. Do not use your own abbreviations.

The danger of including the master chart is that the entire work can be easily plagiarized by others. There have been cases where entire dissertations have been copied.

Precision of numerical data

With the advent of computers it is common to find that the mean value for weight of a group of persons is given as 57.89476 kg and the standard deviation as 7.89760. This kind of spurious precision is not warranted, after all when using a weighing scale, the nearest one would be measuring weight is probably up to one decimal place. Hence, unless someone is actually measuring to that degree of precision, it is prudent to present summary statistics only to one extra decimal place over the raw data e.g., *if while collecting the data, the weight is recorded up to one decimal place then the mean can be reported as 57.89*. The same holds good for the standard deviation or the standard error. When summarizing categorical data from small samples do not give percentages to more than one decimal place. In fact, it can be rounded up to whole numbers.

Presenting results of statistical tests

When giving the confidence intervals it is better to write “5.67 to 17.72” rather than “5.67-17.72” because in the case of one or both being negative numbers it will be confusing. For the ANOVA, it is a good practice to give the F value and the degrees of freedom. The table or figure should clearly reveal the results of the statistical tests that have been applied. As a footnote, mention which values are being compared to what. The common symbols used to represent significance is *, #, @, and so on. Using other symbols should be avoided.

Presenting the P values

With the advent of computers it is possible to compute the exact P values. Hence, they should be given as such, even if they are not significant (omit using NS or not significant). If the statistical software gives P as 0.0000, then it should be written as $P < 0.0001$. If the P value is 0.00038, it can be rounded off as 0.0004 but not written as $P < 0.05$ or $P < 0.01$.

Post-reading Exercises

1. **Comment on the following table**

Table : post operative complications

Complications	Group 1 (acrylic)	Group 2 (PMMA)	Group 3
Increased AC reaction (%)	Nil	6(26.1)	5.324
Presumed non-infectious endophthalmitis (%)	4	2(8.7)	8(30.4)
Pupillary Capture (%)	2(8.7)	16(50.4)*	-
Iris prolapse (%)			0(0)

AC- anterior chamber

2. **Comment on the following figure :**

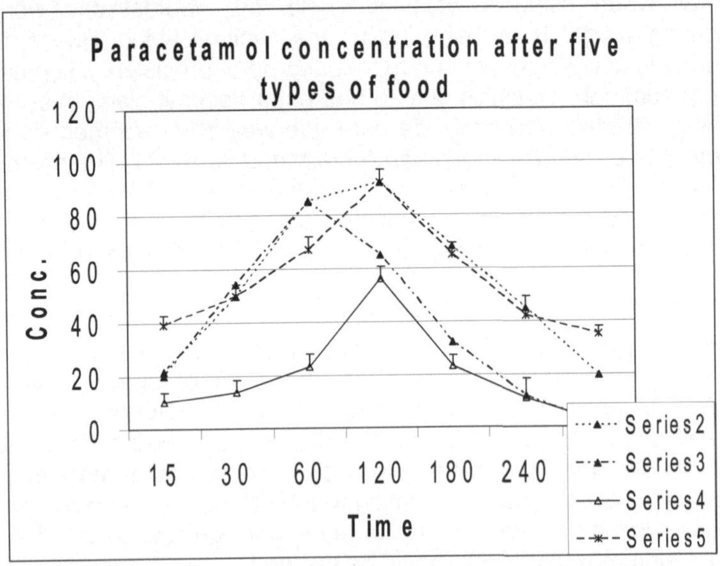

3. **What type of figure would you choose to present the following data?**

Task 1

The number of organ transplantations carried out between 2001 and 2010 in a hospital are given below :

Cornea 764; Liver 124; Kidney 254; Bone marrow 82; Pancreas 48.

Task 2

Blood sugar and endogenous insulin levels were measured in 10 diabetic subjects to find out the relationship between both. The following data were obtained:

Insulin (IU/ml)	20	29	34	25	39	10	18	6	24
Blood sugar (mg%)	282	246	193	256	180	404	264	502	250

Task 3

Blood pressure was measured at regular intervals for 2 years in a patient taking a new beta blocker. The data are given below :

Months	0	3	6	9	12	15	18	21	24
Systolic BP	148	140	132	126	124	126	122	124	126
Diastolic BP	108	106	102	96	92	96	90	92	94

Task 4

The marks scored by students in a class are given below.

Marks scored	No. of students scored
0 – 9	2
10 – 19	3
20 – 29	7
30 – 39	13
40 – 49	19
50 – 59	23
60 – 69	17
70 – 79	9
80 – 89	4
90 – 99	1

Task 5

Three new drugs were tried in anemic patients to improve the hemoglobin levels. The results are given below.

	Mean Hb (g%)	
	Males	Females
Baseline	7.3	5.1
Standard drug	14.3	12.7
Drug 1	9.9	13.1
Drug 2	15.4	7.4
Drug 3	11.6	11.9

Chapter 22

Discussion

Further hints on write-ups

1. In any collection of data, the figures that most closely confirm the theory are wrong.
2. No one you ask for help will see the mistakes either.
3. Any nagging intruder who stops by with unsought advice will see them immediately.
4. If an experiment works, you must be using the wrong equipment.
5. An experiment may be considered successful if no more than half the data must be discarded to agree with the theory.
6. No experiment is ever a complete failure. It can serve as a bad example.
7. Always leave room, when writing a report, to add an explanation if it doesn't work (Rule of the Way Out).

From http://www.xs4all.nl/~jcdverha/scijokes/8_1.html#subindex

22. Discussion

The role of discussion

Writing the discussion is one of the most difficult tasks one would face as a postgraduate. The reason is that postgraduates do not get any training on how to write one and also because, some guides themselves may not be sure how to go about it. A well written discussion is a pleasure to read, because it places the results of the study in context with the objectives, justification and future implications. The discussion is meant to interpret the results and give directions for future work.

When to write the discussion?

The discussion can only be written when all the data collection and analysis have been done and the results have been written. Only if there is a very clear picture of the results and their interpretation, one will be in a position to begin writing the discussion.

How to go about it?

Split up the discussion into the various parts as dictated by convention (see Box 22.1) and write one or two paragraphs under each heading.

Box 22.1 **Structural conventions of the discussion**

1. State the main findings
2. Relate the results of the study to the research hypothesis
3. State the strengths and weaknesses of the study
4. Compare the results with other studies
5. State the conclusions
6. Indicate implications for future research

1. **State the main findings:** Begin the discussion by stating the main findings of the study. This should not be a verbatim repetition of what was given in the results. State those findings which are statistically and clinically significant. In case there are no results which are statistically (or clinically) significant, that can also be stated (relating to the primary objective). If there are any surprising (unexpected) findings, write about them too.

2. **Relate the results of the study to the research hypothesis:** State whether the results proved or disproved the hypothesis and give reasons e.g. *if the results of a clinical trial proved no difference between the test drug and control drug, the outcome should be discussed in the light of post-hoc power analysis to show whether or not the power was sufficient to detect a difference.*
3. **State the strengths and weaknesses of the study:** No study can be perfect, therefore, listing the strengths and weaknesses of the study will show the readers (or examiners) that the results have been interpreted in the light of the strengths and weaknesses. Explain (either as a strength or limitation) the sample size, selection bias (inclusion/exclusion criteria), power and drop-outs/non-responders (reasons). In case it is a study based on laboratory findings like analyzing samples – state whether the study used duplicates or triplicates or internal controls and whether equipment was calibrated.

4. **Compare the results with other studies:** This is where a good literature search comes in handy. If there are many studies on the same topic, choose the more important ones especially the landmark studies and compare them on important parameters. A table listing the studies and the points of comparison can be made. A difference in outcome from the other studies could be due to methodology used, definitions of outcome, sample size or statistical methods. To give an example, *resistance patterns of bacteria to antibiotics will vary widely depending on whether the samples were taken from the community or hospital (methodology), the minimum inhibitory concentrations and the zone of inhibition used as cut-off values (definitions of outcome) and the size of the sample (larger samples may give different results from studies using very small samples).* Keep in mind that this opportunity should not be misused to review the literature but critically compare the results of the study with the published ones.
5. **State the conclusions:** Only those conclusions which can be supported by data should be stated. If there are any recommendations (as an outcome of the study) they too can find a place here.
6. **Indicate implications for future research:** Do not give a blanket statement like more research should be done in the future. These generalizations are not useful to anybody. Rather the direction of future research should be spelled out.

How many pages?

A discussion can be five to six pages or more if necessary. However, one must aim to present a crisp discussion which is to the point. Use as many references as necessary to argue your point of view. The references should be up to date (current) and it would be a good idea to search literature once again before starting to write the discussion.

Other tips...

Focus the discussion to the topic studied. Do not permit other issues and sub-topics remotely linked to the main topic to intrude. Try to extract useful information from the data, rather than simply stating the results as you find them e.g. *there may be a highly significant difference between the treatment (with a new drug) and control (standard drug) groups in the prophylaxis of a disease.* However, on estimating the Number Needed to Treat (NNT), if it was found that only on treating 150 patients with the new drug one person would be prevented from developing the disease, the discussion should be based on the cost of the new drug versus old drug, risk versus benefit, cost versus benefit and so on. It is simply not enough to state that one has got a significant result; an effort must be made to explain the significance in terms of clinical utility.

It is also important to maintain a logical sequence. When predicting from the results, make sure not to extrapolate findings which are not supported by data and statistical analysis. One should speculate intelligently and always avoid speculating beyond results. Correlation/association does not mean causation and hence make a careful evaluation of risk factors. One should be very careful in concluding on such lines.

After writing the discussion show it to your peers and guide well in advance to give them adequate time to make corrections. Many drafts may have to be written before getting it just right.

Chapter 23

References

'And the rest'

et al. is an abbreviation of the Latin term et alii which means "and the rest". When there are many authors, it may be difficult to name all of them when listing a reference. Hence et al. is used after naming a few authors to indicate that there are more authors who contributed to the referenced source.

The words et cetera (etc.) and et al. are used in the same way though they do not mean the same thing. While etc. refers to a list of objects, et al. refers to a list of people. The word 'and' should not be used in front of et al. (e.g. Ramasamy N, Karthik B and et al.) because et al. includes 'and' and it is redundant if used. Since et al. is an abbreviation it should end with a period but need not be italicized or underlined. But many journals italicize et al. in the articles and instruct the contributors to do so in the manuscripts submitted.

23. References

- Terminology
- Reference styles
- Sources of references
- Manual referencing
- Software

What is a reference?

A reference is defined as "a set of elements describing a document or part of a document which is sufficiently precise and detailed enough to enable a potential reader to identify and locate it". Therefore, a typical reference citation should, identify the source precisely and describe it in sufficient detail so that it can help readers easily locate and obtain the document. The sources should be described in an accurate and consistent manner. It must be indicated within the text of the dissertation/paper where the particular source was used.

Why cite references?

The framework of scientific writing requires professional citation of the sources of information used in the preparation of a manuscript. Unless the writer acknowledges the documents used to establish his arguments and criticisms, there is a possibility that one may be accused of plagiarism. Besides, one of the key functions of publication is to enable others to assess your work. Unless the sources used for your ideas, opinions and methodology are known, that will not be possible. Further, others who want to work in a similar field will find the references very useful.

What kind of information needs a reference?

This is a common dilemma. A general rule of thumb will be to give a reference for information which is not common knowledge e.g. *aspirin has analgesic and anti-inflammatory properties* – no reference needed. *Milwaukee protocol has saved a few patients from rabies* – reference needed.

Terminology

The list of references which is found near the end of the dissertation is referred to by the same name or as "reference list" and should contain all the sources mentioned in the text of the document. The term "bibliography" is used to indicate the list of all the sources of information as well as the background material which were referred and formed the basis of the written document and may or may not be cited in the text. In a sense, bibliography will also include those books and treatises consulted for the paper but which does not necessarily find a place in the text.

Referencing consists of two components:

1. In-text citation: The way the source is acknowledged and referred to (cited) in the text.
2. List of references: The way the sources are listed at the end of a dissertation/paper to enable identification, i.e., bibliography / reference list

   The key to good referencing is to stick to the selected style of referencing throughout the dissertation or paper.

Which sources can be used for referencing?

Any source which can be authenticated and the reference located can be used. Text books, review articles, original papers (including research letters) from journals, electronic sources, web resources, monographs, theses are the common sources for dissertations. Preferably, do not use newspaper clippings, articles ""in press", articles from lay magazines and personal communications since these do not have the legitimacy one associates with scientific writing. Abstracts of papers presented in scientific conferences are also to be avoided since the full paper cannot be obtained by the reader and they are usually not peer reviewed.

What are reference styles?

A reference style is the manner in which references are cited within the text and then listed at the end of the manuscript. The two commonest and well known styles of referencing in the biomedical fields are Vancouver and Harvard.

Vancouver style

This is the style that is being promoted by the International Committee of Medical Journal Editors (ICMJE). The style gets its name from the city in which the meeting of ICMJE was held in order to evolve a common style which could be adopted by all the major journals and also used for cataloguing. It is also rarely referred to as Citation-order, Citation-by-reference or Author-number system. It is the most commonly used system at present.

In the Vancouver style, references are numbered consecutively in the order in which they are first mentioned in the text. They are identified by Arabic numerals in parentheses in text, tables, and legends. Each reference will be listed only once, since the same number is used throughout the dissertation or manuscript. The titles of the journals are abbreviated according to the style used in Index Medicus/PubMed.

Box 23.1 **Vancouver style**

An example of in-text citation in the Vancouver style :	Cultural attitudes are known to influence compliance (1-3).
However, journals which follow this style are permitted to make their own modifications. For instance, the same example might appear in the journal as :	Cultural attitudes are known to influence compliance.[1-3] OR as: Cultural attitudes are known to influence compliance.[1-3]
An example of the listing of a paper in a journal :	Parkin DM, Clayton D, Black RJ. Childhood leukaemia in Europe after Chernobyl: five year follow-up. Br J Cancer 1996;73:1006-12.

List each author's last name and initials. Do not include full first and middle names. List all authors, but if the number exceeds six, give the first six followed by "*et al.*" meaning *"and the rest"*. What one should note is that every space, comma, colon and full stop is important. The usual mistakes postgraduates make is that they don't pay enough attention to details. The list of examples in the Vancouver style is given in Appendix 3. However it would be a good idea to check on the ICMJE website (www.icmje.org) which gives the link to the Vancouver style of formatting references and see whether you have the most recent updated version.

Harvard style

This was first introduced by the American Psychology Association and hence also known as the APA system, Author-Date / Name and Year style. It was very widely used till the introduction of the Vancouver style when its popularity began to wane. However, many journals still continue to use it. This system uses the primary author's last name and year of publication in the body of the text as given in Box 23.2

The reference list (at the end of the paper or dissertation) is arranged alphabetically by the author's names. Journal names are given in full and are italicized, as are book names.

Box 23.2 **Harvard style**

An example of in-text citation in the Harvard style :	Previous studies by Marshall (1968), Smith *et al.*(1977) and Harvey (1983) have shown that cultural attitudes influence compliance. Or Previous studies have shown that cultural attitudes influence compliance (Marshall 1968, Smith et al.1977 and Harvey 1983).
An example of the listing of a paper in a journal:	Annas, G.J. (1997), 'New drugs for acute respiratory distress syndrome', New England Journal of Medicine, vol. 337, no. 6, pp. 435-439.
A book would be listed as:	Grinspoon, L. & Bakalar, J.B. (1993), Marijuana: the forbidden medicine, Yale University Press, London.

For further examples on the Harvard style of referencing may be obtained from websites. All one has to do is to search Google with search terms '*Harvard style referencing examples*'.

Which style to choose?

In the absence of any guidelines we would advise the readers to choose the Vancouver format since this is the style that is being followed by the major biomedical journals of the world. Hence in case you want to publish your dissertation there need not be additional effort to change the style.

Using the examples

If you go through http://www.nlm.nih.gov/citingmedicine, it would become clear that an example of almost every possible type of document is represented. If it is the first time you are using these examples, it would be a good idea to get some help from the guide. The abbreviations for the titles of journals can be accessed from PubMed (http://www.ncbi.nih.gov/entrez/query.fcgi). After connecting to PubMed, click on "journals database" and then enter the full title (name) of the journal to view its abbreviation.

How many references...?

Most postgraduates seem to think there is a specific number that "must" be listed in order to impress the examiners. There is no obligatory number. However between 75-100 would be an appropriate number for a dissertation. A thesis will require much more since the length of the thesis will be much longer. This does not mean that one cannot have only 60 references. The number should be decided by the write-up, which in turn will be decided on the topic, how much work has been done on the topic and so on.

Citing from abstracts and cross references

The dictum for referencing is "never cite a reference which you have not read". This means that one should cite only those references for which he has found the full text of the paper and has read it completely. Citing after reading only the abstract is not a good practice since there may be discrepancies between the full paper and its abstract which will lead the reader to misquote the reference. It is also not good practice to list a reference of a paper after having read about the contents of it from the cross reference and without having read either the abstract or the full paper which is being cited. Therefore, in case there is a need to cite a paper which could not be retrieved or read, but the information appeared in a review article (or any other paper type), then cite only the review article which you have read as the source of information. Postgraduates commonly cite and list papers written in early 1900s by reading some review articles. There is a remote chance that even the writer of the review never read the original articles which appeared in the 1900s.

The common excuse given by postgraduates is that full papers are difficult (but not impossible) to collect. We would suggest that you write to the author, email him, contact friends working in the same institute or having access to better libraries, post a request on egroups/ forums or use inter-library services for getting the full reference. Generally, not enough effort is put into obtaining a full reference. Perhaps the only time when an abstract can be used (cited) is when the publication is in another language, and only the translated abstract is available from Pubmed.

How current should references be?

References should be as current as possible. Many postgraduates cite references which are more than one or two decades old. It is generally desirable to have a good number of references from work published within the previous five years. Search thoroughly just before writing the dissertation for any recent articles on the topic which may have been missed.

Which references to avoid?

Never cite a retracted paper unless you are writing about that paper or on the topic. Articles published in websites meant for general public and personal communications must not be listed as references in a scientific article.

Tips on referencing manually (Vancouver format)

If you are not using a bibliography managing software and would be managing your references manually, then the following tips will be useful (only if you have chosen the Vancouver format).

1. Type all your references carefully in the Vancouver format. Do not bother about the order of appearance at this point of time. Check them for errors.
2. Give each reference a number. (If you are using MS Word, do not use the option of numbering automatically). The numbers must be serially typed in.
3. When you write your dissertation, cite the corresponding numbers of the references, even if they do not happen to be in order.

4. Once all the corrections are over and the final draft is ready, now arrange the references in the reference list according to the order in which they appear in the text and renumber them serially (without deleting the original numbers given to them). At this point of time each reference in the reference list will have two numbers, i.e., one which is the old number and one which has been given after arranging it in the order of appearance according to the text.
5. Change the numbers of the in-text citations to match with the new numbers of the reference list.
6. Now delete the 'old' numbers in the reference list.

In case you type the references in the order in which they appear and give the numbers in this order too, you will find that during corrections you may decide to delete, add or change the place of appearance of the references. This will necessitate you having to redo the order of all references and change the numbering too. Hence, keep this for the very last when the final version of the dissertation or thesis is ready.

Software to manage bibliography

There are, at present, excellent software packages which are commercially available, to manage bibliography. Reference Manager® (also called Refman), EndNote®, Procite®, Library Master®, are some, to name a few. Freeware such as MyNotes, Scholar's Aid, Gelit, Biblio Express and Zotero are also downloadable from the internet. These bibliography database managers can be used for the following purposes:

1. Generating a list of selected references from the database (electronic or online such as Medline) in a format required for publication.
2. Prepare instantaneous formatted in-text citations and bibliographies during manuscript preparation
3. Building a database of references to journal articles, books, and other research publications, using both manual and electronic input methods
4. Searching the created database by author, subject, journal name, and other criteria
5. Format references in multiple bibliographic styles, to meet the requirements of scholarly publications.

There are obvious advantages in using these software packages. We would encourage all PG students to familiarize themselves with at least one of them and use it in the preparation of the dissertation.

The limiting factor is the cost of some of the software. However, cheaper rates are available for students and one could avail this offer. Zotero is a free online software and it is recommended for PGs.

References – Much ado about nothing?

Many postgraduates think that references do not form an important part of the dissertation. One should remember that it is very easy for the examiner to check the veracity of the reference by going online and doing a PubMed search. In case the reference is wrongly cited, it creates a bad impression of the student and the guide and examiners will tend to infer that if the referencing was sloppy, then maybe the research work too was sloppy.

Missing references: References that are cited in the text but are not listed in the list of references or listed but not cited are called missing references. These should be avoided at all costs.

Ghost references: Those references in the list which cannot be traced or do not exist. If examiners find even a single ghost reference the credibility of the dissertation will be at stake.

Duplicate references: Sometimes the same reference will be listed twice, with different identifying numbers. This will easily happen with the Vancouver style, especially if there are a large number of references which are manually managed. One should take every effort to make sure this does not happen.

Common myths

There seems to be a general unwritten rule among some academics, that it is impossible to collect the full text of all listed references in a PhD thesis or in a dissertation if the number of references listed is very large. There should be no compromise on this issue. If you are citing a reference after reading only the abstract, it should be written (abstract) within parentheses after the citation in the list of references. It is perhaps acceptable if the paper is in another language and only the abstract is in English. But for all other references there is really no excuse. The dictum is *"cite only those papers which you have read completely"*. The ultimate aim of a dissertation or thesis is mastery of the subject which you can hope only if you have read widely.

Important skill

Referencing is an important skill which is the keystone of scientific writing. The principles of correct referencing have to be followed even though use of bibliographic database managers makes the job much easier. Practice will certainly make one proficient in this area.

Post-reading Exercises

1. Write a journal article reference in Vancouver and Harvard styles using the following information :

   Title : Efficacy of anti-scorpion venom serum over prazosin in the management of severe scorpion envenomation

   Authors: VS Natu, SB Kamerkar, K Geeta, K Vidya, V Natu, S Sane, R Kushte, S Thatte, DA Uchil, NN Rege, RD Bapat

   Year : 2010

   Volume : 56

   Issue : 4

   Page : 275-280

2. Write a book reference in Vancouver and Harvard styles using the following information :

   Title : 3D and 4D Ultrasound: A Text & Atlas

   Authors: Ashok Khurana, Nirvikar Dahiya

   Year : 2004

   Edition : First

   Publisher : JAYPEE BROTHERS MEDICAL PUBLISHERS (P) LTD.

   Place of publication : New Delhi

3. Comment on the format of the references given below:

   (a) Turner RH, AK Kurban, Ryan T John. Fibrinolytic activity in human skin following epidermal injury. Journal Invest Dermatol 1969;53:458-62.

   (b) Nishioka K & Ryan. Inhibitors and proactivators of fibrinolysis in human epidermis. Br J Dermatol 1971;85:561-565.

   (c) Bhadal N, Wall IB, Porter SR, Broad S, Lindahl GE, Whawell S, Lewis MP. The effect of mechanical strain on protease production by keratinocytes. Br J Dermatol 2008; 00:396-8.

(d) Ogura Y et al. Plasmin induces degradation and dysfunction of laminin 332(laminin 5) and impaired assembly of basement membrane at the dermal-epidermal junction. British Journal of Dermatology 2008;159:49-60.

(e) Ryan TJ and Mallon EC. Lymphatics and the processing of antigen. Clin Dermatol 1995;13:485-9234.

(f) Elephantiasis and chronic wound healing, 19th century and contemporary viewpoints that are relevant to hypotheses concerning lymphoedema, leprosy, erysipelas and psoriasis. 2009;42:19-25.

(g) SR, Ryan TJ, Mahadevan E, Bose KS, Prasanna KS. Lymphology 2007 40 3-13.

(h) Mortimer PS, Cherry GW, Jones RL, Barnhill RL, Ryan TJ. The importance of elastic fibres in skin lymphatics. British J Dermatol, 1983,108, 566-561.

Chapter 24

What not to do?

You cannot get away.....

An MD student, a PhD student, and their guide (professor) are walking through a city park and they find an antique oil lamp. They rub it and a Genie comes out in a puff of smoke.

The Genie says, "I usually only grant three wishes, so I'll give each of you just one."

"Me first! Me first!" says the MD student. "I want to be in the Bahamas, driving a speedboat with a gorgeous woman who sunbathes topless." Poof! He's gone. "Me next! Me next!" says the PhD student. "I want to be in Hawaii, relaxing on the beach with a professional hula dancer on one side and a Mai Tai on the other." Poof! He's gone. "You're next," the Genie says to the professor. The professor says, "I want those guys back in the lab after lunch."

From http://home.sprynet.com/~owl1/psych.htm

24. What not to do?

Error free document
Plagiarism
Playing with data
Improper acknowledgements
Trouble with references
Discrepancies
Publication

Error free document

In writing a dissertation, it is not only important to know what to do but, also, what not to do. While writing a technically sound dissertation may not award a student laurels, a bad one could land him in trouble. As a student one should always expect the examiner to look for mistakes and the main goal should be in producing an error free document without any inconsistencies.

Plagiarism

Plagiarising is literally playing with fire. Anyone who is smart enough (or devious enough) to copy-paste paragraphs or portions of text from other articles without proper attribution to the author from where the text is taken, is laying himself or herself wide open to their thesis being rejected by the examiner. Some of the more knowledgeable and stricter examiners will reject if large portions are copied and the reference is given. This is because when copying large amounts of text verbatim it should be placed within quotes, and anyone failing to do this would, in the strict sense be accused of plagiarism.

Playing with data

Giving wrong information: One of the most common experiences which postgraduates face when they have completed data analysis is to find that there is nothing significant which comes out of the study. Rather than trying to explain their results in terms of the reasons for the findings, some of them tend to indulge in data massaging. Let me illustrate with an example.

In a study on the effect of a drug on serum melatonin levels, the standard deviations for the serum melatonin values were very wide making the comparison between the two groups (placebo and drug treated) as not statistically significant. However, on removing the extreme values (and justifying the exclusion as outliers, though, in real terms they were not) the results became significant. The dilemma here is should the values be excluded when they cannot be labeled outliers? Definitely not, because biological variation is quite a well known phenomenon and especially when it comes to hormonal levels, these are known to fluctuate quite a lot even for the same individual. Hence, sanitizing the data should never be an option, since the conclusions drawn would not reflect the true picture. One may get the 'p' value he wanted but it would lead to misinformation. Therefore, playing with data is not only unethical but completely unscientific as well.

Hiding unfavorable results: At times results throw up unexpected outcomes and part of the data may suggest outcomes that are not in keeping with the hypothesis. The obvious knee-jerk action by most would be to hide it, and not make a mention of it; after all, it would save the student the trouble of having to explain this data. But we should remember that in science we are mandated to reveal the truth and the whole truth. There are many instances in the past where pharmaceutical companies have suppressed data regarding adverse outcomes and published only the conclusions favourable to sell their product. This has led to major undesirable outcomes for patients which have led to products being withdrawn from the market.

So what should be done about unfavourable results? Report them as they are and try to explain them. If you cannot find an explanation you can think of speculating, intelligently in the light of what is known. If even that is not possible, say you cannot explain this finding at this point of time and when drawing conclusions, make sure they are guarded.

Improper acknowledgements

Not acknowledging those helped: Most dissertations will have an acknowledgement section running to one to ten pages at least. While postgraduates are keen to acknowledge their parents, spouses and even God they are irresponsible in not acknowledging those who helped for fear of offending their head of the department or guide. Many dissertations are done with the help of a person who is low down in the pecking order, who may not be in the good books of the guide or head of the department. Acknowledging their help officially is ethical and considered good scientific practice.

Not acknowledging funding/donors of drugs: If drugs or other consumable like kits, chemical other materials are given by pharmaceutical companies or funding agencies, they must be acknowledged. There is a trend to refrain from acknowledging pharmaceutical companies, for fear of having to declare conflict of interest when writing the paper. There is no logic behind this sort of thinking.

Redundant data presentation

The idea of presenting data is to inform the reader of what was found in relation to addressing the objectives. In any clinical study one may end up collecting a lot of data which are not going to support the hypothesis or objectives (non-significant results). This data need not be elaborately presented in the form of tables and figures. One may add two or three sentences in the text that this data are not significantly different. But leaving them out without a mention is also not correct.

Presenting the same data in tables and figures (sometimes more than one type of figures) should never be allowed. Use either a table or any one type of the most appropriate illustration for one set of data.

Tricks (not to be followed)

Postgraduates have a mistaken notion that dissertations are valued by their size. In order to increase the number of pages, many resort to cheap tricks such as writing 10 lines to a page, leaving two inch margins, using font size of 14, double or triple spacing, inserting one small table or figure in a single page with no other text in it. In these times of ecological awareness one should not resort to these tricks.

Trouble with references

Whenever possible, quote only from references for which one has been able to obtain the full paper. In case of references in other languages such as Spanish or French, the translated abstract may be used and cited. However, it should be clearly indicated (such as 'Abstract; article in Spanish') in the reference list when an abstract is cited. The reason for this is because many abstracts do not reflect the original paper accurately and never cite a reference which you have not read.

It is a good policy to check each and every reference against the cited version on Pubmed. The complex nature of some names where it is difficult to figure out which is the surname and which is the first name as well as abbreviations for journal names can be easily sorted out.

Ten minutes after the examiner started reading my dissertation he threw it out.

Why the delay? Ten minutes is too long.

Discrepancies

The whole process of a scientific report rests on its consistency. In a dissertation this would translate as the title matching with the objectives, the methodology designed to address the objectives, the results and discussion to compliment each other and conclusions to match the objectives. The incongruence usually creeps in at the writing stage because this is not done in one sitting. Many postgraduates tend to copy and paste the methodology they had submitted with their proposal to the ethics committee or research committee. At that time the proposed sample size would be different from the final sample size. Corrections in the results section may not get reflected in the discussion or in the summary. The box 24.1 gives a check list to help eliminate the discrepancies.

Summary and main text: We would recommend that the summary and conclusions are written after the initial corrections by the guide are over. It is important to update the summary, once the text has been corrected and final draft has been made. Check whether the objectives, methods (e.g. *data collection procedure, sample size*), numerical results and conclusions in both the summary and the respective sections of main text are matching. The numerical data must be identical.

Tables/Figures and Results section: The common discrepancies seen in this section are:

- the wrong table/figure number is cited in the text when referring to a particular table/figure
- the number of tables/figures listed in the annexure in the list of tables/figures do not match with the number/order/title of the tables/figures in the results section
- the table/figure is not cited within the text of the results

All of these can be easily spotted and rectified by careful revision and proof reading.

Box 24.1 **Discrepancies in the dissertation**

Title *Vs* Main text	The title in general may not be appropriate. Part of the title may be irrelevant. e.g. *The title "Clinical, laboratory and histopathological profile of ....." may not be relevant if histopathological results are not reported.*
Abstract *Vs* Main text	Objectives, methodological details, numerical results, conclusions may not match
Objectives Vs Conclusions	Check whether a conclusion is spelt out for each objective. Check each conclusion whether it answers research question or matches with the objective.
Tables/Illustrations *Vs* Results	Check all numerical data. Text description such as 'increased' and 'decreased' under Results must be reflected in the table/figures.
Discussion *Vs* Results	Description of results and numerical values of results if any mentioned under Discussion should match with those under Results.
Conclusions *Vs* Data	Only those conclusions for which data are presented must be retained. Others should be removed.
Reference list *Vs* Citation in the text	Ghost references : Reference cited but not listed; reference listed but not cited Citation does not match the listed reference. Author name/year cited does not match with that of the reference listed.

Mismatch between objectives and conclusions: When starting the work the objectives are clearly listed. However, by the time it is over and the results are analysed more ideas could have crept in and the data may reveal or give some insight into other aspects of the study. The mismatch between the objectives and conclusions appear when one starts to extrapolate the data and speculate. While speculating intelligently is permissible within the context of the discussion one cannot form a conclusion based on speculation.

If the only objective of the study was 'to evaluate the efficacy of drug A as an antihypertensive in young adults with hypertension' the conclusions cannot be any of the following:

- drug A may be a good antihypertensive in elderly age group
- drug A can be effective in pregnancy related hypertension
- drug A is a safe and cheap antihypertensive
- the adverse effect profile of drug A is very favourable

It should be noted that unless the secondary objectives of the study focused on any of the conclusions above like observing the adverse effects or cost, these conclusions cannot and should not be made. As a rule of thumb, for each objective – just write one conclusion. Most importantly the conclusions must be supported by the data.

Publication

The effort and interest shown by many postgraduates to complete their dissertation is not shown when it comes to publishing their work. If you believe you have found something useful and the work is publishable – it should be sent for publication. The important thing is to do it immediately after the exam so that the work will be fresh for you to write it up. Guides often become disillusioned with postgraduates for not writing up their dissertations and submitting it to journals. At the time of passing the examination many postgraduates do not realize the value of a publication. It is only when they appear in interviews that the importance given to an original publication will be felt. Hence, do not put off trying to get the work published.

Chapter 25

Research Misconduct

Mike Adams, Natural News

Thursday, February 18th, 2010

http://www.naturalnews.com/028194_Scott_Reuben_research_fraud.html

It's being called the largest research fraud in medical history. Dr. Scott Reuben, a former member of Pfizer's speakers' bureau, has agreed to plead guilty to faking dozens of research studies that were published in medical journals.

Now being reported across the mainstream media is the fact that Dr. Reuben accepted a $75,000 grant from Pfizer to study Celebrex in 2005. His research, which was published in a medical journal, has since been quoted by hundreds of other doctors and researchers as "proof" that Celebrex helped reduce pain during post-surgical recovery.

There's only one problem with all this:

No patients were ever enrolled in the study!

Dr. Scott Reuben, it turns out, *faked the entire study* and got it published anyway.

It wasn't the first study faked by Dr. Reuben: **He also faked study data on Bextra and Vioxx drugs, reports the Wall Street Journal.**

As a result of Dr. Reuben's faked studies, the peer-reviewed medical journal *Anesthesia & Analgesia* was forced to retract 10 "scientific" papers authored by Reuben. *The Day* of London reports that 21 articles written by Dr. Reuben that appear in medical journals have apparently been fabricated, too, and must be retracted.

25. Research misconduct

What is research misconduct?

The definition of research misconduct given by the Office of Research Integrity, USA (ORI;http://ori.dhhs.gov/misconduct/definition_ misconduct.shtml) is self explanatory:

Research misconduct means fabrication, falsification, or plagiarism in proposing, performing, or reviewing research, or in reporting research results.

(a) *Fabrication is making up data or results and recording or reporting them.*

(b) *Falsification is manipulating research materials, equipment, or processes, or changing or omitting data or results such that the research is not accurately represented in the research record.*

(c) *Plagiarism is the appropriation of another person's ideas, processes, results, or words without giving appropriate credit.*

(d) *Research misconduct does not include honest error or differences of opinion.*

Intellectual honesty is the minimum standard expected of a researcher. Lack of integrity could lead to a disastrous outcome affecting the scientific community and the general public. The Joint Consensus on Misconduct in Biomedical Research, Edinburgh 1999 stated that *"Every single case of fraud and misconduct reduces public confidence, abuses the use of public and charitable funds and causes insult and frustration to the vast majority of careful and honest workers"*. Hence it is essential that researchers should strictly adhere to the rules regulations, guidelines, commonly accepted professional code of conduct and ethical norms which guide research.

Breach of ethical requirements

The above definition of the ORI does not include violation of ethical requirements which is also considered serious research misconduct. For example, *carrying out a research project or a procedure without the permission of ethics committee and not obtaining informed consent as explained in the protocol* come under misconduct which also includes intentionally violating any of the basic ethical principles such as 'autonomy', 'equality and justice' and 'beneficence or non-maleficence' during the conduct of research.

Misuse of funds and safety violations are also construed as research misconduct. There are many reasons for researchers to indulge in misconduct; some of them are listed in Box 25.1.

He did not recruit even a single subject for his study but faked the entire data and published it. When he got caught he had the audacity to claim that he did the study with robots......

Box 25.1 **Reasons for research misconduct**

Guide related – poor mentoring

Student related – apathy, ambition

Incentives – better job, promotion, grant

Pressure to meet deadlines, regulatory requirements.

Psychiatric illness

Prestige, competition, ego

Beware of the consequences

Research misconduct damages the name and fame of the researcher who indulges in it and he is finally left with shame. Every researcher should be careful not to get into a situation where he is charged with research misconduct. PGs should be doubly careful because, for many of them dissertation is their first research project and they may not be familiar with the rules of the game. Claiming ignorance may not protect the researcher who has committed an act of misconduct, since it is akin to a driver on a road who when caught for a traffic violation says he did not know the rules. Getting caught is relatively easy due to the extensive reach of the internet. It is simply not worth risking ones career. It is, therefore, essential for PGs to go through the GCP/GLP and ethical guidelines thoroughly before starting the work. They should make sure the guidelines are followed in letter and spirit when conducting research.

Chapter 26

Ethics of Human Research

Who was more unethical?

Everyone remembers unethical research conducted by Nazis but a very few are aware that Japanese Military Unit 731 conducted equally atrocious experiments on the prisoners during World War II. Men, women, children, and infants were dissected alive without anesthesia and some of them were infected with various organism. The stomachs were surgically removed in some prisoners and the esophagus was sutured to the intestines. Parts of the brain, lungs, liver and other organs were removed all in the name of research. Syphilis and other venereal diseases were induced in prisoners and studied. Air was injected to determine the onset of embolism. Some of the prisoners were exposed to heavy doses of X-rays. Some of them were placed into centrifuges and spun till death. More details on such utterly unethical and inhuman experiments can be read from Wikipedia.

When the Japanese surrendered, the Americans took over the country. But the doctors, scientists and officials who were responsible for inhuman experiments were not brought to book. The Americans offered them immunity in exchange for the data collected from the experiments. They realised that they would never be able to conduct such experiments in the US and the data must be kept away from the Russians. That was how the Japanese war criminals got immunity and were never even tried.

So, who was more unethical? Japanese or Americans?

Based on :

http://en.wikipedia.org/wiki/Unit_731

http://curiosity.discovery.com/question/medical-research-obtained-unethical-conditions

http://news.bbc.co.uk/2/hi/programmes/correspondent/1796044.stm

26. Ethics of Human Research

- Biomedical ethics
- Guidelines
- Informed consent
- Ethics committee
- Applying for permission

What is biomedical ethics?

Ethics (from the Greek word "ethikos" meaning arising from habit, morality) is that branch of philosophy concerned with the distinction between right and wrong, with moral choices, duties and obligations. Biomedical ethics deals with the values and guidelines that should govern judgments in medical practice including research. The main principles of biomedical ethics are Autonomy (right to choose, respect for human rights, dignity and freedom), Non Maleficence (do no harm), Beneficence (do good), Justice and Equality.

Guidelines for research in human subjects

The Nazi trials at Nuremburg highlighted the need for a set of guidelines which could be used to govern medical research on human subjects. The Nuremberg Code was a set of ten principles which laid down the norms for research involving humans. This was primarily drawn up to protect human subjects against such instances of torture, cruelty and exploitation being carried out in the name of medical research. The Helsinki Declaration, adopted by the World Medical Association (WMA) General Assembly in 1964 at Helsinki, Finland, is a document consisting of the general principles and specific guidelines for medical research involving human subjects. The latest version (2008) can be downloaded from the WMA's official website at www.wma.net.

The Indian Council of Medical Research has brought out "Ethical guidelines for biomedical research on human subjects" in the year 2006. This document provides authoritative information on the ethics of conducting research in human subjects in India. We would recommend all PGs to read this document to have a thorough understanding of the ethical aspects that have to be considered when planning, conducting and reporting research done on humans. This document is freely downloadable from http://www.icmr.nic.in/bioethics.htm. Those who want to study the social aspects of health care should read the "Ethical guidelines for social science research in health" which can be downloaded from http://www.cehat.org/publications/ethical.html.

How to get ethics clearance

In case the study is to be done on humans, make sure the study is based on a sound scientific rationale and is designed properly. Make sure it satisfies all the ethical criteria which are necessary such as: an investigator who has the requisite background and competence to carry out such research is included in the team; that the risks to an individual are outweighed by the potential benefits to him or to society or by the importance of the knowledge to be gained; that the rights and welfare of human subjects on whom experiments are carried out are adequately protected and so on. Then prepare a complete study protocol and get the approval of the research committee of the institute.

Once this is done, clearance from the institutional ethics committee (IEC) should be sought. A model form is given in Appendix 2. Submit the details of funding, volunteer payment if any and the informed consent form, including a translation in case it will be in the local vernacular. The study protocol should also be included in the submission to the ethics committee. Contact the member secretary of the committee and get details of the number of copies that have to be submitted and other details such as the format for submission since this may vary from place to place and IEC to IEC. These details may be available on the website of the institute. After the meeting of the IEC, in case any clarifications are requested, respond promptly. File all your correspondences with the IEC including the clearance when it is obtained.

Informed consent

The informed consent is a process by which permission is obtained from the subject (or patient) for the conduct of the scientific investigation. It implies that all the details of the investigation and the risks involved therein have been explained by the investigator, has been understood by the subject/patient and consent has been given without undue duress or coercion. Informed consent also implies "fully informed consent" which means that all relevant information regarding the study, including those of the probable risks involved in the project has been given to the subject. It is mandatory for the subject to sign a document in the presence of one or two witnesses who are unrelated to the project (written informed consent). These forms should be carefully filed until the study has been published.

He thinks we are registering him for some kind of benefit scheme and demands that his wife and two children should be included.

What is partial consent?

"Partial consent" means that some part/s of the experimental procedure is/are not explained to the subject since it will have a bearing on the outcome. This is done only in the rarest of rare instances and that too only with the full approval of the IEC.

In India, providing the form in the local vernacular may not be enough, since many patients and subjects participating in a study cannot read. In such instances, explaining the form orally and using pictures, flip charts, and explaining the study to them and getting their left thumb print is enough. It is a good idea to also have witnesses in the room while getting consent.

Informed consent of special groups

Consent for doing experiments in children is usually taken from their parents or legal guardians. However, we must keep in mind that the rules for testing any new therapy or drug in children are very rigid. It is now becoming a routine in the West to get informed consent (or assent) from children. This is because many children are able to understand what is being done and there is an increased trend towards recognizing children's rights. For mentally ill patients who are not in a position to give consent, it is usually taken from the legal guardian. But every effort should be made to explain the procedure to the patient once the patient is better.

Pregnant women are another special group in which one should not attempt any intervention. Unless the drug or procedure has been shown to prevent a negative outcome in these women beyond reasonable doubt, it is unethical to use them as subjects. People with diminished autonomy need special protection and it is for this reason that research being done on them requires additional safeguards to protect their interests. Box 26.1 lists those who belong to special groups.

Box 26.1 **Special groups**

Extremes of age – elderly, children
Students
Pregnant women
Military personnel
Uneducated persons
Employees
Poor people
Institutionalized persons
Prisoners
Mentally ill people
Tribal people

Do all studies need clearance from ethics committees?

Any scientific study in which data is collected from human subjects for the purpose of research (including the use of their tissue, biological fluids or subjecting them to questions) requires clearance from the IEC. This includes epidemiological studies, microbiological, and pathological studies. There is a misconception that studies which are done by the basic science departments and those which do not involve invasive tests do not require clearance by ethics committees.

All studies must get clearance from the IEC. For e.g., *if the food preferences of a group of people are to be studied using a questionnaire, the study should get clearance.* If the blood sugar level of a group of people are to be studied IEC clearance is needed. Each of the individuals answering the questionnaire should give informed consent as should each subject giving a sample of blood. All research studies, even though they may involve only routine procedures which are usually done as a part of the treatment (e.g., *biopsy and blood tests*) require ethics clearance. It may seem an excessive caution to get ethics clearance when one is doing a study where only throat swabs are to be taken. However, one should remember that ethics clearance not only indicates that the project is ethical in all respects but also indicates that the need for research is justified which makes the research in itself ethical.

The interim analysis of my results clearly indicates 85% of the patients who received placebo got significantly better in comparison with 40% of those in the drug group.Is it ethical to continue with the drug or should I switch all patients in drug group to placebo.........

How to decide what is unethical?

There is no clear line to demarcate what is ethical from what is unethical. Many studies done in the past by many great names in medicine would never have been passed by the ethics committees of today. One way of solving ethical dilemma is to employ an ethical self-test such as asking oneself "Would I conduct this study on myself or my child (or parent)?" If the answer is yes, go ahead plan the study.

A study planned in JIPMER, Pondicherry, but to be conducted in a remote village in Punjab should go through the ethics committee of JIPMER as well as the ethics committee of the collaborating institution in Punjab. This is because cultural norms and social practices vary from place to place and what is ethical in Pondicherry need not be so in Punjab.

What are ethics committees?

This is a committee which is formed of a group of people who will go through the research protocol and state whether or not the proposal is ethically acceptable. The main responsibility of an ethics committee is to prevent unethical research, and protect the interests of the human subjects. Clearance from an ethics committee not only protects volunteers and patients participating in clinical research from being exposed to unjustified risks, but it also safeguards the scientists, institution and even the country from being maligned later on, provided, the research was being conducted in the exact manner in which it was described in the protocol and accepted by the committee. These committees also have the responsibility to see that the investigators conduct their research according to ethical norms. Ideally the committee should meet at least once a month to clear any proposal pending ethics clearance so that investigators need not have to wait for a long time before starting their project.

In India, ethics committees have a further responsibility of educating researchers about ethical issues involved and the importance of submitting proposals for permission. The committee should function purely to assess the ethical implications of the projects submitted without any personal bias. This is the reason why most ethics committees disallow the investigators or anyone with a vested interest in the project to be present at the meeting. Ethical queries which arise as a result of the discussions of such a meeting will be forwarded to the investigator, who will be asked to defend/modify his protocol.

Who are the members of an ethics committee?

It consists of experienced scientists who have been doing clinical research, lawyers, lay persons and (in some countries) the clergy. The scientist who has sent the proposal or any other person on that team (or closely associated with the team i.e., *Head of the department concerned*) should not be present at the meeting. This is to prevent projects with vested interests (such as those being sponsored by drug companies) being cleared as a result of the position of the member of the board. The standard operating procedures (SOP) for ethics committees are given in the ICMR website. Readers are encouraged to read the document for information.

How to apply for ethics clearance?

First of all find out whether your institute has an ethics committee and if so, contact the secretary of the committee and obtain the following information:

1. When is the next meeting of the Ethics committee?
2. When is the deadline for submission of the protocol?
3. How many copies of the protocol are to be submitted?
4. To whom should the copies be submitted?
5. Format for submission or prescribed form if any available

As in writing up any protocol, pay attention to the methodology. Give the detailed methodology, leaving nothing out. Do not try to hide any aspect of the study. A copy of the informed consent form should also be submitted along with the protocol (see Appendix 2 for a model of the proforma application and informed consent form). A paragraph on the ethical considerations of the proposal will be appreciated. In this, outline any special areas which may be discussed at the meeting. If there are any groups with a special interest in the outcome e.g., *drug companies - make a mention of this too.* If payment will be made to volunteers or patients for the study, the amount and source from which it is going to be met must be mentioned. The ethics committee will decide whether the amount is acceptable or not. Some studies may require patients coming for repeated follow-ups. In this case the investigator may decide to pay the travel allowance which again should be mentioned.

What to do when there is no ethics committee?

Convince your Head of the Department that the proposal has to be cleared by an Ethics committee. Ask him to approach the Dean or the Director of the institute and request them to set up such a committee. Independent ethics committees that are functioning in the country may be approached for clearance. But the researcher or his institute must be willing to pay the fees charged by the independent ethics committee.

Problems of getting informed consent for studies in India

When one of us was doing our dissertation, we needed to give the subject antipyrine and collect saliva for estimating its levels. The subjects needed to be healthy women aged between 35-60 years of age. We decided to request the lady faculty members of a medical institute to participate in this study. Despite the fact that we explained about antipyrine being relatively free of adverse effects, that there was no need for the subject to be hospitalized and that we needed only salivary samples and not blood, only one faculty member came forward. If this is the attitude of highly educated people towards research, one can forgive the common man for refusing to participate in something he cannot even begin to understand. Many of us may feel disgusted and irritated when subjects refuse to give informed consent. Most patients are frightened of giving 10-20 ml of blood or taking a new drug. At least 50% of subjects will refuse permission when trying to get fully informed consent. Therefore most investigators get partial consent and pass it off as fully informed consent. At times even that is not done. Patients are threatened that if they do not agree for the study they will not get treatment. Some investigators tell subjects that if they give 10 ml blood in return they will be given a black tablet (ferrous sulphate) or a blood red injection (B complex) which will increase the quantity of blood in their body. The methods adopted by investigators to recruit subjects for their study range from being frankly unethical to marginally acceptable. But the fact remains that no matter what the educational level of the subjects, Indians are reluctant to participate in clinical studies. It is time this problem was looked into, and remedies are sought. Since one of us has done clinical studies in the U.K. we cannot help contrasting the attitude of patients and normal subjects there and here.

Post-reading Exercises

Comment on the ethical aspects of the following research studies :

1. A scientist was doing a project on perinatal transmission of HIV. He wanted blood samples from the infant and the mother. Since all the women admitted for labour had to give a sample of blood for various tests, the patients were not informed of the tests being done for HIV but additional blood was drawn from them.

2. A study on gastric carcinoma was being conducted. All patients coming to the surgery OPD with complaints of dyspepsia were subjected to endoscopy and gastric biopsy after taking informed consent that the test ***may*** reveal a malignancy. From each patient 12 biopsy samples were collected (normally 3-4 are taken).

3. The Head of the Department of Pharmacology wanted to conduct a bioavailability study on a well known antibiotic. He asked the undergraduate (3rd and 4th semester) students and postgraduate students to participate in the study as healthy volunteers. Written informed consent was taken from all volunteers.

4. A clinical trial on antiretroviral drugs was conducted in AIDS patients from a small slum in Mumbai. The trial was funded by an organization from a developed country. The drugs were very effective and the interim analysis showed a significant improvement in those treated with the drugs. The study was abandoned immediately and the drugs were used for the treatment of AIDS in the country which funded the research.
5. A study required estimation of neurotransmitters from foetal brain. The investigator collected brains of aborted foetuses. No permission was sought from the parents of the aborted foetuses.
6. A study comparing the antidepressant effect of a drug and electroconvulsive therapy was done on patients with major depression. Informed consent on behalf of the patients was taken from whoever brought the patient to the hospital.
7. A trace element was to be tried for its effect on pregnancy induced nausea and vomiting. Animal studies showed no teratogenic or toxic effects. Educated women in their first trimester were enrolled for the study. All gave written informed consent.

Chapter 27

Ethics of Animal Research

The Hindu

Saturday, Jan 16, 2010

http://www.hindu.com/2010/01/16/stories/2010011656181800.htm

Reduce use of animals in experiments: Jairam Ramesh

NEW DELHI: Expressing concern over the increasing use of animals for **clinical trials**, Minister of State for Environment Jairam Ramesh on Friday advocated alternatives. He hoped that India would become a pioneer in reducing the use of animals in experiments by adopting alternative methods.

Inaugurating a national conference of the Committee for the Purpose of Control and Supervision of Experiments on Animals (CPCSEA), Mr. Ramesh said India was taking certain steps in that direction.

"Recent trend shows the use of primates in experimentation is on an upward climb. With the development of human genome research, activities of commercial units and industries and modern methods, there is growing demand for primates in experimentation. But, we need not open the floodgates to use animals in experimentation in the name of academic knowledge," he said.

....

....

P.S. : The bold emphasis is ours

27. Ethics of animal research

Animal rights

Three Rs

IAEC

General ethical principles

Animal rights

A group of animal rights activists protested in front of a premier research institute in Hyderabad against the inhuman (or should we say inanimal) treatment of animals. Animal rights activists have reportedly gone on rampage in Europe and the U.S.A. destroying equipment and valuable data collected over many years - all in the name of freedom for animals. It is important to nurture the correct scientific temper towards the use of animals in scientific research and make sure that we do not allow a similar situation to develop. Hence researchers have to be familiar with ethical principles governing animal experiments. The use of animals in research is unavoidable; but this does not give researchers freedom to use animals as they like. They are expected to follow the ethical guidelines for the use of animals in research. In India the guidelines were drawn and are being enforced by the Committee for the Purpose of Control and Supervision of Experiments on Animals (CPCSEA). These guidelines deals with ethical aspects of animal experimentation and should be consulted to avoid the use of unethical procedures for transport, blood collection, anesthesia, euthanasia and disposal of animals (the guidelines can be downloaded from the website of ICMR).

Three Rs

In 1959, two British scientists, Russell WMS and Burch RL in their book entitled "*The Principles of Humane Experimental Technique*" classified humane techniques under the headings of **replacement**, **reduction**, and **refinement**--now commonly known as the **three Rs.**

Refinement: Refinement techniques include those methods that prevent or minimize potential pain and distress and enhance animal well-being. Any technique that is used on animals must not cause undue pain or discomfort. Refined techniques which cause least pain and discomfort should be preferred to old or conventional ones.

Reduction: As far as possible the smallest number of animals that does not compromise the validity of the study must be used for experiments. Techniques which require lesser number of animals should be employed and statistical methods may be used to reduce the number of animals. It is unethical to use more number of animals than required for a research project. Greater the number, higher will be the cost and larger will be the number of animals subjected to discomfort or suffering.

Replacement: Replacement refers to those methods that would achieve the purpose without conducting experiments or other scientific procedures on animals. Animal experimental methods should be replaced if suitable non-animal alternative methods are available. For example *computer assisted learning modules can replace animals used for teaching or training purpose*. Similarly in research too some alternative methods which can replace animals fully or partially are used i.e., *use of mathematical and computer models; use of plants and microorganisms; use of in vitro methods such as tissue cultures and use of human volunteers and epidemiological studies.*

Fourth R: Rehabilitation of used animals is considered fourth R. Leaving animals uncared for after the experiment is over is unethical.

It is important that researchers should follow the 4Rs principles while planning research on animals. Personnel using experimental animals have a moral responsibility for animals after their use. The cost of aftercare/rehabilitation of animals post experimentation is a part of research costs and the study should be budgeted accordingly while it is being planned.

Care and maintenance of animals

Ensure there is adequate space, ventilation, food and water for the animals. Cages should be cleaned daily, husk changed, sick or dead animals should be removed. During the weekend or on holidays make sure that someone comes in to look after the animals. Learn how to handle animals from a technician or a senior person.

He is so scared of CPCSEA and animal rights activists. He stopped using animals and is doing research using 'bonsai humans' which he cloned and developed.

Experimentation

Most animals need to be acclimatized to the place where the experiment is being conducted. If the animals are received from a central animal house, collect the animals 4-5 days in advance. House them in the laboratory or animal room (where experiments are conducted) for these 4-5 days. During experimentation animals should be handled carefully and as minimally as possible. Unnecessary handling, rough handling, noisy environment can all modify the outcome of the experiment. Do not subject the animal to unnecessary pain. If the experiment involves surgery, adequate anesthesia should be given prior to the procedure. Only the ethically acceptable procedures/agents for blood collection, anesthesia and euthanasia should be used. The general ethical principles to be followed in any animal experiment are listed in Box 27.1 and some of the unethical research practices are given in Box 27.2.

Ethics committees for animal experiments

Any study which uses animals or its tissues should obtain prior permission from animal ethics committee. For studies involving small animals such as mice, rat, guinea pig, and rabbits, clearance should be obtained from the Institutional Animal Ethics Committee (IAEC). For large animals, the permission should be obtained from the Sub Committee on Large Animals (SCLA - constituted by CPCSEA) after approval by the IAEC.

Every institute which conducts animal experiments should have an IAEC. The IAEC is composed of a biological scientist, two scientists from different biological disciplines, a veterinarian involved in the care of animals, the scientist in charge of animal facility of the establishment concerned, a scientist from outside the institute, a non-scientific socially aware member and a representative or nominee of the CPCSEA.

Box 27.1 **General ethical principles**

The study design and the procedures used should be as humane as possible and the well being of the animal should be given due consideration.
Painful and aversive stimulation leading to overt distress of animal is not acceptable.
Whenever alternative procedures that minimize discomfort to the animal are available, such procedures should be used.
As far as possible, animals should be anesthetized during the painful procedures and adequate post-operative analgesia should be ensured.
When restraining the animals, only the type(s) of restraint that is (are) acceptable in the guidelines should be used. It must meet the approval of the ethics committee too.
Avoid using muscle relaxants alone during surgery, without general anesthesia. It is unacceptable.
Aseptic techniques should be used if surgical procedures are carried out on animals.

There is not even a single vegetarian item except water. Even the pickle is made out of fish......

Box 27.2 **Unethical research practices**

Lack of justification for the study

Inappropriate number of animals

Not obtaining ethics committee permission before starting the study

Using animals when alternatives are available

Procuring animals from the unauthorised sources

Not taking care of animals – housing, feeding, health and environment

Not using trained personnel and causing unnecessary pain and discomfort

Not using approved procedures for experimentation, fluid collection and euthanasia

Not meeting the current standards while transporting animals

How to apply for permission?

Researchers should fill in the appropriate forms and submit them to the member secretary of the IAEC before starting the study (the forms are available at http://moef.nic.in/modules/public-information/proforma-forms/). The IAEC will meet and the researcher may be called to present his protocol. Queries, if any by the members of the committee should be answered by the researcher. The committee then will discuss the proposal and grant or deny permission depending on the merits or demerits of the proposed study. The IAEC will look into the research as well as the ethical aspects of the study before approving it.

Some tips :

1. Plan the study to use the phylogenetically lower forms of animals as far as possible
2. Do not start the study till the clearance is received in writing
3. Apply well in advance
4. Fill in the forms properly and do not leave any section incomplete
5. Do not ask for more animals than that required for the study
6. Make sure the protocol/procedure does not violate any part of the CPCSEA guidelines for animal experimentation
7. Remember that the CPCSEA nominee may not be a medical person or a researcher but is vested with veto power to reject the proposal. He must be convinced of the need for using animals for the project presented.

8. Be thorough with the details of the proposal and answer the queries confidently with simple explanations.

Post-reading Exercises

Comment on the following :

1. In a medical college, dogs were used for demonstrating the actions of drugs. On questioning, it was said the Institute Animal Ethics Committee has given permission to use dogs.
2. A proposal to carry out the toxicity studies of a plant was submitted to the IAEC. The CPCSEA representative opined that since the plant was widely used for suicidal purposes in humans, the toxic effect of the plant can be observed in patients when they are alive or after death and hence the proposal is not ethical.
3. In a college, a large number of rats were regularly used for research studies after obtaining ethics committee permission. After the study was over, the rats were preserved alive and used for experiments to demonstrate the drug actions for the students in the undergraduate practical classes.
4. The CPCSEA nominee did not turn up for the IAEC meeting and she could not be contacted. The chairman and the member secretary decided to go ahead with the meeting and the committee took decisions to permit the studies after discussion.

Chapter 28

Ethics of Publication

Duplicate publication

On October 23, 2007 the Hindustan Times reported that six senior professors and the director of a premier medical institute in India had been accused of committing a fraud by publishing the same research material in two medical journals. The article on the use of stem cells in congenital anomalies was published in 2006 by the authors in the Journal of Indian Association of Pediatric Surgeons and also in the Transplantation Proceedings the following year. A close look at both the articles revealed one author was dropped and replaced by another in the second publication and the order of the authors is also different in both the articles. Harvey Marcovitch, Chairman of the Committee on Publication Ethics (COPE) commented "My personal opinion is that they are based on the same data and come to very similar conclusions. Much of the text is repeated and neither paper cites the other", the newspaper added.

The issue came to light when some pediatric surgeons started discussing the issue on a blog site and referred it to COPE. The corresponding author (for both the articles) reportedly stated that he submitted only to the Journal of Indian Association of Pediatric Surgeons and not to the other. But it appears neither he nor the other authors tried to correct the mistake by writing to the Transplantation Proceedings. Neither of the journals retracted the articles which are still online.

(The above is based mainly on the news item in the Hindustan Times)

28. Ethics of publication

Why is publication ethics important?

Research does not stop with completion of laboratory or clinical work. The results/findings should be communicated to other scientists/medical professionals for various reasons and the best way to do this is to publish the findings in a journal. Published findings have been the basis for many treatment decisions. In the current scenario, publications play a major role in fetching promotions, funds for further research, awards, recognition apart from name and fame to the authors. Hence what is published in a journal should be a honest work communicated in a truthful manner. The system of scientific publication is based on integrity and trust. Ignoring these values in publication process and indulging in unethical practices will seriously affect the progress of medicine. One must realize that ethical concerns apply not only to research methods but publication process also and the authors should be careful enough not to violate the ethical principles while trying to communicate their research findings.

PGs beware

A manuscript that violates the ethics of publication is likely to be detected by the journal editors. Even if it escapes and manages to get printed evading the editorial scrutiny, it is unlikely to escape the attention of the readers. In that case it would attract severe criticisms the consequences of which could be detrimental to the career of the authors. It is said that major frauds in publishing are rare but subtle violations of ethics are not uncommon. Generally no postgraduate student or researcher is formally taught what is ethical and what is unethical. One is expected to learn somehow and yet if caught for some unethical practice, he is not pardoned for the act even if it is the result of sheer ignorance. Since the onus is on the authors, it is important for the PGs to be thoroughly aware of the unethical practices in publishing and avoid them. Many PGs may be stepping into the world of publication for the first time and they must be extra-careful not to slip up.

Unethical publication practices

Publication ethics deals with the code of conduct for authors, editors, reviewers and publishers. This chapter briefly discusses only the practices of authors which are considered unethical. They are listed in Box 28.1.The list is not exhaustive but covers the commonly encountered unethical practices which PGs should be aware of and avoid.

Box 28.1 **Commonly encountered unethical publication practices**

Multiple submission
Guest Authorship
Fudging the content/data
Conflicts of interest
Redundant publication
Plagiarism
Inappropriate acknowledgements

Submission:

Almost all biomedical journals insist that the manuscript submitted for review should not be under consideration elsewhere which means a manuscript must be submitted to only one journal at a time. It is unethical to submit a manuscript to more than one journal thinking that even if one journal rejects it, the response from the other could be favourable. If for some reason authors want to submit a manuscript to another journal when it is already under consideration by one, they should inform both the editors giving the reasons.

Not taking the approval of the final version of the manuscript from all the authors will also be considered unethical. It is the responsibility of the corresponding author who should make sure that all authors have read the final version of the manuscript and approved it. It is unethical to submit a paper without the knowledge and consent of anyone included as an author.

Authorship:

There is no universally accepted guidelines on who should be given authorship and who should not be. However it is widely agreed that those who make significant intellectual contribution to a study should be given authorship. One should be able to differentiate the intellectual contributions to conception, design, analyses and writing of the study from the routine work such as collection of data and laboratory investigation. If no intellectual task can be attributed to a person, he should not be given authorship.

Authorship means not just credit but responsibility also. Those who are credited with authorship should take public responsibility for the content of their paper. They should be in a position to defend the work in case of any disputes occurring after publication of the paper. If the paper is of multidisciplinary nature, the authors should take responsibility for at least the part of the work they have carried out. For example *it may not be possible for a statistician who has intellectually contributed to the design of a study (and been credited with authorship) to take responsibility for decisions regarding laboratory analytical procedures.*

I am planning to publish my dissertation and everyone in the department including the secretarial assistants demand authorship........

The following will be considered unethical :

- not giving authorship to those who have made significant intellectual contribution,
- giving authorship to those who have NOT made significant intellectual contribution,
- refusing to take public responsibility for the content.

One must be careful about offering authorship to:

- chairman/head of the department as a routine practice,
- the sponsoring agency or its employees,
- those who do routine work such as laboratory technicians.

If there is no intellectual contribution, the above category of people do not deserve authorship. But it is important that those who help the authors conducting the study must be acknowledged. In some situations the authorship disputes are difficult to resolve i.e., *it is difficult to say whether the contribution by a person is intellectual or not and significant enough to give authorship*. To avoid such problems, it is better to decide who will do what, who will get the authorship and who will be acknowledged, at the beginning of a study.

Content:

A manuscript must present the truth, nothing but the truth and the whole truth. The following acts will be considered unethical :

1. intentionally hiding the crucial information

   so that the drawbacks/limitations of the study are not known to the readers
2. making false statements

   to strengthen the conclusions drawn or support wrong conclusions
3. intentional alteration of data

   to achieve the desired results
4. misquoting others work

   to discredit others or support the author's findings
5. not quoting previous important work

   not to give credit to an earlier worker
6. too many self citations (not relevant to the study)

   Some have the habit of quoting their earlier publications whether it is relevant or not to the context of the paper. Here the intention may be to increase the citation index of their papers. It is highly undesirable.

7. publishing the photographs of patients without consent

   If the article contains clinical photographs, authors should get explicit permission from the patients. Some journals insist that consent letters from the patients should be submitted along with the manuscripts.

8. not concealing the identity of patients (in the text as well as the photographs)

   Getting consent from the patient does not absolve the authors of not concealing the identity of the patients. The eyes in the photograph must be blackened and any other marks (such as hospital number or name) must be concealed. The text describing the case histories should not reveal the identity of patients.

Conflict of interests:

Interests other than scientific – commercial, political, personal, academic, religious or financial - may influence publication. Such interests may introduce an element of bias in the presentation of results, discussion and conclusion. Hence the authors who have conflicting interests (competing interests as they are otherwise called) must declare them to the editor. If a researcher receives funding/fees from a drug company for publishing a review about a drug manufactured by the company, he is duty bound to declare it as a conflicting interest. The readers should know about such interests of the authors so that they do not feel hoodwinked when they came to know about them later. Not declaring it at the beginning could lead to suspicion and the consequences could be ugly for the researcher. The readers of research/review papers have every right to know the competing interests of the authors to help them arrive at their own conclusions about the credibility of the paper.

Will other interests really affect the judgment of the authors? It is futile to claim that *"I am honest and nothing can affect my writing".* Whether a competing interest has had an effect or not, it must be declared for the reasons that (a) bias is subtle and the author might not be able realize its influence and (b) justice must not only be done but should appear to be done.

Oh my God!! Instead of sending the photograph of the patient to the journal, I have sent mine by mistake.........

Redundant publication :

Publishing an article that has already appeared in the same or different journal amounts to scientific misconduct. If the articles share the same hypothesis, data, discussion points, or conclusions, it will be considered unethical. Such redundant publications must be avoided. Any biomedical journal would like to publish only new information. A manuscript is expected to add new knowledge or modify the existing knowledge. Rephrasing one's own already published research article and publishing it again with minor modifications in another journal for the sake of increasing the number of publications is unethical. If there are some compelling reasons to do so, the editors and the readers must be informed by prominently citing the original publication.

Plagiarism :

Plagiarism is stealing others ideas and contents of a paper (written or illustrative material) and passing it as one's own. Copying large portions **verbatim** from other papers is plagiarism even if references are given. Citing references does NOT give any author the right to reproduce portions verbatim from the cited article. When a reference is cited, it means the view/information given by the authors is supported by the cited work(s). Definitely it does not imply that the authors have copied verbatim from the cited publication. An article must be the original work (write up) of the authors supported by references.

When it is required to include small portions (may be a few lines) verbatim from a source, it should be made distinctly visible by quoting the authors and/or the source in the running text and printing the copied portions in italics within inverted quotes. If it is a paragraph it may be slightly indented. Apart from being unethical, copying large portions verbatim, even with proper acknowledgment will breach copyright if prior permission from the copyright owners has not been obtained. One would have noticed acknowledgments stating, "reproduced with permission from ......" under the tables/figures reproduced from published sources.

Acknowledgements :

The sponsoring/funding agency whether it is governmental or private should be acknowledged. Not acknowledging them may not be in good taste and it is certainly unethical too. Any help received from others should be acknowledged. However routine work or duty cannot be considered a help and need not be acknowledged. For example *the work of a technician or a secretary employed for the purpose need not be acknowledged*. Similarly acknowledging the head of the institute for granting permission to carry out the work is not required.

[A slightly different version of the above article was published as a chapter by one of the authors (RR) in Medicine Update, Vol 7, APICON-ASSAM 2003, Dibrugarh]

Post-reading Exercises
Read the situation and comment on it : 1. A paper which was published in a journal was found to be published already in an international journal. When asked, the author explained that he submitted the paper to both the journals so that the paper will be widely read and both national as well as international readers will be benefited. Is the justification of the author correct? Explain. 2. In a review submitted for publication, it was found that a few paragraphs were copied verbatim from another review published earlier in another journal. When the author was asked to explain, he said he had listed those articles under references and cited them in the running text and hence he can use the paragraphs word by word in his review. Is the justification of the author correct? Explain.

3. A review about a new drug and its controversial uses in some diseases was submitted by an author. After the publication it was brought to the notice of the editor by a reader that the author who is a faculty member in medical school is also a paid consultant to a drug company which is the sole manufacturer of the drug.

   Did the author commit any unethical act? If 'yes', explain how it could have been avoided.

4. An author submitted a paper with partial data when whole data were available. After publication he submitted the entire data to the drug control authority with a conclusion different from the one he drew in the paper published in the journal.

   Is what the author has done acceptable? Explain.

5. When a paper was about to be published, the authors wrote to the editor of the journal (A) that he would like to withdraw the paper. The reason given was that he submitted the paper to another journal (B) earlier but he did not hear from them for a long time. His many letters to B requesting the status of his manuscript did not receive a reply. Hence, he decided to submit the paper to A but he subsequently found that the paper was published in B and hence the withdrawal.

   Is what the author has done acceptable? Explain.

6. When a paper on a clinical trial was published from a clinical pharmacology department, the research nurse who had helped the researchers in the conduct of the trial objected that she was not given authorship. She argued that since she is a research nurse and not a ward nurse, not including her name as an author would affect her career.

   Is the argument of the nurse acceptable? Explain.

7. A paper published by a senior researcher contained fabricated data. When the editor asked the researcher she admitted the data were false but her junior did it without her knowledge. Her statement was found to be true on enquiry.

   Should the senior researcher still take responsibility for submitting the fabricated data? Explain.

8. A faculty member in a medical college received an acknowledgement from a journal for submitting a research paper. The faculty member replied to the editor that she did not submit any paper and hence she could not take any responsibility for the paper. It was found that her

former student submitted the paper without her knowledge. The work was carried out in her lab and the student included her name as a corresponding author.

Did the faculty member do the right thing? What would you do if you were the faculty member?

What should the former student have done?

Chapter 29

Computers and Internet in Research

The reliability of medical information on the internet

A study by Scullard et al. to assess the reliability and accuracy of medical advice found on the websites reveals the extent of reliability of information obtained from the internet (Googling children's health: reliability of medical advice on the internet, *Archives of Disease in Childhood, doi:10.1136/adc.2009.168856)*. The Results section of the abstract says "*39% of the 500 sites searched gave correct information; 11% were incorrect and 49% failed to answer the question. Where an answer was available, 78% of sites gave the correct information. The accuracy of information varied depending on the topic and ranged from 51% (mumps, measles and rubella and autism) to 100% (breast feeding with mastitis/the sleeping position of a baby). Governmental sites gave uniformly accurate advice. News sites gave correct advice in 55% of cases*".

There are tools available to check the reliability of internet health information and the following sites provide those tools which can be used by the readers :

1. "Checklist for evaluating websites" (http://staff.library.wisc.edu/instruction/instmat/Custom/evalweb.pdf)
2. "DISCERN" (www.discern.org.uk)
3. "HONcode" (www.hon.ch)
4. "Healthy Wisconsin People" (www.healthywisconsin.org)
5. "Medline Plus" (www.medlineplus.gov)
6. "Healthfinder" (www.healthfinder.gov)
7. "BadgerLink" (http://www.badgerlink.net/)

29. Computers and internet in research

Computer is no more a mystery and internet is on the verge of becoming a part and parcel of our life. No self respecting researcher can afford to say he does not know how to use computers or internet. Since both are very familiar to most of us, this chapter skips the description and basic aspects but explores the effective use of these tools.

Software for research

Computers can be useful in planning and executing the study. For example *sample size calculations and random allocation of subjects to different groups can be carried out using computer software*. Doing these tasks manually is not really necessary unless one wants to understand the process and get a taste of it. In that case doing it manually once would suffice. While executing the study, data storage and retrieval may require a computer especially when the volume of data collected is large. Apart from the above uses, there may be situations where the use of computers is needed. For example *calculation of dose based on the body surface area for each patient might be carried out with ease if software for the same is available.*

Where to get the software?

Many software packages are available from commercial software companies. But free software programs are also available and they can fulfill a large proportion of the needs. Sometimes they prove better than their commercial counterparts. Google search can be used to find out where/how to get free software. The following sites will let the users download the free software for sample size calculation and randomization:

1. PS - http://biostat.mc.vanderbilt.edu/wiki/Main/PowerSampleSize
2. Randomisation - http://mahmoodsaghaei.tripod.com/Softwares/randalloc. html
3. Rando - www.indphar.org

There are many websites which can carry out data analysis online when the data are entered. The web page **http://statpages.org/** gives links to numerous sites to carry out online statistical analysis, calculate sample size, determine statistical test and generate random assignments. These tasks are carried out by online software which cannot be downloaded and used on your PC. These services can be used only if the PC is connected to the internet. The biggest advantage is most of them are free and may not even require user registration.

Data storage and retrieval

For handling data, the use of a spreadsheet may be sufficient if the volume is not very large. Otherwise, one should use a database program and create a database for the study. Spreadsheet and database programs are easily available. Any 'Office' package will include these two. For example *Microsoft Office package includes Excel spreadsheet and Access database system*. Many free spreadsheet and database programs are also available on the internet and it is not a must that one should use the commercial software always. It is better to go for freeware available on the Net rather than using the pirated commercial software.

Using a database system for data storage and retrieval has definite advantages. It makes life easy on adding, editing, deleting and searching the data. Later the data may be easily transported to a data analysis system such as statistics software for transformation of data and data analysis.

Literature search

Medical information databases abound on the internet. The details of databases on the internet and strategies for searching the internet for articles and other information are discussed in chapter 3. Not all information is freely accessible. While many journals follow various models of 'open access' policy, a lot other journals demand payment for online access of research articles. PubMed is free whereas other indexing databases charge the users. Some sites are authentic sources and some are not. For example, *Wikipedia contains a whole lot of information on a wide variety of subjects. The content in Wikipedia is provided by its users. Anyone can contribute any topic and anyone can edit it too. Relying too much on Wikipedia content and citing it as a reference to support the scientific content of a study is not quite acceptable to many*. The same is true with a lot other sites displaying medical information for common man. Evaluate the content before using it for a scientific or medical purpose.

Data analysis

As discussed earlier, data may have to be analysed to derive a new set of data which will be subjected to statistical analysis. Software programs may be used, if available to derive new data from the collected data. For example *pharmacokinetic software packages are available for deriving pharmacokinetic parameters such as t-half, clearance and volume of distribution of a drug from plasma concentration-time data*. Some of these programs employ some complex calculations (algorithms) for non-linear kinetics which cannot be done manually. In such cases, it is important to use a software program; otherwise the results may not be acceptable if some simplified, less accurate manual methods are used to derive the parameters. If any software for data analysis is mentioned in the literature, a copy of the same may be obtained and tried. Again Google might be of help to locate the place of availability or email the author of the paper (where the software is mentioned) to get information or the software itself. Those who are proficient in programming can write a program and use it.

Plenty of software packages for statistics is available on the Net. Some are absolutely free, some are demo versions and some are available only on payment. Beginners can download a free/demo version of a software and practice it. There is a statistical package called Instat which we recommend for the beginners. A free demo version of Instat is available at www.graphpad.com. The program is very user friendly and intuitive as the name suggests. Tests of significance can be carried out without any difficulty. The demo version in which a few features of the software such as printing are disabled can still be used for data analysis. If the user finds it useful, he can purchase the regular version which will have all the features.

There is a popular commercial package called SPSS (Statistical Package for Social Sciences). It is very costly and beginners will find it difficult to use. It is better to get some training on how to use the software and how to interpret the results displayed by the software at the end of analysis. A demo version is available (at the company website) and interested readers can try it. Some other popular statistical software packages are Prism, Statistix, Minitab, Statgraphics and SAS.

There are sites where the titles and availability of statistical software (free as well as commercial) are listed. Along with the title, a brief description may also be available. Interested readers may browse the lists at www.statistics.com. These lists include some online calculation sites which will perform statistical calculations online only. Those who want to use the facility should visit the site and enter the data while the internet connection is on. The readers may make use of such sites if they find it comfortable to use.

Preparing a dissertation

There is no option other than using a computer; because universities have started asking students to submit their dissertation in electronic format (on a CD) along with copies in print (bound dissertation books). All one needs is a good word processor and a data management software that is capable of producing good scientific graphs and figures. MS Word (word processor) and MS Excel (spreadsheet) both from Microsoft will be suitable for the above requirements. Bibliographic software, if available would prove very useful.

Cheer up man!. Our problems are over.
He is downloading a software that can write the entire dissertation when you feed the data.

Type the text in the word processor and correct the mistakes. Do not rely too much on the spell checker. The software may not recognize many scientific terms and it cannot detect some mistakes at all. For example, *'hear' instead of 'heart' will never be identified as a mistake by the spell checker.* Tables can be made using the features available in many word processor packages. An option for drawing the tables is available on the menu bar of the MS Word and neat tables can be made with help of it. See to that the table is complete in all aspects such as title, column and row titles, units for the figures (numbers) and foot notes. Pay attention to vertical and horizontal alignment of figures.

If data are already entered in a spreadsheet, graphic representations of the data such as bar chart, line graph and scatter plot can be made and cut and pasted in the text at appropriate places. Before cutting and pasting, make sure the figure is complete is all aspects – title, graduation of axes, markers and asterisks to indicate significance. MS Excel gives a range of options for different types of graphs and it would be sufficient for most of the projects.

Bibliographic software packages can store references. They eliminate the use of index cards for storing references. One can enter the details like authors' names, title of the article and title of the journal and the software makes a database of these items. It is easy to retrieve the information later. The software can also arrange the references in alphabetical order or in any desired order. It can print the references in any style/format. Some bibliography packages use in-built styles i.e. *when the journal name is specified the references will be arranged in the style required by the particular journal.* Some packages are very versatile in the sense they can read the manuscript (on a word processor), cite the references at appropriate places and pick up the references automatically from the database (of references created by the user) and arrange them in the desired style. One such package is called RefMan (Reference Manager) available in India at a cheaper rate for students. Some free bibliographic packages are also available on the internet. A free, online application called Zotero (http://www.zotero.org/) which works with Firefox browser is an easy-to-use reference management software. It includes almost all the sophisticated functions claimed to be present in the commercial software packages.

Use a good printer for printing the dissertation, preferably a laser printer. The printer must be compatible with the software used. Otherwise what is seen on the screen is not reproduced on the printer as expected. One should check the print-outs and make sure the alignment of page and tables are perfect and as seen on the screen. It is better to read the final print out at least once to check whether any lines or pages are missing and whether the print quality of text, tables and figures are acceptable. Colors, if any used should be reproduced properly.

Scientific communication

Two decades back submitting a paper for publication was time consuming and costly especially if the journal office is located in a foreign country. Even getting the acknowledgment would take about a month after posting the manuscript. Nowadays the whole process of article publication is made electronic and online and that too at a fraction of the cost borne by the researchers of yesteryears. One can submit the manuscripts online by visiting the journal web site and clicking the 'online submission' option. When the submission is over, the acknowledgement along with the manuscript reference number is received instantaneously. Many journals now have online review system which enables their reviewers read the articles and post their comments on the journal web site. The editorial board takes a decision quickly and intimates the authors by email. The authors can also use the online tracking system provided by the journal to find out the progress of their manuscripts.

Checking for plagiarism

In this age of internet, plagiarism is easy to commit. Sometimes it happens unintentionally/accidentally or lack of awareness. Hence it is a good idea to check one's own written material using online plagiarism detection resources. Such a check will avoid embarrassments later after the write up/article is published. The websites which provide facilities to check which sentences/portions of your write up resemble the already published material is given in Box 29.1. One can use these tools to detect plagiarism in articles published by others too.

Box 29.1 **Online tools for detecting plagiarism**

Free	Commercial
http://www.dustball.com/cs/plagiarism.checker/	http://www.plagiarismdetect.com/
http://www.duplichecker.com/	http://plagiarism-detector.com/
http://www.plagiarismchecker.com/	http://www.plagiarismsearch.com/
http://www.crossrefme.com/	http://www.universitydissertations.com/
http://www.articlechecker.com/	http://www.scanmyessay.com/index.php
http://searchenginereports.net/articlecheck.aspx	http://www.canexus.com/
http://etest.vbi.vt.edu/etblast3/	http://www.iplagiarismcheck.com/

It may be noted that the authors do not vouch for the reliability or the efficacy of the any online tool as they have tried none of the commercial sites but only a few free sites. The readers are advised to try and choose the one that suits them. Many offline software packages are also available for checking plagiarism. A Google search will reveal more information on these packages.

Registering clinical trials

All clinical trials conducted in India must be registered with The Clinical Trials Registry- India (CTRI). The details can be obtained from http://www.ctri.in/Clinicaltrials/. With effect from 15th June 2009, registration of all clinical trials conducted in the country has been made mandatory by the Indian government. The registration can be done online. The readers are advised to log on to the above website and read the FAQs at http://www.ctri.in/Clinicaltrials/do/login1?action=toFAQ.

Precautions

Software: If used for the first time, it is better to test the software with a worked out example illustrated in a text book or other authentic sources. This is to make sure the software works as expected and it is being operated properly. It is better to read the software manual, if one is available. Still better would be to get some training from a well informed user of the software.

Data entry and storage: Any data entered must be checked at least twice with the source document. It is easy to make mistakes when the volume of data is large and the data are entered fast. The system used for storage (database / spreadsheet software) must have facilities to edit, search and import from and export data to other software. The software may not check the validity of the data though validity checks can be programmed to a certain extent in some software packages. For example *the user can be prevented from entering the age in years <0 or >150*. But the software will not complain if '52' is entered instead of '25'.

Backup: Remember to have at least two backups of data, files, software, pictures/photographs and whatever is stored on a computer. Apart from the main computer (say Desktop PC), a copy may be stored on a pen drive and a laptop PC. Backups must be done at regular intervals or whenever the changes are made. Software backups must be installation files rather than installed run files. If a software gets corrupted in the middle of the work, backups come handy. Do not keep the data and the files only on pen drive or laptop as these gadgets can be easily misplaced or stolen.

Security: Secure all the files and data using a password (to avoid data theft), if necessary. But make sure the password is safely stored and is not forgotten.

Computer: Take proper care of the computer used for doing/storing the work. Viruses can crash the computer and corrupt the files. Pirated software can also create problems. If the same computer is used for browsing the internet, beware of malware, spyware, viruses, worms and phishing attempts. Visiting strange web sites and downloading and installing software from such sites must be avoided. A good antivirus software and a firewall package will keep the computer healthy.

Print outs: Check whether symbols such as alpha and beta are reproduced properly. Some printers do not recognise Greek/Latin characters but replace them with strange characters. Printer's behavior would be unpredictable if it is not 100% compatible with the software i.e. *software and printer are not able to communicate properly with each other.* Color reproduction will be a problem which can be sorted out by trial and error only.

Internet: Simply because some information is available on the internet, it does not automatically become authentic. Evaluate the content in terms of who is hosting the website, who has provided the content, whether the content is peer reviewed or not and whether there are any declared or undeclared conflicts of interest of webhost(s) or authors.

Computers and common sense

It is true the computers appear to be very intelligent machines. They are best described as `stupid but super fast machines'. One must not forget that computer is only a tool which executes what we order it. It is not difficult to program a computer to yield a result of 5 when it is asked to multiply 2 and 2. Computers have no brain of their own and it is the human brain which programs it to do things. *`Garbage in, garbage out'* is one of the popular quotes about the computers. If garbage is fed, the result given by a computer will be garbage too. So one should not lose his common sense and believe whatever a computer says is true. This is especially important in data analysis and interpretation of results by the computers. Use of software cannot compensate the lack of knowledge in research methodology and statistics since certain amount of understanding and knowledge of these subjects is essential for appropriate use of software and to understand and interpret the output of the software at the end of a task.

Appendix 1

General Structure of a Research Project

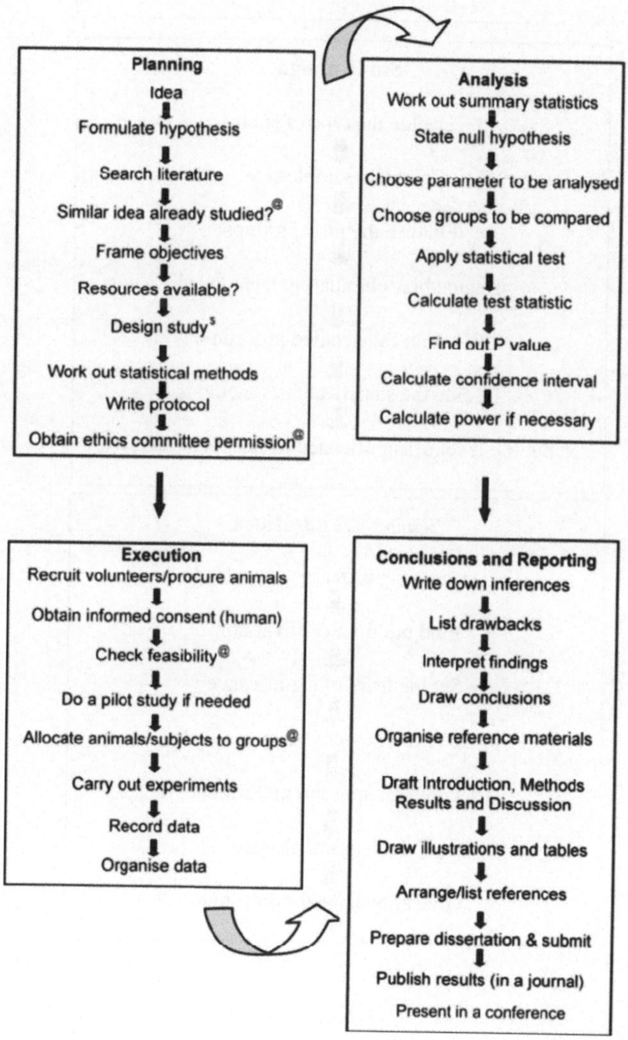

@Modify	
If a similar idea has already been tried (or) if the study is not feasible →	Go for a new idea
If there are ethical objections on aims, design & methodology →	Modify the objectives/ design/ methodology

$Study design

Decide the type of study

↓

Calculate sample size#

↓

Finalise the no. of groups

↓

Decide bias eliminating techniques

↓

Workout the detailed procedure

↓

Decide the statistical tests/methods

↓

Set the level of significance (if not set already)

#Sample size calculation

Decide the difference expected

↓

Find out the SD of variable

↓

Set the level of significance

↓

Set power (1-beta)

↓

Choose an appropriate formula

↓

Calculate sample size

↓

Give allowance for drop-out

Appendix 2

Model form* to be Filled by the Principal Investigator (PI) for Submission to Institutional Ethics Committee (IEC)

1. Proposal Title

2. Details of investigators

	Name, Designation & Qualifications	Address, Tel & Fax Nos. Email ID
Principal investigator Co-investigators		

3. Brief description of the study : Introduction, review of literature, aim(s) & objectives, justification for study, methodology describing the potential risks & benefits, outcome measures, statistical analysis (maximum 500 words):		
4. **Intervention :** **i.** Does the study involve use of : Drug ☐ Devices ☐ Vaccines ☐ Indian Systems of Medicine/ Alternate System of Medicine ☐ Any other ☐ NA ☐		
ii. Is it approved and marketed In India ☐ UK & Europe ☐ USA ☐ Other countries, specify ☐		
iii. Does it involve a change in use, dosage, route of administration? **If yes**, whether DCGI's /Any other Regulatory authority's Permission is obtained? **If yes,** Date of permission :	Yes Yes	No No
5. Subject selection: i. Number of Subjects:		
ii. Duration of study		
iii. Will subjects from both sexes be recruited	Yes	No
iv. Inclusion / exclusion criteria given	Yes	No
v. Type of subjects Volunteers ☐ Patients ☐		

vi. Vulnerable subjects Yes ☐ No ☐

(Tick the appropriate boxes)

pregnant women	☐	children	☐	elderly	☐
fetus	☐	illiterate	☐	handicapped	☐
terminally ill	☐	seriously ill	☐	mentally challenged	☐
economically & socially backward	☐	any other	☐		

6. Use of biological/ hazardous materials	Yes	No
i. Use of fetal tissue or abortus		
ii. Use of organs or body fluids	Yes	No
iv. Use of pre-existing/stored/left over samples	Yes	No
v. Collection for banking/future research	Yes	No
vii. Use of Infectious/biohazardous specimens	Yes	No
viii. Proper disposal of material	Yes	No

7. Consent : Written ☐ Oral ☐ Audio-visual ☐

i. Consent form : (tick the included elements)

Understandable language	☐	Alternatives to participation	☐
Statement that study involves research	☐	Confidentiality of records	☐
Sponsor of study, if any	☐	Contact information	☐
Purpose and procedures	☐	Statement that consent is voluntary	☐
Risks & Discomforts	☐	Right to withdraw	☐
Benefits	☐	Consent for future use of biological material	☐
Compensation for participation	☐	Benefits if any on future commercialization eg., genetic basis for drug development	☐
Compensation for study related injury	☐		

ii. Who will obtain consent ? PI/Co-PI ☐ Nurse/Counsellor ☐ Research staff ☐ Any other ☐

8. Is there compensation for participation?	Yes	No
If Yes, Monetary ☐ In kind ☐ Specify amount and type:		

Checklist for attached documents:

Project proposal ☐

Patient information sheet ☐

Informed Consent form ☐

Place

Signature & Designation of PI/Co-PI

Date:

**Modified from model form suggested by Indian Council of Medical Research, New Delhi*

Appendix 3

Examples of References

Writing references in the correct format (of a chosen style) is a tedious job mainly because there are many types of sources which could be referred and the format varies with each. Even for a single type of source, there are many formats to be used depending on certain conditions related to the individual source. For example, the format of journal references varies depending on the pagination policies of the journals, types of authorship (personal, organization etc.) and many such variations. There are more than 70 formats to be used when citing journal articles.

The different types of sources which are referenced are given below:

1. Published Print Documents

Journals
Books
Conference Publications
Scientific and Technical Reports
Dissertations and Theses
Bibliographies
Patents
Newspaper Articles
Maps
Legal Documents

2. Unpublished Material

Forthcoming ("in press")
Papers and Poster Sessions Presented at Meet
Letters and other Personal Communication
Manuscripts

3. **Audio and Visual Media (audiocassettes, videocassettes, slides, photographs, etc.)**

    Books and other Individual Titles in Audiovisual Formats

    Journals in Audiovisual Formats

    Prints and Photographs

4. **Material on CD-ROM, DVD, or Disk**

    Books and other Individual Titles on CD-ROM, DVD, or Disk

    Journals on CD-ROM, DVD, or Disk

    Databases on CD-ROM, DVD, or Disk

    Computer Programs on CD-ROM, DVD, or Disk

5. **Citing Material on the Internet**

    Books and other Individual Titles on the Internet

    Journals on the Internet

    Databases/Retrieval Systems on the Internet

    Web Sites

    Electronic Mail and Discussion Forums

The above list, the examples of reference formats for each of the above sources and their variants are given in Citing Medicine@ (http://www.nlm.nih.gov/citingmedicine or http://www.ncbi.nlm.nih.gov/bookshelf/br.fcgi?book=citmed) published by the National Library of Medicine, US. The examples are not printed here for lack of space. The readers may visit the site and view the examples. The PDF files of the same may be downloaded for later consultations. The above book also gives following information which will be useful for writing references:

Abbreviations for commonly used English words in journal titles

Additional sources for journal title abbreviations

Abbreviations for commonly used English words in bibliographic description

ISO country codes for selected countries

Two-Letter abbreviations for Canadian provinces and territories and U.S. states and territories

Notes for citing MEDLINE/PubMed

The following paragraphs are reproduced verbatim from ***Citing medicine: the NLM style guide for authors, editors, and publishers***@

Application

Although this publication permits a number of variations in format, the user should be consistent in applying them throughout a reference list. For example, if the full journal title is used instead of the title abbreviation in one reference, it should be used in all journal article references.

When citing any type of format, one rule is primary: an author should never place in a reference list a document that he or she has not seen. The medical literature is full of references that have been cited from other references, serving only to perpetuate erroneous information. If a document is important enough to be cited in a reference list, it is equally important to examine the original for citation information.

Internet publication has created the new complication of citing the version seen. Many publishers are producing documents such as books and journals in multiple versions - in print, CD-ROM or DVD, and the Internet. These versions may appear identical in content, but because errors or other changes may have been introduced in the conversion from one format to another, they may in fact differ in significant ways. Also, once a document is in electronic format, changes and additions can easily be made that further distance the content from the more fixed print version. Always cite the specific version seen. In particular, do not cite a document as if it were a print one when the electronic version was used.

@Patrias, K. Citing medicine: the NLM style guide for authors, editors, and publishers [Internet]. 2nd ed. Wendling, Daniel L., technical editor. Bethesda (MD): National Library of Medicine (US); 2007 [2008/8/8]. Available from: http://www.nlm.nih.gov/citingmedicine

[Examples of reference formats are reproduced below as given in Citing medicine: the NLM style guide for authors, editors, and publishers. Only selected variations are given. The readers may visit the NLM website for more examples].

Examples of Citations to Journal Articles

1. **Standard journal article**

   Petitti DB, Crooks VC, Buckwalter JG, Chiu V. Blood pressure levels before dementia. Arch Neurol. 2005 Jan;62(1):112-6.

Jun BC, Song SW, Park CS, Lee DH, Cho KJ, Cho JH. The analysis of maxillary sinus aeration according to aging process: volume assessment by 3-dimensional reconstruction by high-resolutional CT scanning. Otolaryngol Head Neck Surg. 2005 Mar;132(3):429-34.

Meneton P, Jeunemaitre X, de Wardener HE, MacGregor GA. Links between dietary salt intake, renal salt handling, blood pressure, and cardiovascular diseases. Physiol Rev. 2005 Apr;85(2):679-715.

2. **Journal article with many authors**

Rastan S, Hough T, Kierman A, Hardisty R, Erven A, Gray IC, Voeling S, Isaacs A, Tsai H, Strivens M, Washbourne R, Thornton C, Greenaway S, Hewitt M, McCormick S, Selley R, Wells C, Tymowska-Lalanne Z, Roby P, Mburu P, Rogers D, Hagan J, Reavill C, Davies K, Glenister P, Fisher EM, Martin J, Vizor L, Bouzyk M, Kelsell D, Guenet JL, Steel KP, Sheardown S, Spurr N, Gray I, Peters J, Nolan PM, Hunter AJ, Brown SD. Towards a mutant map of the mouse--new models of neurological, behavioural, deafness, bone, renal and blood disorders. Genetica. 2004 Sep;122(1):47-9.

3. **Journal article with optional limit to the number of authors**

to 3 authors

Rastan S, Hough T, Kierman A, et al. Towards a mutant map of the mouse--new models of neurological, behavioural, deafness, bone, renal and blood disorders. Genetica. 2004 Sep;122(1):47-9.

or

Rastan S, Hough T, Kierman A, and others. Towards a mutant map of the mouse--new models of neurological, behavioural, deafness, bone, renal and blood disorders. Genetica. 2004 Sep;122(1):47-9.

to 6 authors

Hallal AH, Amortegui JD, Jeroukhimov IM, Casillas J, Schulman CI, Manning RJ, et al. Magnetic resonance cholangiopancreatography accurately detects common bile duct stones in resolving gallstone pancreatitis. J Am Coll Surg. 2005 Jun;200(6):869-75.

or

Hallal AH, Amortegui JD, Jeroukhimov IM, Casillas J, Schulman CI, Manning RJ, and others. Magnetic resonance cholangiopancreatography accurately detects common bile duct stones in resolving gallstone pancreatitis. J Am Coll Surg. 2005 Jun;200(6):869-75.

4. **Journal article with organization as author**

American Diabetes Association. Diabetes update. Nursing. 2003 Nov;Suppl:19-20, 24.

Parkinson Study Group. A randomized placebo-controlled trial of rasagiline in levodopa-treated patients with Parkinson disease and motor fluctuations: the PRESTO study. Arch Neurol. 2005 Feb;62(2):241-8.

Merritt, Hawkins & Associates. 2004 survey of physicians 50 to 65 years old. J Med Assoc Ga. 2004;93(3):21-6.

Institute of Medical Illustrators. Photography of cleft audit patients. J Audiov Media Med. 2004 Dec;27(4):170-4.

Sugarterapias es Onkologiai Szakmai Kollegium. [Methodologic recommendations of the Oncology and Radiotherapy College. Protocol for oncology care. Diagnostic algorithms in the course of patient follow-up]. Magy Onkol. 2004;48(4):339-47. Hungarian.

8. **Journal article with governmental body as author**

National Institutes of Health (US). End-of-life care. National Institutes of Health statement on the state of the science. AWHONN Lifelines. 2005 Feb-Mar;9(1):15-22.

12. **Journal article authors with designations of rank within a family**

King JT Jr, Horowitz MB, Kassam AB, Yonas H, Roberts MS. The short form-12 and the measurement of health status in patients with cerebral aneurysms: performance, validity, and reliability. J Neurosurg. 2005 Mar;102(3):489-94.

13. **Journal article authors with compound last names (give as found in the article)**

Bruno-Ambrosius K, Yucel-Lindberg T, Twetman S. Salivary buffer capacity in relation to menarche and progesterone levels in saliva from adolescent girls: a longitudinal study. Acta Odontol Scand. 2004 Oct;62(5):269-72.

14. Journal article author names with particles, prepostitions, prefixes (give as found in the article)

O'Neill GM, Catchpoole DR, Golemis EA. From correlation to causality: microarrays, cancer, and cancer treatment. Biotechniques. 2003 Mar;Suppl:64-71.

de Pouvourville G, Ulmann P, Nixon J, Boulenger S, Glanville J, Drummond M. The diffusion of health economics knowledge in Europe: The EURONHEED (European Network of Health Economics Evaluation Database) project. Pharmacoeconomics. 2005;23(2):113-20.

15. Journal article authors with romanized names

Nyporko AIu, Demchuk ON, Blium IaB. [Analysis of structural characteristics of alpha-tubulins in plants with enhanced cold tolerance]. Tsitol Genet. 2003 Nov-Dec;37(6):3-11. Russian.

Ni H, Qing D, Kaisa S, Lu J. [The study on the effect of LBP on cleaning hydroxygen free radical by EPR technique]. Zhong Yao Cai. 2004 Aug;27(8):599-600. Chinese.

16. Journal article with no author provided

Pelvic floor exercise can reduce stress incontinence. Health News. 2005 Apr;11(4):11.

Drug-resistance tuberculosis among the foreign-born in Canada. Can Commun Dis Rep. 2005 Feb 15;31(4):46-52. English, French.

18. Journal article in a language other than English

in a roman alphabet

Berrino F, Gatta G, Crosignani P. [Case-control evaluation of screening efficacy]. Epidemiol Prev. 2004 Nov-Dec;28(6):354-9. Italian.

Bechade D, Desrame J, Raynaud JJ, Algayres JP. [Oesophageal ulcer associated with the use of bacampicillin]. Presse Med. 2005 Feb 26;34(4):299-300. French.

in a non-roman alphabet

Zhao L, Li H, Han D. [Effects of intestinal endotoxemia on the development of cirrhosis in rats]. Zhonghua Gan Zang Bing Za Zhi. 2001 Jul;9 Suppl:21-3. Chinese.

Paroussis D, Papaoutsopoulou C. [Porcelain laminate veneers (HI-ERAM)]. Odontostomatol Proodos. 1990 Dec;44(6):423-6. Greek.

30. Journal article with year having a supplement

Draghici S, Khatri P, Shah A, Tainsky MA. Assessing the functional bias of commercial microarrays using the onto-compare database. Biotechniques. 2003 Mar;Suppl:55-61.

38. Journal article volume with supplement

El Shehaby A, Ganz JC, Reda WA, Hafez A. Temporary symptomatic swelling of meningiomas following gamma knife surgery. Report of two cases. J Neurosurg. 2005 Jan;102 Suppl:293-6.

Lee A, Chan EC, Ho M, Wong WS, Ng PP. The importance of needs assessment in planning health promoting schools initiatives: comparison of youth risk behaviours of two districts in Hong Kong. Asia Pac J Public Health. 2004;16 Suppl:S7-11.

49. Journal article issue with supplement

Crawford M, Mullan J, Vanderveen T. Technology and safe medication administration. J Infus Nurs. 2005 Mar-Apr;28(2 Suppl):37-41.

Fabregas B. [Ethics and gerontology. The dialyzed elderly patient: until when? For what terminal goals?]. Soins. 2003 Oct;(679 Suppl):18. French.

58. Journal article with no volume or issue

Schwartz-Cassell T. Feeding assistants: based on logic or way off base? Contemp Longterm Care. 2005 Jan:26-8.

60. Journal article with roman numerals for page numbers (upper or lower case as found)

Giger JN. Human genetics: can we really eliminate health disparities. J Natl Black Nurses Assoc. 2003 Jun;14(1):vii-viii.

65. Journal article that is a retraction notice

Chen C, Li Q. A strict solution for the optimal superimposition of protein structures. Retraction. Acta Crystallogr A. 2004 Nov;60(Pt 6):640. Retraction of:Chen C, Li Q. Acta Crystallogr A. 2004 May;60(Pt 3):201-3.

66. **Journal article retracted**

Chen C, Li Q. A strict solution for the optimal superimposition of protein structures. Acta Crystallogr A. 2004 May;60(Pt 3):201-3. Retraction in: Chen C, Li Q. Acta Crystallogr A. 2004 Nov;60(Pt 6):640.

67. **Journal article that is an erratum notice**

Scuderi A, Letsou A. Amnioserosa is required for dorsal closure in Drosophila. Dev Dyn. 2005 May;233(1):249. Erratum for: Dev Dyn. 2005 Mar;232(3):791-800.

68. **Journal article having an erratum**

Scuderi A, Letsou A. Amnioserosa is required for dorsal closure in Drosophila. Dev Dyn. 2005 Mar;232(3):791-800. Erratum in: Dev Dyn. 2005 May;233(1):249.

70. **Journal article with an indication it may be found in PubMed**

Amalberti R, Auroy Y, Berwick D, Barach P. Five system barriers to achieving ultrasafe health care. Ann Intern Med. 2005 May 3;142(9):756-64. Cited in: PubMed; PMID 15867408.

71. **Journal article with DOI provided**

Bhutta ZA, Darmstadt GL, Hasan BS, Haws RA. Community-based interventions for improving perinatal and neonatal health outcomes in developing countries: a review of the evidence. Pediatrics. 2005 Feb;115(2 Suppl):519-617. doi:10.1542/peds.2004-1441.

73. **Journal article accompanied by a videocassette, CD-ROM, or other visual medium**

Sathananthan AH, Tarin JJ, Gianaroli L, Ng SC, Dharmawardena V, Magli MC, Fernando R, Trounson AO. Development of the human dispermic embryo. Hum Reprod Update. 1999 Sep-Oct;5(5):553-60. Accompanied by: Video on CD-ROM.

Orchard JW, Alcott E, James T, Farhart P, Portus M, Waugh SR. Exact moment of a gastrocnemius muscle strain captured on video. Br J Sports Med. 2002 Jun;36(3):222-3. Accompanied by: Video available at http://www.bjsportmed.com

74. **CD-ROM published as a supplement to an issue of a journal**

9th United European Gastroenterology Week. Amsterdam 2001. Abstracts of presentations [CD-ROM]. Gut. 2001 Nov;49 (5 Suppl 3): [1 CD-ROM].

Examples of Citations to Volumes of Books with a Separate Title for the Volume but Without Separate Authors/Editors

1. **Standard volume of a book without separate authors/editors**

   Tos M. Manual of middle ear surgery. Vol. 3, Surgery of the external auditory canal. Stuttgart (Germany): Georg Thieme Verlag; 1997. 305 p.

   Cicchetti D, Cohen DJ, editors. Developmental psychopathology. Vol. 1, Theory and methods. New York: John Wiley & Sons, Inc.; c1995. 787 p.

2. **Volumes of books without separate authors/editors following an edition statement**

   Krachmer JH, Mannis MJ, Holland DJ. Cornea. 2nd ed. Vol. 1, Fundamentals, diagnosis and management. Philadelphia: Elsevier Mosby; 2005. 1409 p.

   Voet D, Voet JG. Biochemistry. 3rd ed. Vol. 2, The expression and transmission of genetic information. New York: J. Wiley & Sons; c2004. p. 1107-560.

3. **Volumes of books without separate authors/editors following an edition statement and secondary authors**

   Moller TB, Reif E. Pocket atlas of sectional anatomy: computer tomography and magnetic resonance imaging. 2nd ed., rev. and enl. Telger T, translator. Vol. 2, Thorax, abdomen, and pelvis. Stuttgart (Germany): Thieme; 2001. 226 p.

4. **Volumes of books without separate authors/editors following a content type**

   Merbach W, Muller-Uri C. Lead in the environment [bibliography]. Pt. 3, Distribution of the environmental lead. Halle (Germany): Universitats- und Landesbibliothek Sachsen-Anhalt; 1993. 211 p. English, German, French, Spanish, Polish, Italian.

5. **Volumes of books without separate authors/editors with numbers labeled other than volume**

   Merbach W, Muller-Uri C. Lead in the environment [bibliography]. Pt. 3, Distribution of the environmental lead. Halle (Germany): Universitats- und Landesbibliothek Sachsen-Anhalt; 1993. 211 p. English, German, French, Spanish, Polish, Italian.

7. **Volumes of books without separate authors/editors continuously paginated**

Oppenheim JJ, Feldmann M, Durum SK, Hirano T, Vilcek J, Nicola NA, editors. Cytokine reference: a compendium of cytokines and other mediators of host defense. Vol. 2, Receptors. London: Academic Press; c2001. p. 1437-2260.

Goldstein RE, Haywood VA, editors. Esthetics in dentistry. 2nd ed. Vol. 2, Esthetic problems of individual teeth, missing teeth, malocclusion, special populations. Hamilton (ON): BC Decker Inc; 2002. p. 471-884.

Examples of Citations to Volumes with a Separate Title and Separate Author/Editors

1. **Standard volume with a separate title and separate authors/editors for each volume**

Bays RA, Quinn PD, editors. Temporomandibular disorders. Philadelphia: W.B. Saunders Company; c2000. 426 p. (Fonseca RJ, editor. Oral and maxillofacial surgery; vol. 4).

Frank RG, Baum A, Wallander JL, editors. Models and perspectives in health psychology. Washington: American Psychological Association; c2004. 641 p. (Boll TJ, editor. Handbook of clinical health psychology; vol. 3).

Stephens D, editor. Adult audiology. Oxford (UK): Butterworth-Heinemann; c1997. 657 p. (Kerr AG, editor. Scott-Brown's otolaryngology; vol. 2).

2. **Volume with optional full first names for editors**

Gottsch, John D.; Stark, Walter J.; Goldberg, Morton F., editors. Ophthalmic surgery. 5th ed. London: Arnold; c1999. 506 p. (Carter, David C.; Russell, R.C.; Pitt, Henry A., editors. Operative surgery; vol. 6).

4. **Volume with author(s), not editor(s)**

Reichart PA, Philipson HP. Oral pathology. Hassel T, translator; Hormann J, illustrator. Stuttgart (Germany): Thieme; 2000. 285 p. (Rateitschak KH, Wolf HF, editors. Color atlas of dental medicine).

Pott S. Medizin, Medizinethik und schone Literatur. Berlin: Walter De Gruyter; 2002. 284 p. (Sakularisierung in den Wissenschaften seit der Fruhen Neuzeit; bd. 3). German.

5. **Volume with author/editor affiliation**

Schachat AP (Johns Hopkins University and Hospital, Baltimore, MD), editor. Medical retina. 4th ed. Philadelphia: Elsevier Mosby; c2006. p. 873-1889. (Ryan SJ, editor. Retina; vol. 2).

Poppas D (New York Hospital-Cornell Medical Center, New York, NY), Retik AB, editors. Pediatric urology. Philadelphia: Current Medicine, Inc.; c2003. 182 p. (Vaughan ED Jr, Perlmutter AP, editors. Atlas of clinical urology; vol. 4).

10. **Volume with edition**

Kaufmann SH, Steward MW, editors. Immunology. 10th ed. London: Hodder Arnold; c2005. 1033 p. (Topley and Wilson's microbiology & microbial infections; vol. 7).

Freedman DX, Dyrud JE, editors. Treatment. 2nd ed. New York: Basic Books; c1975. 1009 p. (Arieti S, editor. American handbook of psychiatry; vol. 5).

11. **Volume with secondary author(s)**

Guyuron B, editor. Aesthetic surgery. Kanasz J, illustrator. St. Louis (MO): Mosby; c2000. p. 2427-887. (Achauer BM, Eriksson E, Guyuron B, Coleman JJ 3rd, Russell RC, Vander Kolk CA, editors. Plastic surgery: indications, operations, and outcomes; vol. 5).

Reichart PA, Philipson HP. Oral pathology. Hassel T, translator; Hormann J, illustrator. Stuttgart (Germany): Thieme; 2000. 285 p. (Rateitschak KH, Wolf HF, editors. Color atlas of dental medicine).

12. **Volume with well-known place of publication**

Reves JG, editor. Cardiothoracic anesthesia. Philadelphia: Churchill Livingstone; c1999. (Miller RD, editor. Atlas of anesthesia; vol.8).

13. **Volume with geographic qualifier added to place of publication for clarity**

Sudarshan SR, editor. Diseases and their causes. Taredo (India): Popular Prakashan; 2005. 319 p. (Encyclopaedia of Indian medicine; vol. 6).

Adams DA, Cinnamond MJ, editors. Paediatric otolaryngology. Oxford (UK): Butterworth Heinemann; c1997. (Kerr AG, editor. Scott-Brown's otolaryngology; vol. 6).

14. Volume with government agency as publisher

Jones FD, Sparacino LR, Wilcox VL, Rothberg JM, Stokes JW, editors. War psychiatry. Falls Church (VA): Department of the Army (US), Office of the Surgeon General; 1995. 508 p. (Lounsbury DE, editor. Textbooks of military medicine).

15. Volume with unknown publisher

Alizai S, Zia A. [Chanesar Goth and Landhi]. Islamabad (Pakistan): [publisher unknown]; [1993?]. 53 p. (Gender differentials in access to health care for Pakistani children; vol. 3). Study conducted for Unicef in November 1990.

16. Volume with date of publication

Sudarshan SR, editor. Diseases and their causes. Taredo (India): Popular Prakashan; 2005. 319 p. (Encyclopaedia of Indian medicine; vol. 6).

Belar CD, editor. Sociocultural and individual differences. New York: Pergamon; 1998. 384 p. (Bellack AS, Hersen M, editors. Comprehensive clinical psychology; vol. 10).

17. Volume with date of copyright instead of date of publication

Renninger KA, Sigel IE, editors. Child psychology in practice. 6th ed. Hoboken (NJ): John Wiley & Sons, Inc.; c2006. 1073 p. (Damon W, Lerner RM, editors. Handbook of child psychology; vol. 4).

Wilcox CS, editor. Hypertension and the kidney. Philadelphia: Current Medicine, Inc.; c1999. (Schrier RW, editor. Atlas of diseases of the kidney; vol. 3).

20. Volume with standard pagination

Harrison SI, Eth S, editors. Clinical assessment and intervention planning. New York: John Wiley & Sons, Inc.; c1998. 832 p. (Noshpitz JD, editor. Handbook of child and adolescent psychiatry; vol. 5).

25. Volume with series title having a subtitle

Guyuron B, editor. Aesthetic surgery. Kanasz J, illustrator. St. Louis (MO): Mosby; c2000. p. 2427-887. (Achauer BM, Eriksson E,

Guyuron B, Coleman JJ 3rd, Russell RC, Vander Kolk CA, editors. Plastic surgery: indications, operations, and outcomes; vol. 5).

Examples of Citations to Parts of Books

1. **Standard chapter in a book**

   Riffenburgh RH. Statistics in medicine. 2nd ed. Amsterdam (Netherlands): Elsevier Academic Press; c2006. Chapter 24, Regression and correlation methods; p. 447-86.

   Reed JG, Baxter PM. Library use: handbook for psychology. 3rd ed. Washington: American Psychological Association; c2003. Chapter 2, Selecting and defining the topic; p. 11-25.

   Goldstein RE. Esthetics in dentistry. 2nd ed. Vol. 1, Principles, communications, treatment methods. Hamilton (ON): B.C. Decker; c1998. Chapter 13, Composite resin bonding; p. 277-338.

2. **Chapter in a book with optional full first names of authors**

   Speroff, Leon; Fritz, Marc A. Clinical gynecologic endocrinology and infertility. 7th ed. Philadelphia: Lippincott Williams & Wilkins; c2005. Chapter 29, Endometriosis; p. 1103-33.

3. **Standard figure in a book with number**

   Lashley FR. Clinical genetics in nursing practice. 3rd ed. New York: Springer Publishing Company; c2005. Figure 2.5, Meiosis with two autosomal chromosome pairs; p. 27-8.

   Thibodeau GA, Patton KT. Anatomy & physiology. 5th ed. St. Louis (MO): Mosby; c2003. Figure 6-13, Onycholysis; p. 179.

   Munro BH. Statistical methods for health care research. 5th ed. Philadelphia: Lippincott Williams & Wilkins; c2005. Exercise figure 14-1, Factor analysis of IPA items; p. 347.

   Lancaster FW, Joncich MJ. The measure and evaluation of library services. Washington: Information Resources Press; c1977. Figure 9, Questionnaire used in U.K. catalog use study; p. 47-50.

8. **Standard table in a book with a number**

   Larone DH. Medically important fungi: a guide to identification. 4th ed. Washington: ASM Press; c2002. Table 15, Characteristics of some of the "black yeasts"; p. 200.

   American health: demographics and spending of health care consumers. Ithaca (NY): New Strategist Publications, Inc.; c2005.

Table 11.19, Percent distribution of hospital discharges by diagnosis and age, 2002; p. 395-6.

Burant CF. Medical management of type 2 diabetes. 5th ed. Alexandria (VA): American Diabetes Association; c2004. Table 3.12, Sample regimens for achieving glycemic control; p. 68.

Moore KL, Persaud TV. The developing human: clinically oriented embryology. 7th ed. Philadelphia: Saunders; c2003. Table 6-1, Criteria for estimating fertilization age during the fetal period; p.103.

Examples of Citations to Contributions to Books

1. Standard reference to a contributed chapter

Whiteside TL, Heberman RB. Effectors of immunity and rationale for immunotherapy. In: Kufe DW, Pollock RE, Weichselbaum RR, Bast RC Jr, Gansler TS, Holland JF, Frei E 3rd, editors. Cancer medicine 6. Hamilton (ON): BC Decker Inc; 2003. p. 221-8.

Rojko JL, Hardy WD Jr. Feline leukemia virus and other retroviruses. In: Sherding RG, editor. The cat: diseases and clinical management. New York: Churchill Livingstone; 1989. p. 229-332.

Kone BC. Metabolic basis of solute transport. In: Brenner BM, Rector FC, editors. Brenner and Rector's the kidney. 8th ed. Vol. 1. Philadelphia: Saunders Elsevier; c2008. p. 130-55.

Appendix 4

Further Reading

I Electronic resources (Free)

Resource title	Available at
Ethical Guidelines for Biomedical Research on Human Participants (2006) Ethical guidelines for research in social sciences and health (1998 -2000)	http://www.icmr.nic.in/human_ethics.htm
Approved Guidelines by CPCSEA on the norms and practices for regulation of Animal Experimentation CPCSEA Guidelines for Laboratory Animal Facility National Science Academy (INSA) Guidelines for Care and Use of Animals in Scientific Research ICMR Guidelines for use of Laboratory Animals in Medical Colleges	http://www.icmr.nic.in/animal_ethics.htm #Guidelines
Russell, W.M.S. and Burch, R.L., The Principles of Humane Experimental Technique. Methuen, London, 1959. Reprinted by UFAW, 1992: 8 Hamilton Close, South Mimms, Potters Bar, Herts EN6 3QD England. ISBN 0 900767 78 2	http://altweb.jhsph.edu/pubs/books/humane_exp/het-toc

Resource title	Available at
CONSORT (CONsolidated Standards of Reporting Trials) The CONSORT "Explanation and Elaboration" document	http://www.consort-statement.org/
ARRIVE (Animal Research: Reporting *In Vivo* Experiments)	http://www.jpharmacol.com/article.asp?issn=0976-500X; year=2010; volume=1; issue=2;spage=94;epage=99;aulast=Kil Kenny; type=2
CHERRIES(Checklist for Reporting Results of Internet E-Surveys)	http://www.jmir.org/2004/3/e34/
MOOSE(Meta-Analysis of Observational Studies in Epidemiology)	http://jama.ama-assn.org/cgi/content/full/283/15/2008
STARD(Standards for Reporting of Diagnostic Accuracy)	http://www.clinchem.org/cgi/reprint/49/1/7.pdf or http://www.clinchem.org/cgi/content/full/49/1/7/
STROBE(Strengthening the Reporting of Observational Studies in Epidemiology)	http://www.strobe-statement.org
TREND(Transparent Reporting of Evaluations with Nonrandomized Designs)	http://www.ajph.org/cgi/content/full/94/3/361/ or http://www.trend-statement.org/asp/documents/statements/AJPH_Mar2004_Trendstatement.pdf
Reporting of Observational Longitudinal Research	http://aje.oxfordjournals.org/cgi/content/abstract/161/3/280
HyperStat Statistics Textbook	http://davidmlane.com/hyperstat
Statistics at Square One 9th Edition	http://www.bmj.com/collections/statsbk/
VassarStats: Web Site for Statistical Computation.	http://faculty.vassar.edu/lowry/VassarStats.html
Citing medicine: the NLM style guide for authors, editors, and publishers	http://www.nlm.nih.gov/citingmedicine

Note: The URLs (site addresses) indicated above were verified and found to be correct at the time of going to press.

II Print resources - Books:

Research Methodology

1. Jagadeesh G, Murthy S, Gupta YK, Prakash A. Biomedical Research: From ideation to publication. 1st ed. New Delhi: Wolters Kluwer Health; 2010.
2. Greenberg RS, Daniels SR, Flanders WD, Eley JW, Borin JR 3rd. Medical epidemiology. 4th ed. New York: McGraw Hill; 2005.
3. Duley L, Farrell B. Clinical trials. 1st ed(Indian). New Delhi: Viva books private limited; 2003.
4. Schulz KF, Grimes DA. The lancet handbook of essential concepts in clinical research. 1st ed. Edinburgh: Elsevier; 2006.
5. Hulley SB, Cummings SR, Browner WS, Grady D, Hearst N, Newman TB. Designing clinical research. 2nd ed. Philadelphia: Lippincott Williams Wilkins; 2001.

Statistics

1. Swinscow TDV, Champbell MJ. Statistics at square one. 10th ed(Indian). New Delhi: Viva books private limited; 2003.
2. Glaser AN. High yield biostatistics. 1st ed. Baltimore: Williams & Wilkins; 2000.
3. Sundar Rao PSS, Richard J. Introduction to biostatistics and research methods. 4th ed. New Delhi: Prentice Hall of India; 2006.
4. Dawson B, Trapp RG. Basic & clinical biostatistics. 4th ed. New York: McGraw Hill; 2004.
5. Petrie A, Sabin C. Medical statistics at a glance. 3rd ed. Oxford: Wiley-Blackwell; 2009.
6. Norman GR, Streiner DL. Biostatistics: the bare essentials. 2nd ed. Hamilton: B.C.Decker Inc.; 2000.
7. Glantz SA. Primer of biostatistics. 6th ed. New York: McGraw Hill; 2006.
8. Sundaram KR, Dwivedi SN, Sreenivas V. Medical statistics: principles and methods. 1st ed. New Delhi: B.I. Publications; 2010.
9. Gravetter FJ, Wallnau LB. Statistics for the behavioural sciences. 5th ed. Belmont: Wadsworth; 2000.

Scientific writing

1. Hall GM. How to write a paper. 3rd ed(Indian). New Delhi: Byword Viva; 2004.
2. Peat J, Elliott E, Baur L, Keena V. Scientific writing easy when you know how. 1st ed(Indian). New Delhi: Byword Viva; 2004.
3. Caro S. How to publish your PhD. 1st ed(Indian). New Delhi: Sage; 2009.
4. Oliver P. Writing your thesis. 2nd ed(Indian). New Delhi: Sage; 2009.